D1213067

EDWARD W. BARRETT

TRUTH

IS

OUR

WEAPON

1953
NEW YORK :: FUNK & WAGNALLS COMPANY

To Mason, my wife—and to hundreds of other wives who have tolerated and encouraged propagandist husbands in the frustrating toil of trying to convert men to the cause of freedom.

*There is nothing so powerful as
truth — and often nothing so strange.*
—Daniel Webster, 1830.

Acknowledgments

T O a large number of friends in government service and in private media of information, I express deep thanks for supplying information, suggestions, and criticisms.

Particular thanks go to Thurman L. Barnard, Elmer Davis, Albert Pickerell, Francis A. Jamieson, Davidson Taylor, Mark A. May, George H. Lyon, Justin Miller, Howland H. Sargeant, Robert E. Sherwood, William Benton, Robert Lang, Wallace Carroll, Edward Klauber, Raymond Moley, James Webb Young, Arthur Goodfriend, Porter McKeever, Serge Gagarin, Pierre Bedard, Joseph B. Phillips, and Frank Rounds, Jr.—for ideas, suggestions, and, in some cases, criticism of particular chapters. Blame, however, attaches to none, since the finished product is the author's alone.

To dozens of others, who are in national or international public service and prefer to remain anonymous, I express equally deep appreciation.

Thanks for various ideas on international persuasion, growing out of many discussions in the past, go to Senators Alexander Smith, William Fulbright, Lister Hill, Karl Mundt, Ralph Flanders, and Mike Mansfield; to Representatives John McCormack, A. S. J. Carnahan, John Rooney, John Vorys, and Prince Preston; to former Representative Daniel Flood; and to Messrs. Allen Dulles, George Kennan, C. D. Jackson, and Frank Wisner.

Unusually enthusiastic thanks go to David Penn for help in reading the final manuscript, to Mrs. Edwin K. Fox for research and copy assistance, and to Miss Frances M. Barry for shepherding the whole manuscript from the first notes through the printed proofs.

Introduction

DWIGHT D. EISENHOWER and HARRY S. TRUMAN agreed on at least one thing. They said it in substantially the same words in 1952, "We cannot hope to win the cold war unless we win the minds of men."

This book is written out of deep personal conviction that we can progressively win men's minds but that the job is extraordinarily difficult.

A gigantic war of ideas is now going on. It will be a long-drawn-out war. It could easily outlast even the present cold war —with, say, Mao Tse-Tung ultimately replacing Malenkov and Company as the prime foe, much as Stalin replaced Hitler. The issues of the conflict, however, will remain basically the same: freedom and human dignity versus slavery and expansionist tyranny. The great, prolonged war of ideas must be waged with as much skill, professional competence, and steadfastness as are needed in any military conflict.

In the contest for men's minds, truth can be peculiarly the American weapon. It cannot be an isolated weapon, because the propaganda of truth is powerful only when linked with concrete actions and policies. To date, we Americans have treated the weapon of truthful international persuasion with absurd fickleness. Yet, because truth is generally on our side, it can be our decisive weapon if we will only profit from past lessons and employ it with wisdom, consistency, and responsibility.

The answer does not lie just in spending tens of millions on propaganda apparatus, essential though that may be. Nor does it lie in sonorous talk about "taking the psychological offensive." And it certainly does not lie in permitting irresponsibles periodically to dismantle the whole complex mechanism of international persuasion in public.

ix

The job of international persuasion is far from a cinch. Indeed, it is inordinately complex. Simply transplanting the highly developed American techniques of advertising and public relations to foreign lands can produce gross blunders. What sells soap in Indiana can unsell democracy in India. What amuses Czechs can offend Chinese. Mere boastfulness can alienate others. International name-calling may be fun, but it rarely accomplishes anything.

This book attempts to show why a highly skilful and substantial campaign of truth is as indispensible as an air force. It traces the nation's faltering progress to date in international information. It outlines the obvious strategy of Malenkov and his Kremlin colleagues and depicts the incredible mechanism they now devote to the Big Lie. It seeks to show how the propaganda of truth—when linked with firm diplomatic, economic, and military policies—can yield vast returns. And it endeavors to plot some basic guidelines for the future.

Nature, of course, has endowed me with no Olympian vision. Happenstance simply provided me with as wide experience in the complex field of international persuasion as perhaps any American has had. I hope my hindsight can strengthen the foresight of others.

My own experience started in the last war with a brief span in General William J. Donovan's organization that later became O.S.S. Subsequently, that experience included setting up the world-wide news network of the O.W.I. and helping with the original Voice of America and the first United Nations Radio. It embraced much Allies-wide propaganda planning, including that for D-day. It included leaflet work and other combat propaganda with Eisenhower's AFHq. in the Mediterranean. It involved early postwar planning for UNESCO. Finally, it covered two hectic years (1950-52) as Assistant Secretary of State in charge of all international information and educational exchange activities.

Before, between, and after these official assignments, I have served in journalism and radio, as Editorial Director of *Newsweek* magazine, and as a consultant in news and publishing. Politically, I have been a mugwump—an independent who is far more interested in finding ways to combat Communist imperialism than in furthering the political fortunes of either party. While holding official jobs, I naturally have had my share of abuse—from the ultra-nationalist press and politicos—have been honored by the slander of *Pravda* and the Moscow Radio, and have been commended by two congressionally established commissions, and by a substantial number of Democrats and Republicans in Congress. I am sure the plaudits were exaggerated; I believe the denunciations were. At any rate, as one no longer in government, perhaps I can now speak frankly without having my motives questioned.

The next few years hold enormous international dangers for America and for the cause of freedom. Happily, they also hold opportunities of a sort unparalleled in years. The recent emotional purge of a great national election and the presence of relatively new faces in Washington still provide the opportunity for carrying through an intelligent, firm, and imaginative psychological campaign. There is still the chance of removing the whole range of psychological operations from the political football field and entrusting its supervision to capable and responsible leaders in the executive and legislative branches. That could well mean the difference between winning and losing the current world conflict.

In the past, many members of Congress have been sincere and constructive about this vital problem. Some have not. Indeed, we Americans have heard a few of our Congressmen spend hours debating non-essentials of the Campaign of Truth —including the particular musical tunes used to lure foreign radio listeners. We have heard one Representative seriously beseech his colleagues to halt Voice of America broadcasts unless the editing is done by a committee of the Daughters of the

American Revolution. We have witnessed ridiculously lop-sided "hearings" on television. We have heard long debates on whether any information program at all is needed. And once we saw the whole effort nearly demolished because one maga-zine on the shelves of American libraries abroad contained a piece critical of a powerful Senator.

We can no longer afford the luxury of such nonsense. The time has come to stop squandering energy in debating whether we need a Campaign of Truth on a sizable scale. It is urgent for us to agree on that and to channel the energy of the Congress, the Executive Branch, and the citizenry into a responsible effort to make sure that the job is done well.

If these chapters help toward that end, they will have been worth many times the extensive work and research that have gone into them.

Contents

PART I

WE BEGIN TO LEARN

PART II

THE FOES WE FACE

Part III

THE TIME TO WAGE PEACE

Part I

WE BEGIN TO LEARN

1

Our Peril—and Our Chance

AT TIMES recently America has seemed to conduct psychological warfare against its own people instead of against the Soviet Union.

Never before in history have the American people been so bombarded and so confused by news about international propaganda as in the year 1953. Some of the developments have been irresponsible and baffling. Others have been important and constructive.

The President wisely set up a new commission of private citizens to take a fresh look at the whole complex field of psychological strategy. He made a masterful speech putting peace squarely up to the Soviet Union and calling for "deeds" not "words." Statesmen made vague speeches about "mobilizing the minds of men." Senator Joseph R. McCarthy staged certain televised hearings featuring the sensational tales of a few disgruntled employees of the Voice of America. And, under outside prodding, the government temporarily did some silly things in propaganda, but it soon corrected most of these.

Because extreme charges make bolder headlines than do constructive developments, the net effect was to generate more heat than light. Charges and countercharges about alleged waste or about personal habits of a few individuals obscured far greater issues of national interest and national safety. They

3

overshadowed the grave central question of how best to use international persuasion to head off a hot war and win a cold war.

EVERY American who in recent years has gone into a top position in the State Department or the defense establishment has been shocked into a deep sense of urgency. Given access to Top Secret papers appraising Soviet capabilities and Soviet intentions, he has felt his worst fears were confirmed—or multiplied. These papers, like one monumental job prepared by the National Security Council, are not just memos batted out by two or three bureaucrats. They are enormously detailed studies drawing upon the data collected by all intelligence agencies of the U. S. Government.

The new top official finds that Soviet capabilities are astounding—in troops, in submarines, in military production, in airplanes, and even in probable ability to cripple American industry in a matter of days. He becomes aware that Kremlin efforts at subversion in other lands are enormous. On Soviet intentions, he finds disagreement among the most experienced intelligence experts, but he finds none optimistic. As of this writing, most are extremely skeptical of "friendly" gestures from the Soviet rulers. A few see the Kremlin still planning an all-out war. More see a systematic Soviet program for progressive world conquest through the *threat* of war, combined with subversion, trickery, and enormous propaganda—plus tactical retreats whenever expedient. And they see, at least, a Kremlin readiness to *risk* war in pursuing its aims. As if these dangers were not enough, the freshman official learns that the new and shaky system of alliances between free nations is jeopardized by even more economic, political, and public-opinion forces than he ever realized.

If the newcomer is unusually perceptive, he soon recognizes that the mass opinions of large groups or of entire populations, abroad and at home, have far more impact on international developments than in years gone by. In country after country the views of ordinary citizens are altering major policies.

In Italy, he learns, the Italian Government dares not take a major step which it knows is vital because it fears Italian mass opinion. It seems the step involves a commitment to the United States, which Italian opinion fears is trigger-happy. In Burma, leaders want to go along on a major project but fear Burmese opinion still suspects America of too close ties with hated "colonial powers." Another government publicly rebukes the United States, then privately explains it had to do so because the voters felt it was letting Americans push it around. Occasionally, even a satellite government foregoes a drastic move because a similar action earlier had produced too much popular grumbling. And in Washington, a constructive measure agreed on by all informed officials is watered down for fear of being interpreted as "appeasement" by voters and by those Congressmen who are less informed on the subject.

THE NEW and growing impact of public opinion on international policy reflects a natural evolution. In Washington today there are still some of the weathered diplomatic notes written out in handsome longhand by Thomas Jefferson as Secretary of State. He conducted foreign policy by sitting down and personally writing a message to another government. Then he would have it sent down and put aboard ship. Weeks later an American ambassador would receive it, put on his fanciest breeches, and deliver the message to the foreign minister. Six weeks later, if the matter was urgent, Mr. Jefferson would get a reply. The American people paid little attention to goings on in this élite world of diplomacy. Most voters in most lands viewed foreign affairs as a complex matter to be left to a little group of experts known as diplomats. What a change has occurred! Today the grim knowledge that a rash diplomatic move could unleash forces of appalling destruction has radically altered the citizens' role. They insist, quite properly, that international relations are their business too.

Too few experienced diplomats clearly recognize this basic world-wide trend. Those that do recognize it too often view it as just a frustrating factor. A minority, fortunately a growing minority, look upon this potent new force as a challenge and an opportunity. When the aims and basic policies of a nation are decent, non-imperialistic, and relatively just, it is clear that public opinion around the world *could* become a gigantic force in support of those aims and policies.

Unless we Americans are bent on suicide, we have no wise choice but to master the techniques of international persuasion. This does not mean going hog-wild, misconstruing propaganda as a substitute for action. It does not mean adopting, under pressure from immature headline-hunters, such shrill and strident techniques as to alienate at the outset those we seek to win over. It doesn't mean confusing volume with effectiveness. And it certainly does not mean periodic public statements which say, in effect, "Look out, you Communists, we are about to launch psychological warfare to beat all get-out."

The constructive, prudent course does involve having, as a continuing part of government, the mechanism and staff for large-scale international persuasion. It does mean recognizing that massive but well-prescribed doses are sometimes needed— which means, in periods of crisis, augmenting the mechanism just as the Air Force is augmented. And it means entrusting direction of the whole effort to responsible groups in the Administration and Congress, with a minimum of fanfare and boisterous squabbling.

 Totalitarian tyrants are miles ahead of us in recognizing the growing force of mass opinion. Stalin painstakingly built an international propaganda mechanism, from training schools up, that now consumes far more than a billion dollars a year. Our job should be easier and less expensive. We don't have to traffic in distortion and falsehood. If we can wield the truth effectively enough, if we can back our high aims with equally high actions, and if we can tell of them persuasively, we will be well on our way.

Bernard Baruch has wisely said that we can win the peace only if we *wage the peace*. Men as diverse as Paul Hoffman and Mr. Justice Douglas, as Senator Karl Mundt and the late Senator Brien McMahon have agreed that we can wage peace successfully only if we, as a nation, learn to use the weapon of truth effectively.

The performance to date has been only partly effective. If properly interpreted, however, it provides priceless guideposts to the future. If America follows those guides intelligently and boldly, it should be able to make the weapon of truth as powerful as any in its arsenal.

2

Incidents That Point the Way

THE RIGHT WORDS striking the right persons at the right time can change the course of history. Striking masses of peoples, they have caused revolutions. Striking obscure individuals destined for future leadership, they have profoundly altered events years later.

Back in 1908 a young Indian agitator was serving time in Volkrust Prison in South Africa. He borrowed from the prison library a copy of an essay, "Civil Disobedience," by the American, Henry David Thoreau. Years later the Indian recalled: "The masterly treatise . . . made a deep impression on me." By that time he was known to the world as Mahatma Gandhi.

In that case, one brief essay read by one young man affected the course of history in a major area of the world. In many more cases, words heard or read by groups of men or masses of men have changed history.

Within the last decade, the United States has carried out many experiments in planned persuasion. Some had substantial effects. A few instances, major and minor, help point directions for the future.

IN THE EARLY days of World War II, a little group of U. S. Navy officers, taking a suggestion from British colleagues, worked on a hunch that the German submarine service would

8

be particularly susceptible to persuasion. They found most of those in government cynical about the idea but discovered that the Office of War Information was enthusiastic. Soon the O.W.I. and this Navy group, labeled OP-16-W, and headed by Captain Ellis M. Zacharias, had embarked on a systematic campaign to undermine morale in the U-boat service. A German-speaking officer named Lt. Comm. Ralph G. Albrecht was picked as commentator. He went on the air regularly under the name of "Commander Robert Lee Norden, U.S.N." A battery of the O.W.I.'s Voice of America transmitters carried his broadcasts. Occasionally, American or British planes dropped supporting messages in leaflet form over German U-boat bases.

OP-16-W's and O.W.I.'s first job was to gain an audience. To achieve this, Norden was turned into a sort of higher-level Walter Winchell. Officers combed all available intelligence on the German Navy for items to make Norden sound as if he knew more about the U-boat service than the Germans themselves. He started out by reporting on friction within the service, on incidents in the family of Admiral Doenitz, on the sweethearts of Nazi Navy officers in France, and on the defects in new U-boats. He even reported details of how an admiral refused permission to one of his young officers to get married.

The "keyhole" technique proved as infallible for attracting an audience for Norden as it had for the Winchells and Pearsons on the American networks. As soon as secret reports indicated that U-boat crewmen were listening, Norden went to work subtly to undermine the morale of the crews—while sticking to the principle of truth. Finding that exaggerated claims of U-boat successes had helped sustain morale in Germany, Norden started questioning and disproving these claims. He cited facts and figures to show that ships which U-boat commanders claimed to have sunk were still carrying supplies to the battle fronts. He listed the ten U-boat commanders who had done the most extreme falsification of their reports. Soon the Nazis started answering him directly in their home-front propaganda. Finally, they began cutting drastically their claims until they boasted of even less successes than they actually had achieved!

The Norden broadcasts used many other techniques. Intelligence at one time revealed the Nazis were awarding their Knight's Insignia of the Iron Cross to many U-boat commanders but had given only one to an enlisted man. Reciting facts and figures, Norden criticized the unfairness of this. Within a few days, the German Navy announced that two petty officers had just received the award. Norden reported that, too, and took a figurative bow.

When U.S. forces sank one German U-boat, its commander, Lieutenant Heinz Eberhard Müller, resisted to the last. He was finally captured, seriously wounded, and taken aboard an American hospital ship. He had scarcely regained consciousness when he asked an attendant, "Would it be possible for me to talk to Commander Norden?" The interview was ultimately arranged (and Albrecht temporarily given another stripe for the occasion). It provided confirmation that the Norden propaganda was influencing German naval thinking. At the war's end, an official document found at a German naval headquarters in Cherbourg reported that the Norden broadcasts "had a crushing effect on the morale of German naval personnel."

IN THE CRITICAL days between Germany's fall and V-J Day, American prestige was suffering appreciable damage at the hands of one of the most influential newspapers in newly liberated Belgium. By most standards it was a decent paper with an honest, if cynical, editor. But through its columns ran an undertone of sneering at America, its methods, its motives, and its goals.

Shortly, the United States Information Service of O.W.I. arranged for the critical editor to join a group of journalists visiting this country. The visitors saw much of America and talked with leaders in many fields. Wisely, O.W.I. showed them the bad with the good—the worst slums, as well as the best housing developments designed to replace such slums.

When this particular editor returned home, he wrote a thank-you letter. It ended with these words, "I suspect I can best express my thanks by interpreting your country to my fellow citizens as I saw it: fallible, of course, but strong, open, and honest, with a great heart and an unbeatable spirit."

Subsequent clippings showed that his readers got just that sort of interpretation from then on—not saccharine tributes but informative, friendly interpretation; sometimes critical but always fair.

In the years that followed, without doubt, hundreds of such cases illustrated the fact that personal visits to this country could be the most effective single instrument for persuading others of our decency and our physical and moral strength. The Belgian Government generally acted with sympathy toward the United States, partly because it contained three Cabinet officers who had studied here as youths. The most understanding articles about this country appearing in the Latin American press were usually written by young men who had once been brought here as exchange students. What visitors saw here could more than offset the shabby impression sometimes made by our vacationing visitors abroad.

Sometimes a mishap would embitter a visitor—as when an Indian encountered discrimination. But such cases were rare. "Exchange of persons," in at least ninety percent of all cases, helped create sympathetic understanding of this country. It could also serve as a specific treatment for immediate ills. In 1950, for example, U. S. officials were disturbed by wide-spread cynicism in Western Germany about the United States and its motives. First Nazi, then Communist propaganda about American "imperialism," "discrimination," and "downtrodden labor" had left its mark. As part of a broad program, the ECA and the State Department arranged to bring various types of German leaders to America and let them see us for themselves. One of these was a young German labor leader. After his return home, he spoke to labor audiences throughout Western Germany. He started each speech with approximately these words: "When I sailed into New York Harbor, I sneered at the Statue of Liberty as an empty symbol. When I sailed out three months later, I bowed to the old lady because I had found she stood for something truly fine and decent."

ON AUGUST 10, 1945, the Japanese sent word via Switzerland that they were prepared to discuss surrender terms along the lines of the Potsdam Proclamation—lines which, incidentally, had been broadly explained for weeks over the Voice of America in the Captain Zacharias broadcasts. But Tokyo stipulated conditions. Washington responded, rejecting the conditions.

In the following twenty-four hours, the government's monitoring reports revealed a curious fact: the news of Tokyo's surrender offer and of Washington's reply had been announced here and elsewhere in the world—but it had been carefully kept from the Japanese people. The Japanese Government's motive was clear. So long as its own people did not know of the offer, the Tokyo Government could continue fighting, could bargain hard for its conditions, and could even back out of any negotiations.

If, on the other hand, the Japanese people learned of their government's surrender offer, the fighting spirit would go out of them, and the government would find it all but impossible to continue hostilities.

Hurried sessions were held in Washington. State Department specialists on Japan and propagandists in the O.W.I. made a joint recommendation: We should go all out to deliver the news of the surrender offer to the Japanese people themselves. By so doing, we could force the Tokyo Government's hand; we could speed the end of the war and thereby avert the deaths of additional thousands.

James Byrnes, then Secretary of State, took the recommendation to the President. A half-hour later O.W.I. was told to proceed with getting the news through to the Japanese in every possible way. The Voice of America immediately started broadcasting it. By this time, however, the Japanese had an elaborate jamming mechanism to prevent the Voice's being widely heard; they had also imposed severe penalties for listening to the Voice. Clearly, a leaflet campaign was indicated, but the difficulties were enormous. The mere problem of preparing an appropriately worded announcement, translating it, printing leaflets by the millions, and delivering them over Japan would take days if customary procedures were followed. Short cuts had to be found.

O.W.I.'s Japanese section went to work drafting the message. Meanwhile, arrangements were made with the Pentagon for the necessary planes, and messages went to Hawaii and Saipan. There followed an extraordinary example of teamwork.

The Japanese section produced an English-language text in slightly more than an hour. Within two hours it had been worked over and modified slightly by appropriate State Department officials. Within another half-hour it had arrived in Honolulu and was being translated by O.W.I.'s Nisei staffers into bold Japanese characters on a large placard. The placard was cut into four quarters. The Voice of America's 100,000-watt Hawaiian transmitter interrupted its normal broadcasting. Into the circuit engineers hooked an experimental radio-photo machine that happily had arrived in Honolulu a short while before. Over the giant transmitter, now converted to a radiophoto sender, each of the four quarters was wirelessed in facsimile to Saipan, where the O.W.I. base had been alerted only a half-hour earlier—and where there was another new radiophoto machine. There, the four segments were reassembled, plates were made, and the presses started. Simultaneously, superfortresses on Saipan made ready to drop the leaflets over the eight largest Japanese cities.

Within twenty hours after the suggestion had first been made in Washington, natives of Tokyo and seven other Japanese cities were reading 3,000,000 leaflets. The leaflets said in part:

To the Japanese people: These American planes are not dropping bombs on you today. They are dropping these leaflets instead because the Japanese Government has offered to surrender, and every Japanese has a right to know the terms of that offer and the reply made to it by the United States Government on behalf of itself, the British, the Chinese, and the Russians. Your government now has a chance to end the war immediately. You will see how the war can be ended by reading the following official statements.

That cinched the surrender, which became official two days later.

Months later, Japanese officials confirmed that the leaflets had tied the Tokyo Government's hands, giving it no choice but to go through with the surrender on our terms. In 1947, in the *Infantry Journal*, Major Paul Linebarger analyzed psychological warfare's role and wrote that this "one operation alone probably repaid the entire cost of O.W.I. through the war."

SOME THREE years ago, Communist elements were making dangerous headway in one small country, left nameless for obvious reasons. Corruption and ineptness within the government made the Communists' task easier. The little nation's army was shot through with disaffection.

Because the stability of this Country X was of vital interest to the United States, appropriate American officials worked out a comprehensive campaign. First, they quietly insisted that the local government clean up its own house or face loss of American aid. But they did so in utmost privacy, recognizing that any democratic government anywhere will be tossed out of office if it appears to take orders supinely from a foreign power. They provided expert advice to the army and to certain technical departments but did so discreetly; the presence of the American experts was not publicized. Lastly, the nation's government and U. S. officials concocted a joint campaign of persuasion. They formed a steering committee of local editors, churchmen, labor leaders, officers of veterans' associations, and government people. "Advisers" from the U. S. Information Service worked with the committee.

The group took U.S.I.S. material and modified it to meet local needs. Religious organizations distributed over their own names pamphlets and posters exposing the flaws in Communism and promoting the cause of cooperative action by free peoples. A veterans' organization waged a vigorous anti-Communist campaign using U.S.I.S. materials adapted to local tastes. A letter from a nun in a Russian prison camp made a telling poster.

A team of Americans and local citizens began producing nearly a dozen shows a week over the national network. The broadcasts ranged from a straight, honest news program to a hair-raising soap opera. The latter, featuring a villain (Communist) and a clean-cut young hero (anti-Communist), soon became one of the most popular radio shows in the country. Another team produced special films recounting what had happened in nations which the Communists had taken over.

Meanwhile, the part of the U. S. Information Service iceberg that showed above the surface was enlarged. The U.S.I.S. stepped up its normal efforts to combat Communist lies and to explain America's aims and purposes more clearly. Information centers and libraries were expanded. U.S.I.S. officers prepared statements clarifying American policies and persuaded President Truman, Cabinet officers, and members of Congress to issue them. The Voice of America broadcast the statements to Country X, and the U.S.I.S. placed them in the press of the country.

Within eighteen months, the picture in this Country X had

changed markedly. The government had cleaned house. Civilian and military morale had improved. Communist influence had greatly lessened.

Country X, in this case, was a small nation, with a relatively simple economy and social structure. A well-planned, integrated political-military-economic propaganda campaign there was easier than it would be in larger, more complex nations. The experience, however, provided important clues. This campaign worked because a well-coordinated team in the field took the lead, with Washington's approval, in laying out a broad campaign. Then the campaign was executed in detail by competent officials on the scene under the direction of an able ambassador. It worked all the better because there was no American effort to take credit for it.

AFTER the Korean war broke out in mid-1950, a severe wave of jitters swept over Western Europe. Many Europeans took the Communist aggression in Korea as a sign that the Kremlin was about ready to launch an all-out war. Respectable, if timid, Europeans began to "take out insurance"—by getting their names on the rolls of Communist and Communist-front organizations. Western European government officials wavered in their support of the newly formed NATO. Press and public talked openly of the wisdom of "neutralism."

Clearly, a shot in the arm was needed. Those of us concerned with propaganda operations went to the Secretary of State, to Defense Department officials, and to the White House with an urgent plea that General Eisenhower be recalled to service and sent immediately to head the NATO forces in Europe. The proposal was not completely new, but we urged that it be effected immediately. Obviously, "Ike" Eisenhower had an aura of success for leadership and victory that would make him an admirable symbol of the sort of confidence so desperately needed in Europe. The wheels of government turned slowly. Within a few weeks, however, the President announced Eisenhower's designation as Commander of NATO forces. Since the General's personal plans prevented his taking over promptly, the officials concerned wisely agreed that he should make an immediate "inspection trip."

The announcement was scarcely out when the entire Soviet-controlled propaganda machine began spewing forth anti-Eisenhower tirades. He was "a symbol of American imperialist reaction," "a puppet of Wall Street" being sent to "supervise the mass sacrifice of Europe's young men."

Fortunately, the U.S. Information Service had already started work on a pro-Eisenhower campaign to solidify popular support in Europe for the North Atlantic alliance. It served also to combat the Communist barrage. The Voice of America carried daily broadcasts in all European languages contrasting the current Soviet invective with the praise they had heaped on Eisenhower during the war. A typical broadcast repeated Stalin's glowing tribute to Ike in wartime, contrasting it with *Pravda's* current tirades. Britain's B.B.C., France's R.D.F., and others cooperated. U.S.I.S. staff members prepared feature articles and photo collections emphasizing the General's humanitarian side along with his recognized military ability. They placed both in newspapers throughout Western Europe.

In record time, a special film, *Dwight D. Eisenhower,* was prepared and recorded in sixteen languages. It traced the General's entire career, his victories in Europe, and his home life. It stressed his infectious smile and humanitarian qualities. Within ten days, prints of the film were being rushed to twenty countries to pave the way for his tour of Europe. With Italian Government cooperation, U.S.I.S. officials had forty-nine prints of the film being shown in theaters in the major Italian cities within two days. It coincided with the General's arrival. In England ninety prints were rapidly circulated through the theater circuits. Within a few weeks, more than ten million Europeans saw the film.

By the time the General reached most of the countries on his quick tour, the Communist campaign against him had been blunted. In addition, he conducted himself with his usual superb sense of simple public relations. I recall how, before Eisenhower took off, his new deputy, General Alfred Gruenther, telephoned me to say Eisenhower had asked him to get my advice on how to conduct himself. I replied, "Al, we will prepare some written suggestions, but I feel a little as though Babe Ruth had asked me how to bat." I meant it. Of all the American leaders of his era, Eisenhower had the best sense of how to conduct himself among the statesmen and people of other nations. Though often addicted to resounding banalities, he could somehow utter them with a sincerity and a confident smile that made them magic.

The communist-rigged demonstrations against Eisenhower flopped in country after country for want of public support. Presently, diplomatic reports advised that the tide had turned and that Europe's morale was clearly on the upswing.

THE DEVELOPMENTS recorded in this chapter are just a few striking examples. There were failures, too, resulting largely from inexperience. But the successes explain in part why a small group of men and women have battled for years to get the United States Government, and particularly the Congress, to recognize the power of the word and to provide the funds, the manpower, and the consistent support needed. These men and women, representing both parties, have argued that relatively few millions of dollars spent on a continuing campaign of truth could multiply the effectiveness of billions spent on armaments and economic aid. They have admitted that a great propaganda campaign—a "truth campaign"—could have little effect if it were not accompanied by actual accomplishment on the military, economic, and political fronts. But they have insisted that billions spent on guns and factories and farms for the free world will be at least partly wasted if we fail systematically to make the facts known to millions on both sides of the Iron Curtain.

These champions know there is vast danger of oversimplifying the role of propaganda. Sheer volume of output is not enough. Subtlety is essential. By being too shrill, propaganda can defeat itself—as the Soviet's output, happily, has sometimes done. But they know that skilful, large-scale international persuasion can yield enormous returns.

This little group has made progress. Even the Congressional cynics who once sneered at the whole idea of an international information program now profess to oppose it "because it is not properly done." But scores of others in the Congress are still what I have called "foul weather friends" of the program. They support it when the Kremlin rattles the saber, when a Korean war breaks out, or when they are otherwise frightened. When there is a lull on the international scene—the very time when a truth campaign can make hay—they turn lukewarm and slash appropriations.

America's information-program budgets have gone up and down like a yo-yo. When Congress is frightened, personnel is hastily recruited, screened for loyalty and security, and laboriously trained. Then a lull descends, funds are cut, and much of the trained personnel returns to private industry. A few months later, the Kremlin growls again—and up goes the yo-yo. Meanwhile, our top propagandists have been so busy retrenching, expanding, and fighting to preserve any machinery at all that they have had too little time left to fight Soviet propaganda.

Happily, the trend is upward. For the first time in history both parties, in their platforms, have at least endorsed the concept of a Voice of America and related activities. With few exceptions, the men of true stature in both parties and in both houses of Congress give consistent support to the project, though such men are still a minority. We who have long urged such support will be happy if we can help persuade a majority of Congressmen to stay hitched, to approve as a continuing function of government a stable program involving perhaps one tenth of what the Soviet Union spends on propaganda. We will be happy if they will insure the stability needed to perfect an organization and to train manpower in this extraordinarily complex field. We will be happier still if they will recognize that an occasional slip is bound to occur in this work, with which Americans are relatively so unfamiliar. And we will be deliriously happy if Congressmen, when they suspect the Voice of America has a frog in its throat, will get out a bronchoscope, not a guillotine.

We Bumble Through

A WISE old public-relations man once said, "Good public relations is just acting right and letting people know about it."

The United States Government has only begun to learn that lesson. The nation has made strenuous efforts to "act right." Indeed, European historians sometimes say no nation in history has been less motivated, in its international conduct, by desire for self-aggrandizement. Some call it enlightened self-interest; some, international naïveté.

While "acting right," however, Americans have until recently lacked any sustained program for "letting people know about it." They are just beginning to learn what major corporations and organizations learned years ago: that, however good your policies or products, you won't get credit for them without a systematic program for telling about them. If you don't tell your own story, somebody else will tell it for you—and tell it wrong.

In the more distant past, the United States made brief spasmodic attempts at international public relations. Framers of the Declaration of Independence declared it was written out of "a decent respect to the opinions of mankind." Abraham Lincoln, seeking British support for the Union side, exported 1,750,000 booklets and more than 100 lecturers (including

Henry Ward Beecher) to England during the Civil War. President Wilson's Committee on Public Information, headed by George Creel, had the assignment of attempting international, as well as domestic, persuasion in the first World War. Creel worked effectively with Wilson and his Cabinet to achieve public pronouncements that would have the most helpful impact abroad. He set up an embryonic organization for distributing some of this information abroad. It began to register successes. Then the entire effort ended with the war.

The next attempt began with the outbreak of the second World War in Europe. Recognizing that Latin American public opinion was a serious problem, even leaning pro-Nazi-Fascist in some countries, the Administration in Washington undertook to do something about it. President Roosevelt assigned Nelson Rockefeller as Coordinator of Inter-American Affairs to undertake the job—along with much broader assignments in economic, financial, and socio-political fields. Rockefeller rounded up skilled newspapermen, advertising specialists, film executives, and others. A few of their first efforts fizzled. As can so often be the case, the simple transferring of American techniques to alien soil had unhappy effects. Latin Americans laughed at a few early advertisements, prepared by some of the United States' ablest copywriters, which were published in Latin American newspapers.

Soon, however, Rockefeller's people began to learn the pitfalls. More subtle presentation of the United States and anti-Axis cases began to pay off. Articles by distinguished writers on the Good Neighbor Policy were placed in Latin American periodicals. Skilful broadcasts on Latin American radio stations helped. Publications like the well-done *En Guardia,* produced by a private publisher under contract to C.I.A.A., proved effective. From South and Central America Rockefeller brought scores of journalists and specialists to the United States. They were encouraged to take a thorough look-see for themselves. When they returned home, at least ninety percent of them wrote and spoke sympathetically of this nation, its people, and its policies. Rockefeller supervised student-exchange programs. He set up information centers in Latin American cities, wisely putting them under binational auspices. They were financed at the outset largely by American funds but were supervised by a Brazilian-American committee in Brazil or a Mexican-American board in Mexico. Exchanges of radio programs and special movies, deftly created by Walt Disney, began to appear.

Rockefeller's C.I.A.A. (later O.I.A.A.—Office of Inter-American Affairs) emphasized mutual respect, cultural cooperation, and inter-American friendship. Recognizing that joint self-improvement projects can stimulate vast good will, C.I.A.A. information officers exploited the health, sanitation, and economic-development undertakings of their colleagues. But C.I.A.A.'s output was not all sweetness and light. To sway opportunists and bandwagon-jumpers, it hammered away with evidence of U. S. might and with the theme that "an Allied victory is inevitable."

The total impact of the Rockefeller program was unquestionably good. Few impartial students of the operation would deny that the U. S. cultural and information program helped substantially to produce the new era of inter-American good will in the 1940's. Meanwhile, Americans were doing nothing appreciable along that line in the rest of the world.

Then, in the spring of 1941, Robert E. Sherwood, distinguished as a playwright, grew alarmed as he watched propaganda warfare develop in Europe and saw us utterly unprepared. He talked about it with President Roosevelt and with William J. Donovan, whom Roosevelt had authorized to set up a small intelligence operation. Roosevelt liked Sherwood's ideas and arranged for him to head a new "Foreign Information Service" in Donovan's organization. Since Congress had authorized nothing of the sort, the whole arrangement was perhaps illegal.

Nonetheless, Donovan's nebulously defined "Office of the Coordinator of Information" was soon undertaking miscellaneous jobs ranging from cloak-and-dagger work abroad to the dissemination of perfectly open information about America. Its small international information operation was growing and functioning when the Japanese struck Pearl Harbor.

Here, too, American enthusiasm and blatant techniques produced some choice blunders at the outset. Two or three American-type ads appeared abroad and evoked the same kind of snickers as in Latin America. A few glib "experts" wormed their way into the hastily recruited staffs and remained there until they proved conclusively they were experts only at self-promotion. The content of some early broadcasts had dubious value. Occasionally, some new announcer in an exotic tongue would annoy far-off listeners with an accent that made static sound like a mother's lullaby. Too-enthusiastic advertising specialists offended European and Middle Eastern sensibilities with gift packets of candy and needles gaily emblazoned with American flags and slogans.

Inept translations also caused headaches. An occasional publication, hastily produced here in some foreign tongue, had to be pulped when it reached the scene. Perhaps the prize was a translation of the Four Freedoms on match packets for French areas. "Freedom from Want" somehow showed up as "*Liberté Corporale*," which meant only one thing to most Frenchmen. But, with that innate ability of Americans to learn rapidly, Donovan's people were soon doing substantial good work— even while they were weeding out the phonies, sacking bad translators, and abandoning most gift packets.

THE ROOSEVELT ADMINISTRATION, despite its many good points, had its own way of dealing with tough problems: just set up new agencies, then more agencies, then agencies to co-ordinate agencies. Early in the war, the President grew impatient with the stream of conflicting statements coming out of

Washington. So in June 1942, he set up the Office of War Information under Elmer Davis. O.W.I.'s primary assignment was that of coordinating the government's maze of domestic information activities. Almost incidentally, Sherwood's Foreign Information Service ended up in O.W.I. Sherwood and his international propaganda personnel were transferred in toto to O.W.I., while the miscellaneous hush-hush operations stayed in the Donovan office, by then renamed the Office of Strategic Services.

Ineptness and blunders did not automatically cease, though by now most were small in scale. Crates of pamphlets intended for Portugal showed up in Hawaii. A piano-sized packing case, marked "Rush," arrived in London. It contained only air—good Washington air, to be sure. A wireless operator, hastily hired to transmit a daily newsfile for the North African press, tapped the Morse key so crudely that an urgent message came back from far-off Algiers: IF MUST SEND WITH FOOT, PLEASE USE RIGHT FOOT.

As with Rockefeller's operation, the kinks were gradually ironed out. Eager-beaver workers soon learned you don't sell democracy to Danes and Arabs the way you sell soap in Sioux City. In selecting key executives and planners, O.W.I. began to put less emphasis on simple technical skills and more emphasis on first-hand knowledge of the customs, tastes, and susceptibilities of the particular audiences abroad. Ballyhoo experts gave way to area experts.

THE EXECUTIVES in Rockefeller's C.I.A.A., Donovan's C.O.I., and then Elmer Davis's O.W.I. early found it necessary to do something about the eleven short-wave stations broadcasting to overseas audiences. They first effected "voluntary coordination" with the private owners, then took the stations over and welded them into the first official Voice of America. They later added relay stations in Algiers, England, Hawaii, and Saipan. They set up information offices in nearly every accessible country abroad. They employed all standard public-relations de-vices. They devoted vast amounts of time to talking with for-eign editors, correcting false impressions about this country and its aims.

In friendly areas, the O.W.I.'s task was technically more in the field of information (to enlighten) than of propaganda (to influence). It was a job of using facts to combat lies, miscon-ceptions, and distrust. Activities covered the gamut: docu-mentary films of America's growing might amid its continuing freedoms; translations of notable American books; broadcasts, photo displays, and American libraries; talks before leadership groups and exchange-of-persons programs; news releases, press photos, and magazine articles; posters, film strips, and pam-phlets. The costs, great by some standards, were a small frac-tion of one percent of American arms costs.

Operating abroad under the label "United States Informa-tion Service," O.W.I. employees learned to select the tech-niques most effective in each area. They also learned that ingenuity, persistence, and sensitiveness to native tastes in friendly areas paid off; obvious, high-pressure selling did not.

Gradually most American ambassadors changed from skep-tics to warm supporters of the information program. The Brit-ish Minister of Information, Brendan Bracken, studied the quiet but wide-spread activities of the U.S.I.S. in Britain, then described it to the press as "one of the most efficient operations I have ever seen."

MEANWHILE, O.W.I.-trained civilians took the lead in newly formed psychological warfare units in military theaters. They worked with leaflets, loudspeakers, and short-range broadcasts.

Starting out as amateurs, and considered "screwballs" by the military, these units gradually became reasonably profi-cient psychological warfare teams, comprising British and American civilians and military, plus rare representatives from other United Nations. "Sykewar," as it became known, began to develop effectiveness in North Africa, improved in the Italian campaign, and was a smooth-functioning, integrated part of the Eisenhower force by the time of the Normandy invasion.

It rediscovered and perfected techniques, originated in World War I, for firing leaflet shells over particular units. It was widely credited with producing the mass surrender of complete German units, as at Cherbourg. In other cases, as at Aachen, concentrated Sykewar efforts utterly failed to produce such mass surrenders.

O.W.I. airborne newspapers produced in London for French, German, and other audiences were first sneered at by many American military authorities. Originally, they were distributed for O.W.I. only by the Royal Air Force. Long before the war's end they had won such recognition that the U. S. Eighth Air Force had a complete squadron of B-17's occupied exclusively with distributing the papers and three billion O.W.I. leaflets in the European theater.

The B.B.C., the O.W.I.'s ABSIE (American Broadcasting Station in Europe), the Voice of America, and the powerful Radio Luxembourg (which Allied forces had captured intact) came to be relied on by General Eisenhower and his top staff. Indeed, the SHAEF Command prepared a series of eighty-one special messages to be transmitted over these stations. Radio teams were brought in on the top-secret planning of major offensives.

Sykewar also undertook dozens of "special operations," in which Donovan's O.S.S. personnel figured prominently. These operations ranged from campaigns to impair the effectiveness of the Luftwaffe to "intruder broadcasts" which broke in on German home-front programs with disconcerting comments.

Detailed Sykewar plans for D-day alone covered several thousand pages. Prearranged broadcasts of alerts, communiques, warnings, and notices went out over the air. Coordinating their operations with the military timetable, planes dropped twenty-seven million leaflets, divided into seven categories, in

Metropolitan France. Another six million were dropped on other nations. One hundred transmitters carried previously recorded messages in many languages, from generals, presidents, sovereigns, and exiled leaders. Sykewar teams went ashore with the landing forces. Shells packed with leaflets followed by the hundreds. Mobile printing shops were pulled ashore from landing barges. So were loudspeaker units on wheels.

Once ashore, the Sykewar workers went to work with artillery-fired leaflets, loudspeaker messages, and local broadcasting. From Britain, they were backstopped by air-borne leaflets and B.B.C.–ABSIE broadcasts.

Six weeks later, British Foreign Secretary Anthony Eden reported to the House of Commons that seventy-seven percent of captured German prisoners in Europe admitted they had read Allied leaflets, and listened to Allied broadcasts, or both.

As occupied areas were newly liberated, Sykewar "consolidation propagandists" undertook the tremendous job of taking over all newspapers, radio stations, cinemas, and magazines in the country, cleaning them out, starting them up again, and gradually turning them over to trustworthy local personnel. In the case of Germany and Austria, this was necessarily a gigantic and slow process.

In the Pacific, Sykewar was slower in winning recognition from General MacArthur, General Stilwell, and others as a major instrument of warfare. Even here, Secretary of War Robert Patterson ultimately credited leaflets with being "a major factor" in the surrenders of nearly twenty thousand Japanese in the Philippines and on Okinawa. Notable work was done in Burma—even though GI's had to be trained not to shoot surrendering Japanese. The Captain Ellis Zacharias broadcasts to the Japanese élite over O.W.I. transmitters were widely, though not unanimously, hailed as triggering the final surrender of Japan. They demonstrated, as has often been noted, that radio doesn't always have to reach great masses in order to achieve results.

SOCIAL SCIENTISTS have found no way to measure precisely the effect of leaflets, broadcasts, and other Sykewar techniques. It is like trying to measure the precise effect of an Eisenhower speech or a Truman tour on a presidential election. Some of the more elaborate claims for Sykewar are not supported by concrete evidence. It can only be said that most of those who studied available data became convinced that the total Sykewar effort in World War II, errors and waste included, paid for itself many times over in terms of shortening the war and saving lives. Indeed, captured documents showed Field Marshal Guenther von Kluge, German Supreme Commander, reporting to Hitler shortly before the war's end, that Allied psychological warfare had reduced the capacity of German soldiers to fight.

Originally a skeptic, General Eisenhower examined the evidence and at the war's end attested: "I am convinced that the expenditure of men and money in wielding the spoken and written word was an important contributing factor in undermining the enemy's will to resist and supporting the fighting morale of our potential allies in the occupied countries. . . . Psychological warfare has proved its right to a place of dignity in our military arsenal."

WHILE O.W.I. Americans gradually learned the art of persuasion around the world, O.W.I. headquarters officers found the job of persuading Congress more difficult. They were forced to spend the bulk of the war fighting for the existence of the agency. Congressmen, like most citizens, found the very word "propaganda" distasteful. They particularly suspected any agency charged with "coordinating" information on the home front. It smacked of censorship. That background alone would have made the going hard for Davis. Specific developments made it more so.

When the President, in 1942, consolidated information operations in the O.W.I., several influential Americans urged him to name Elmer Davis as director of the agency. Davis had a standout reputation as a C.B.S. news analyst and as a former key member of the New York *Times* staff. He did not want the job but finally accepted in the belief that "in wartime the government has the right to draft any talent it wants."

In retrospect, most of Elmer Davis' wartime colleagues think he did a good job, though modesty often kept him from asserting the authority of himself and his agency as he probably should have. What he lacked in administrative aptitude he made up by appointing capable deputies like Milton Eisenhower, who served briefly, and Edward Klauber. The latter, serving as Associate Director from 1943 on, did a quiet but effective job of untangling snarls and of injecting added effectiveness into the output.

Davis' appointment won effusive praise from most of the press and radio commentators. Many Congressmen lauded him. However, his honeymoon in office proved short-lived. A dozen of the less objective members of Congress quickly singled out O.W.I. as an easy target. In so nebulous a field even the wildest charges could rarely be disproved.

One dyspeptic but powerful House member, who never showed much confidence in the minds of men anyway, took to pot-shotting at Davis regularly in vague but insulting terms. Once, questioned by the press, Davis answered back, "that's exactly what you would expect from him"—and then compared the Congressman's remarks with those of the Tokyo radio. Such *lèse-majesté* was never forgotten by the old man or by some of his colleagues.

Soon many Republicans and some Democrats in the House were voting consistently to cut O.W.I. funds. Once the House voted virtually to wipe out the agency. The appropriation was restored only after the responsible press raised a howl and after the Senate, always more sympathetic and constructive, voted strongly for the agency.

Some of O.W.I.'s habitual critics in and out of Congress frequently and vaguely charged "radicalism" and "disloyal staff," though Davis early set up a personnel loyalty division under a retired admiral, and obtained full assistance from the F.B.I. and other intelligence agencies in checking O.W.I.'s personnel. The critics often charged that O.W.I. was a "collection of incompetents," even though the list of the agency's key men now reads like a Who's Who in the publishing, news, radio, film, and advertising fields. * Critics seemed to favor the epithets "ineffectiveness" and "wastefulness." They sometimes cited an incident or two; more often they cited nothing.

THERE WAS, indeed, some waste and inefficiency in O.W.I. Trial and error, involving some waste, are standard procedures in even well-organized advertising and public-relations businesses. O.W.I. was hardly well organized in its early days. Rather, it was put together on a "crash" basis to meet a wartime emergency. Time was needed to shake down the organization, to replace misfits, and to eliminate ineffective techniques.

By the war's end, I had served in a half dozen O.W.I. and Sykewar assignments in the United States and abroad, ending up as Bob Sherwood's successor in the post of Director of Overseas Operations. When I finally returned to the editing business soon after Japan's collapse, I wrote my O.W.I. colleagues in complete sincerity: "I have seen this team carry on

* Among O.W.I. alumni: the publishers of *Time, Look, Fortune,* and several dailies; editors of such magazines as *Holiday, Coronet, Parade,* and the *Saturday Review;* editors of the Denver *Post,* New Orleans *Times-Picayune,* and others; the heads of Viking Press, Harper & Brothers, and Farrar, Straus and Young; two Hollywood Oscar winners; a two-time Pulitzer prize-winner; the board chairman of C.B.S., and a dozen key network executives; President Eisenhower's chief speech-writer; the editor of the *Reader's Digest's* international editions; at least six partners of large advertising agencies; and a dozen noted social scientists.

with steadfastness and determination in the face of incredibly unjust attacks. And I have seen it carry on with modesty when the vast majority of those who studied its record finally came out in enthusiastic support of its work. I can only say that I never have and probably never shall work in an organization whose members individually and collectively have won my admiration to a greater degree."

In Congress, where a few critics were voluble, nearly all of those who had actually investigated the agency's work abroad finally came to its defense. A notable case involved Representative Everett Dirksen of Illinois, a consistent O.W.I. critic and hardly famed as a friend of Democratic Administrations. He took a trip around the world to "check up" on O.W.I. and other government operations. When he returned home in 1945, anti-O.W.I. forces counted on him to buttress their current move to wipe out the "worse-than-useless" agency. Instead, he shocked them by requesting a chance to testify before a Senate committee and there dropping this bombshell: "I must say that they (O.W.I. men) have done a good job. . . . Area commanders generally were all very high in their praise of the O.W.I. . . . The personnel are all a high type of men. They are doing an efficient job."

A few elements of the extremist press, both right and left, never conceded that the agency did anything well at any time. They ended up with only limited support from responsible papers, however. Among standard newspapers, John S. Knight's Detroit *Free Press* had been particularly skeptical of "O.W.I. boondoggling." By July 30, 1945, even the *Free Press* ran the following dispatch from its featured correspondent, Edwin A. Lahey: "I have had a glimpse of the impact of the O.W.I. on the masses of India and China, and the next wisenheimer in Washington who tries to tell me that O.W.I. is a boondoggle is going to have an argument on his hands. . . . The work will be paying dividends in friendship, understanding, and cash business for the United States when the Congressional hecklers of O.W.I. are ridiculous footnotes in our history text-books."

The New York *Times,* critical at earlier times, editorialized: "As Mr. Davis cleans out his desk he can feel that he has not only done a first-class job in time of war but has established precedents which will be useful in peacetime. . . . O.W.I. gets a 'well done.' "

Such diverse individuals as General MacArthur, Secretary of State Hull, General Eisenhower, and Anthony Eden publicly commended the agency's record. From the late Henry L. Stimson, the respected Secretary of War, came the spontaneous statement, on September 6, 1945: "I feel that the Office of War Information deserves specific praise for the contribution of its psychological warfare program toward the defeat of our enemies. . . . The part played by the O.W.I. . . . was significant in hastening surrender in all theaters, thereby saving the lives of many people in service and conserving our national resources."

4

Wartime Close-ups

A N Y politico supervising a national presidential campaign quickly realizes he cannot rely on any one technique of persuasion. He needs them all: local and national radio and TV, stump speeches, handouts, ads, posters, pamphlets, and billboards. The candidate should stick to consistent lines of argument, but he and his supporters must vary the emphasis according to locality and audience.

Magnify that picture a hundredfold and you get the problem confronting America's wartime operations in the foreign information field. Those of us specializing in international persuasion soon found it to be amazingly intricate business, with techniques and emphases varying from country to country. In each area of wartime operations we made mistakes, we scored successes, and we learned lessons.

The last chapter covered in broad strokes the development of organized persuasion in World War II. To point up the lessons of experience, however, it is worthwhile to examine in detail a few segments of the broad canvas.

AFRICAN TEST TUBE

As THE MISTS rose on the North African coasts on the morning of November 8, 1942, American psychological warfare entered

34

its first large-scale tryout. Aboard the U.S.S. *Texas,* part of a gigantic invasion fleet, a hastily trained crew of psychological warriors, mostly from O.W.I., started broadcasting in French. They used a standard medium-wave transmitter specially installed for the purpose. They told civilians and military in the Casablanca area of the "friendly landings," explaining it as the first step in "the liberation phase of the war." They broadcast previously recorded announcements from Roosevelt and Eisenhower, appealing to the long-standing Franco-American friendship and urging support for the Allied landings.

Meanwhile, similar messages were going out from transmitters in the United States and Britain. In New York, O.W.I. had locked a small group of radio specialists in a large room, told them of the forthcoming landings, set them to work on scripts, and kept them under guard to insure against leaks of information until the first flash came from the invasion fleet. The bulk of their radio output was designed to win the cooperation of the French in North Africa. Subsidiary broadcasts to other areas had other purposes: to apprise the peoples of Europe of the new Allied offensive; to caution resistance groups on the continent against interpreting the news as a signal for coming into the open; to throw the Nazis off balance by implying that there might be Allied landings elsewhere.

In Africa itself there were the kind of flubs to be expected in such novel operations. The U.S.S. *Texas* broadcasts, successful at first, ended abruptly when the ship fired a salvo and knocked out the temporary transmitter. Loudspeakers, mounted on a destroyer coming into Oran, could no longer be heard when shore batteries fired at the landing force. But at three other points, O.W.I. men on landing craft used simple megaphones and persuaded French coastal guards to hold their fire. When the small psychological warfare crews, largely civilians in military uniforms, went ashore, they suffered from inadequate organization and communications. They also suffered from "lack of logistical support"—militarese for the fact that they never could find the radio sets, typewriters, and other equipment that were supposed to be sent there for them.

Nonetheless, in the early days after the landings, they took over the North African radio stations and newspapers. They saw to it that the statements of Roosevelt and Eisenhower were featured. They brought the citizenry up to date on world events which Nazi collaborators had largely suppressed for two years. They seized movie houses and impounded anti-Allied films. They removed German and pro-Vichy posters, replacing them with previously prepared Allied posters. The Eisenhower Command, though baffled by what Chief of Staff Bedell Smith once called "this collection of screwballs," later credited the crew with making the landings and occupation easier for the Allied forces.

It early became necessary to weed out a few prima donnas and to whip this band of psychological operators into something at least approaching a military unit. The job first fell under Colonel C. B. Hazeltine and later was made a part of a broader assignment given Brig. Gen. Robert A. McClure. Both were regular officers having no background in the field. Both were happy choices, however. They recognized their limitations, were willing to bend military rigidity to accommodate such an operation, and proved superb at scrounging the equipment, quarters, and "support" needed. And military rigidity was indeed bent to accommodate the fact that much of the best talent available consisted of a motley collection of 4-F's and other American and British civilians.

On purely military operations, like the firing of leaflets over enemy lines, the traditions of military hierarchy were maintained. On editorial operations, talent alone determined each man's responsibility—and in a way that made the stuffier officers wince. I remember my first impression upon arriving for a special assignment in the Algiers headquarters operation in the summer of 1943. As I entered the newsroom, I found Corporal David Schoenbrun (later a top C.B.S. correspondent) at the editor's desk. The corporal was tongue-lashing a captain for a story the latter had turned in. Later he handed it to a civilian to rewrite.

Enthusiasm for the job, however, soon overcame any hurt feelings. Within weeks the group had organized reasonably smooth news and leaflet operations, plus an intelligence unit to provide the data on enemy morale which is indispensible for such propaganda. Within a few months after the landings, the crew had set up a giant transmitter (formerly WABC, New York) outside of Algiers. It had also taken over two French transmitters and linked the three together into what we called "the United Nations Radio." We used it as the voice of the Allied Forces Headquarters broadcasting to the people of France, Italy, and Germany. It also served to relay important Voice of America and B.B.C. programs aimed at the same audiences.

Soon skeptical field commanders had been persuaded to co-operate in this new-fangled business. They found that where German and Italian forces in North Africa were hard pressed, handsomely printed leaflets labeled "Safe Conduct Passes" led enemy troops to give up in droves, waving the little sheets of paper that guaranteed them safety and fair treatment. Some commanders even became too enthusiastic and expected propaganda to work miracles. They had to learn that Safe Conduct Passes yielded almost no prisoners when the enemy was not under heavy pressure.

Before the Tunisian campaign was over, the Psychological Warfare Branch had printed almost fifteen million leaflets. They were delivered mostly by the air forces; some by leaflet shells. In the last eight days of the campaign, a total of 248,000 German and Italian prisoners gave themselves up, an uncounted number of them waving Safe Conduct Passes. It was a revolutionary development in war. At Stalingrad, Germans had fought to the limit of their endurance and resources. In Tunisia, similar Germans surrendered in droves well before their supplies and strength had been exhausted. Top brass at Allied Forces Headquarters credited psychological warfare with much of the accomplishment.

After that, Sykewar had status. More smoothly functioning P.W.B. teams brought increased successes in the Italian campaign. By the time of the D-day landings in Normandy, General McClure, now a seasoned veteran in the field, had a thoroughly integrated civilian-military organization. It included such O.W.I. veterans as C. D. Jackson, later publisher of *Fortune;* William S. Paley, now chairman of the Columbia Broadcasting System; and William Harlan Hale, one of the ablest German-language propagandists developed by O.W.I. McClure's Psychological Warfare Division, with teams at all levels in the vast invasion force, worked according to an extensive and detailed program which was an integral part of the top military invasion plan.

SIEGE BY LOUDSPEAKER

On June 26, 1944, an American regiment had been pounding at a German unit for two days. The Germans were cut off but fighting fiercely. The American colonel in charge ordered a Sykewar mobile loudspeaker into position, halted his artillery, and told his infantry to cease fire. Then the loudspeaker unit spoke in German in approximately these words:

> Your position is hopeless. If you come over to us, you will be treated as honorable prisoners-of-war. if you persist in fighting you will sacrifice your lives in vain. It is for you to decide whether you desire to see your fatherland again or to be buried here in France. You have ten minutes in which to decide. Should you desire to come over, you will approach this truck with your hands on your heads and showing a white emblem.

The loudspeaker then counted off the minutes. After five, a few Germans with white flags appeared. Soon the number grew to six hundred. Then a captain appeared. He reported that the commanding colonel didn't feel he could "honorably" surrender to a loudspeaker. However, he hinted, the force had no defense against phosphorous grenades. The Americans obligingly threw a half-dozen grenades toward the colonel's position. That obviously constituted "overwhelming force." The colonel came over with the rest of his men.

Next day psychological warfare again was tried—this time against a force of a thousand or so holding out in a strongly fortified arsenal in Cherbourg. Interrogation of prisoners of the previous day had confirmed a lesson of North Africa and Italy: that, to induce a German soldier to surrender, it is wise to assuage his pride and "honor." So the loudspeaker unit added to its message: "You have fought bravely and distinguished yourselves. You have done honor to your country." Again the Germans surrendered en masse—but only after arrangements had been made for the German general in command to be threatened by a tank.

"Seige by loudspeaker" later worked at other points. At still others it failed dismally—notably at Aachen, where commanders and Sykewar units were inexperienced. From successes and failures, the specialists learned lessons: Those writing the messages must have detailed, up-to-date intelligence on enemy morals. Loudspeaker messages must be coordinated completely with other weapons; sometimes bursts of gunfire and persuasion must be interspersed. They should not be tried until the enemy is hard-pressed and preferably not until after leaflets have impressed him with his "hopeless situation." Instead of "threats," Sykewar should give "warnings." Instead of "surrender," it should invite "coming over." It should never (as at Aachen) issue an "ultimatum" or cast doubts on the commander's heroism in the eyes of his troops. It should always make his surrender seem an honorable yielding agreed to only when all hope was gone.

PERSUASION IN ICELAND

WHILE so-called "Sykewarriors" were working on the enemy, other forces were assigned to try techniques of persuasion on citizens in nominally friendly or neutral countries. Again, as in a political campaign, no single technique would succeed universally. All channels of information were needed in varying degrees. The case of one small nation illustrates the point.

Early in the war, U. S. forces, which had been rushed to Iceland to protect it from Nazi invasion, ran into severe public-relations problems. The unmilitaristic Icelanders disliked the presence of American troops, who all but outnumbered the population of the capital city. Also, just as GI's had expected to find igloos instead of modern homes in Iceland, the highly literate Iceland citizens tended to look on Americans as boorish characters out of Western films. Army authorities called on the O.W.I. for help.

Arriving on the scene, a small O.W.I. team talked the situation over with military commanders, Iceland Government officials, editors, and radio representatives. They began supplying the press with articles and photos about U. S. participation in the war. These underscored the reasons for the presence of the troops and their role in maintaining Iceland's security and independence. They presented the GI's as the friendly human beings they are. Plastic printing plates of American photos were supplied to, and printed in, local papers. American books, magazines, and special feature stories were made available to editors and educators. Soon a good deal of the material was appearing in the Icelandic press.

As the American specialists began to show genuine interest in Iceland's own art, education, and medicine, doors were opened all over Iceland. Mutual Icelandic-American projects got under way.

Photo exhibit material was provided to schools and club

groups. An American O.W.I. staff member lectured on American art at the Iceland University. And American classical recordings were lent to the Iceland Broadcasting Service for use in its radio programs.

Radio broadcasts, ostensibly directed to the armed forces, carried messages from U. S. leaders emphasizing common bonds of interest between Americans and Icelanders. Interviews with armed forces personnel, recorded music, news, and information about American life were featured in broadcasts over the Icelandic radio. Recorded interviews with Icelanders in America and live interviews with prominent Icelanders on their specialties were broadcast. The programs attracted and held Icelandic listeners.

O.W.I.'s United Newsreels were included in local theaters' programs, and 16mm. American documentaries were shown by the score in towns and villages throughout the country.

Musicians in the American services won plaudits from the Icelanders for their concerts. The leading actress in Iceland added to her laurels when she was starred in a play with a cast of U. S. service personnel.

Supplementing the work through press, radio, and films, American newsletters on science, agriculture, medicine, education, and the arts roused wonder and won respect for U. S. achievements in these fields. They made a good impression for America because they were "helpful" to Icelanders.

Before long, harmonious relations existed between Icelanders and armed forces. The Icelanders became increasingly aware that the United States was not altogether a nation of uncultured boors. The press (except for a few Communist organs) came to be consistently friendly toward the United States and reported the inevitable "military-civilian" incidents factually and without fanfare.

Once, the chief of the O.W.I. office, chiding a member of the Iceland *Althing* (Parliament) for his skepticism, was told, "We are a tiny nation, and suspicion is our navy." When the same chief, Porter McKeever, finished his tour of duty, a group of Icelanders gave him a farewell banquet. The *Althing* member rose, raised his glass, and proposed a toast to the American information operation, "which has sunk the Icelandic navy."

Perhaps the best testimonial to the whole program came when the Icelandic Government asked the help of the American agency in organizing a similar foreign information service of its own.

VICHY OUTPOST

EARLY in the war, the United States' continued recognition of the collaborationist Vichy Government of France caused prolonged headaches. Throughout Europe, America seemed to average citizens like a nation which mouthed pious principles, then cooperated with the worst forces of reaction. Actually, it was Churchill who had begged Roosevelt to maintain an embassy at Vichy. Over some State Department objections, Roosevelt had gone along. He ordered Ambassador Leahy to fight a rear-guard action there—to try to slow down Vichy collaboration with the Nazis, to block French concessions to Berlin, and to try to keep the French Navy out of German hands.

At least one small by-product of the continued recognition stands out. The chargé d'affairs whom the U. S. kept at Vichy, Somerville Pinkney Tuck, and his assistant, Douglas MacArthur, nephew of the general, did yeoman work in directing the fire of Allied broadcasts to France. They supplied the Voice of America and the B.B.C. with the moving speeches of Herriot and others against the abandonment of republican institutions in France, protests that had been suppressed by the Vichy Government. Broadcast back, these helped immensely to awaken Frenchmen who had been taken in by Vichy. Tuck cabled secret information about Laval's plans to force French workers into service in German war factories. His flow of information, beamed back to France, permitted many Frenchmen to hide out and join the resistance movement before Laval's round-up could catch them.

DARLAN DILEMMA

IF AMERICA's Vichy policy caused headaches, its cooperation with Darlan in North Africa caused all but rigor mortis in the psychological offensive.

Eisenhower, soon after the North African landings, appraised his whole problem: His armed force just about equaled that of the Vichy army in North Africa. Better equipped, it could eventually win out in open warfare against French resistance but only at great cost. French troops, who had taken oaths of allegiance, would obey no one but Admiral Darlan. The best information available indicated that Eisenhower could easily bring North Africa into the war on his side, seize Tunisia, bring Dakar over to the Allies, and perhaps lure the French fleet from Toulon—but only if he had Darlan's cooperation. Without such cooperation, intelligence indicated, the first American drive against Germany and Italy would deteriorate into large-scale police actions against Frenchmen. Eisenhower followed what appeared to be the only course to save American lives—he made an alliance with Darlan.

The strictly military wisdom of his course is undeniable. The politico-psychological drawbacks were enormous. To the majority of Europeans, America itself was collaborating with the worst forces of pro-fascist reaction. After many days of delay, and after much pleading by American propagandists, President Roosevelt publicly labeled the Darlan arrangement "only a temporary expedient justified solely by the stress of battle." "The future French Government," the President added, "will be established, not by any individual in Metropolitan France or overseas, but by the French people themselves after they had been set free by the victory of the United Nations."

That helped to allay fears among America's historic friends, but it came too late to overcome most of the damage already done. Later, Roosevelt, Churchill, and Eisenhower quietly forced Darlan to release political prisoners in North Africa and thwarted his plans to make himself chief of all French representatives and installations outside Metropolitan France. Tragically, however, U. S. officials would say nothing about this to the world. As Wallace Carroll reports in his excellent history of the period, it is probable that only Darlan's assassination by a French royalist student on December 24, 1942, kept the situation from getting worse.

The lesson to be learned is obvious: To win and hold the hearts of men of good will, the U. S. must be wary of individual acts of expediency which seem to belie its fundamental principles. There will, however, be inevitable occasions when concessions to expediency will be necessary, perhaps to save American lives. In these cases, the U. S. must make extraordinary efforts to state its case to the world as promptly and as frankly as possible.

"UNCONDITIONAL SURRENDER"

HISTORIANS will argue from now to doomsday as to whether the Roosevelt-Churchill insistence on "unconditional surrender" by the Germans prolonged the war and cost additional lives. Indeed, they have already filled chapters of history books with the argument.

It had been Roosevelt's idea, first enunciated at Casablanca. He was aware of the way Hitler and Goebbels, in the Nazis' struggle for power in Germany, had made effective use of the legend that Germany had not been defeated in the first World War but had been tricked into surrendering by the "false promises in Wilson's Fourteen Points." Neither he nor Churchill wanted any such legend to come out of this war. They also agreed that the Allied cause would suffer from the existence of any doubts about Allied determination to win the war. Such doubts would leave the way open for Nazi propaganda and "soft peace" advocates to sow suspicion among Allied powers and demoralize resistance movements. So, with the exception of one occasion—when they spoke of "honorable capitulation" in a joint message to the Italian people—the two leaders persistently stuck to the unconditional-surrender position in Europe.

Many Sykewar specialists complained about the term as much as did the majority of American generals. Indeed, I at least helped to pressure the President in 1944 into partly defining the term. The President said: "The German people are not going to be enslaved. Why? Because the United Nations do not traffic in human slavery. But it will be necessary for them to earn their way back into the fellowship of peace-loving and law-abiding nations. And in their climb up that steep road, we shall certainly see to it that they are not encumbered by having to carry guns."

By the war's end, a majority—but not all—of the Sykewar specialists reluctantly agreed that the Roosevelt-Churchill insistence on unconditional surrender had probably been wise in the case of Germany. It had clearly avoided the sort of "fourteen point alibi" with which Germans could plague us in the future. It stimulated the Allied peoples to recognize that this was an all-or-none "war of survival." It encouraged resistance groups in occupied countries to believe that their liberation could never be the subject of negotiations and conditions. It recognized that the Allies had no disposition to negotiate with either the Nazi or the German military hierarchy. And it undermined the rumors that any one of the Allies might break away and make a separate peace with Germany. It doubtless made the Sykewar job tougher, but it still left considerable room for maneuver and, on balance, was probably for the best.

Rarely cited evidence appeared in a postwar study of German attitudes by the U. S. Strategic Bombing Survey. It found that 54% of the sampled German population expressed themselves as having been willing to accept unconditional surrender; 19% had regarded it as inevitable; 16% "didn't know"; and only 11% had been unwilling to accept unconditional surrender.

TARGET: THE ETERNAL CITY

AT THE HEIGHT of the fighting in Italy, the British and American governments found that the gigantic rail yards of Rome were a constant beehive of German activity, seething with German reinforcements and supplies. After long deliberation, they authorized Eisenhower to bomb the yards—but with every precaution taken to minimize the unfavorable repercussions from dropping bombs on the Eternal City.

The U. S. Air Force carefully coached pilots and bombadiers to avoid Vatican City or other cultural and religious structures. On July 3, 1943, they dropped leaflets, warning the people in the capital that continued German use of the rail yards would force the Allies to bomb them as military targets. Elaborate plans were laid to tell the Allied story of the forthcoming bombing before Hitler's propagandists could scream about "atrocities" committed by "Anglo-Saxon barbarians." On the night of July 18, a trusted courier brought to the New York O.W.I. office, where I was then assigned, a sealed envelope on the bombing attack to be made early the next morning. We who were in charge rounded up a crew of script writers and translators and locked them in a room to insure security. For five hours they prepared material in Italian and other languages. At 5:21 A.M., six minutes after the first bomb had fallen on Rome, the Voice of America interrupted all its radio programs to Europe to announce the news, followed by carefully prepared announcements of the reasons for the bombing and the efforts to avoid non-military areas. Immediately thereafter, the O.W.I. radiophoto network began transmitting around the world a map showing the rail yards and their distance from Vatican City and other shrines.

It developed that the bombers had badly damaged the rail yards but unfortunately did some damage to a nearby religious building. Careful propaganda handling, however, eased the psychological effect. Reaction even in heavily Catholic areas of the world was mild. Most Catholics welcomed the news as an indication that the Allies were fighting an all-out war but were doing so decently and responsibly. The morale effect in Italy was even more helpful than anticipated. Coming on top of the Allied landings in Sicily, the daylight raid on the Rome rail yards was a final shock to the Mussolini regime. Within six days, the Fascist Grand Council had turned against Mussolini. The king had accepted his resignation, and Badoglio began seeking a peace with the United Nations.

A FLEET SURRENDERS

AT 5:30 P.M. on September 8, 1943, General Eisenhower announced over the United Nations Radio at Algiers that the Italian Government under General Badoglio had surrendered. The Italian fleet, however, had not surrendered. It was still intact. In Algiers, Maurice Pierce, an O.W.I. engineer, ingeniously switched the wave length of one transmitter to the international distress frequency, to which all naval vessels are supposed to listen. News of the surrender and instructions to the Italian fleet were broadcast over this frequency every fifteen minutes. Within three days the Italian fleet from Spezia sailed into Britain's naval base at Malta. It was then that Admiral Cunningham turned to an aide and said with gracious hyperbole, "Tell General McClure [Sykewar head] that they've accomplished in one day with propaganda what I've been trying to do for three years."

ONE MEASURE OF IMPACT

RARELY was O.W.I. able to gage with any accuracy the impact of American propaganda. In the first place, Sykewar operators were too busy for elaborate post mortems. Secondly, there was almost no field of human endeavor so difficult to measure. In one notable case, however, it was possible to gage the impact of the "propaganda of truth."

Shortly after the war, O.W.I. prepared and printed "K–Z," an extensively illustrated factual booklet on the horrors of Buchenwald, Belsen, and other Nazi concentration camps. We in O.W.I. felt that such carefully documented evidence of Nazi brutality, distributed by the millions among Germans, would help convince them of Nazi war guilt.

As a test, we gave copies of the booklet to 127 German prisoners in Europe. Then we selected a control group of 127 others so carefully matched that every man in the first group had a counterpart in the second as to age, occupation, and education. The second group did not see the booklet. We then gave both groups identical questionnaires.

Only 49% of those who had not seen the booklet admitted that Germany was more to blame than Great Britain or America for starting the war. Of those who had read the booklet, 68% said that Germany was more to blame than the other nations.

Only 35% of the control group said that German treatment of Jews was unjustified. Of the group who had read it, 57% answered "yes." Those who had read the booklet were asked whether they believed the atrocity facts as presented: 77% said they did; 3% called the booklet propaganda; 20% expressed no opinion.

GIFT PACKETS

As NOTED earlier, the tendency of American advertising specialists to spread gift packets over foreign countrysides usually kicked back.

Some O.W.I. hands tried shipping to Iceland batches of candy bearing a message of friendship from the children of the U. S. to the children of Iceland. Fortunately, representatives on the scene tried out the items on a few citizens. The Icelanders were incensed; they could provide candy for their own children, thank you, and they didn't welcome such patronage. The candy was hastily stashed away by the O.W.I. staff.

The idea, however, was not invariably a dud, proving again that every idea has to be gaged by local tastes and mores. A young Briton, hired by the O.W.I. in Burma because of his intimate knowledge of the people and dialects of the area, tried the give-away scheme in another guise. He found that the Japanese occupying parts of north and central Burma had consumed all grain and left the tribesmen without seeds for their next planting. The Allies needed the good will of these tribesmen to help in the rescue of aviators lost on Hump flights, to pave the way for the eventual reopening of the Burma Road, and to help with the Wingate commando operation.

Guided by the savvy young Briton, O.W.I. procured American seeds and had packets printed in India bearing Shan and Kachin instructions and good-will messages. Then, without bothering the high brass, O.W.I. persuaded a couple of bomber pilots to drop the seed packets on jungle trails as they returned from missions. The Shans and Kachins thereafter became sympathizers, helped downed U. S. aviators, assisted commando operations, and began to sabotage the Nipponese. The Japanese, troubled by all this, made a typical propaganda error. They told the natives the seeds would not grow and that the plants would prove poisonous. They added that the seeds, in fact, were taboo. The natives found the seeds did grow and that the produce was highly edible. So the Japanese had lied, they concluded. Moreover, they didn't like outsiders telling them what is or is not taboo.

The "packet racket" confirmed old lessons: that tactical propaganda decisions made on the spot are usually far better than those made in Washington offices; that friendly, helpful propaganda is particularly effective among primitives; that if people think in terms of villages, it is necessary to talk to them, not in cosmic terms but on a village level.

We Start Over

EVEN before General Douglas MacArthur, aboard the battleship *Missouri,* intoned the words that officially ended World War II, American citizens and politicos had begun to cry for "bringing the boys home" as quickly as possible. In Washington the same voices that called for immediate disarmament began demanding prompt disbanding of "all those war agencies." As for international information work: "Well, we've sure shown the world plenty. We shouldn't have to spend a lot of tax dollars telling 'em things."

A number of journalistic specialists on foreign affairs had begun to call for a continuing campaign of persuasion abroad if the U. S. was not to lose the peace. A minority in Congress also saw the need for, and urged, some permanent information agency. The majority, however, tended almost as much toward disarmament in the international information field as in the military field.

It was against this background that most of us who had been asked to make recommendations on the future of international information urged that the O.W.I. and O.I.A.A. organizations be cut down and transferred to the Department of State. That seemed the logical place for such work. Moreover, we felt that putting it under the cloak of an old-line agency afforded the best way for preserving at least those minimum functions which were sure to be necessary if the United States were not to lose what it had won through enormous military sacrifice. The State Department was then under ex-Senator James Byrnes, who was still popular in the Congress and whom no one accused of leftist leanings even though he was still energetically trying to cooperate with the U.S.S.R. There were other reasons for recommending that the State Department should take over future information work. Just as wartime Sykewar had to be dovetailed with the military effort, so peacetime persuasion needed to be tied in as closely as possible with foreign policy. Indeed, the Army's own General Board at the end of the war reported, "In its broader aspects, propaganda warfare is more properly a State Department than a War Department problem."

That same Army General Board report pointed to another reason for putting the work in the State Department: the urgent need for awakening the Department to the needs of twentieth-century diplomacy. "Peacetime propaganda," the Board reported, "is a neglected and ineptly used political and diplomatic weapon." We propagandists could only say Amen. Some men in the Department had begun to recognize the weapon. Many of the more traditional career men disliked the idea, didn't think it was necessary, and preferred to have nothing to do with it. If only they could be forced, we reasoned, to take the orphan of international information into the family, they would come to know it, recognize its worth, and learn to put it to work.

Out of this reasoning came the President's Executive Order 9608 of August 31, 1945. It transferred the overseas information functions of O.W.I. and O.I.A.A. to an Interim International Information Service in the Department of State. It asked the Secretary of State to study the problem of a permanent service and make recommendations. It added, "The nature of present day foreign relations makes it essential for the United

States to maintain information activities abroad as an integral part of the conduct of our foreign affairs."

Actually, many Departmental officers were not so sure the President was right. Secretary Byrnes himself, though astute in domestic public relations, had little appreciation for international information. Many in Congress were extremely skeptical.

It was into this jumbled picture that William Benton was tossed in August of 1945, when President Truman and Secretary Byrnes put him into the position of Assistant Secretary of State for Public Affairs. He had made a small fortune in advertising (Benton & Bowles), then turned college executive (University of Chicago), publisher (Encyclopædia Britannica), and purveyor of music (Musak). All these careers added together, he later said, presented about one one-hundredth of the problem of his new job.

Sensing the Congressional mood, Benton carried much further the cutbacks already started by O.W.I. and O.I.A.A. He dropped all the wartime magazines like *Victory, En Guardia, Voir,* and *Photo Review,* with the exception of the Russian-language *Amerika.* He dropped O.W.I.'s radiophoto system, cut the overseas news service by eighty percent, slashed radio programming, and began a large-scale reduction of personnel.

Benton and his colleagues later concluded that he had gone too far. He didn't even get from the Bureau of the Budget and from Congress the credit he anticipated. The Bureau cut his budget still further. Instead of commending him for the sort of wholesale reductions that oratorical economizers perennially shout for, a group in Congress then went to work on his budget with a vengeance. But by painstakingly explaining the program to one Congressman after another, Benton stemmed the tide. In a long and drearily complex series of Congressional proceedings, Benton barely managed to save his skeleton information operation.

Meanwhile, he found his international information service

in the traditional role of the illegitimate child at a family re-
union. Only a minority of key State Department officials recognized its value or saw any use for it. Many of them ultimately
came around, but the going was slow.

BENTON'S battle for a permanent information service took
place against an international backdrop that seems curious
today. The United States had come out of the war with top
leaders hoping and often believing that the Soviet Union
would cooperate, that it would maintain a practical working
relationship permitting unity of the great powers within the
framework of the United Nations. Walter Lippmann had not
yet popularized the phrase "cold war." Almost no one challenged Truman when he sought to work cooperatively with
the U.S.S.R. No one publicly questioned Eisenhower when
he told a Congressional committee that "there is no one thing
that guides the policy of Russia more today than to keep
friendship with the United States." Only a few hands like
Ambassador Averell Harriman and former Ambassador Lau-
rence Steinhardt, who had tried to work with the Kremlin
masters in Moscow, voiced serious warnings.

In retrospect, the United States was probably sound in its
course, sound in at least trying to work with Soviet Russia. If
America had not made full-scale and patently honest efforts to
cooperate, other nations of the world would never have supported the United States when it was finally forced to give up
that course and embark on a great program of collective security. If one never even tries to get along with neighbor Jones,
he will have little sympathy from other neighbors when bricks
start flying over the back fence. America's mistake, it is now
evident, was not in trying to work with the Kremlin. That was
a necessary first step. The error lay, first, in throwing away the
nation's armed strength. It lay, second, in failure to plan a
long-term alternative to cooperation.

That latter course should have been reasonably clear. It was to strengthen the nation's bonds with like-minded allies, to convince their citizens and governments that their aims and America's were alike, to help them recover, and to agree with them on maintaining reasonable armed strength at least until there was firm evidence that the Soviet bloc would work with the free nations. It should have been clear then, as it is now, that the characters in the Kremlin are most likely to cooperate when they realize the other party has somewhere else to turn.

Instead, we Americans behaved for two years almost as though we wished to deprive ourselves of any alternative course. Administration and Congress, yielding to enormous public pressure, disarmed the nation as rapidly as was humanly possible. At the same time, in matters of international good will, we seemed almost to be striving to do the Kremlin's work for it.

The most promising of all U. S. alliances in wartime was probably that with Britain. No single American action had done more to win British hearts than Lend-Lease. Yet immediately after the Japanese surrender President Truman abruptly announced the end of Lend-Lease. He had to end it quickly under the law. He did not have to do so without any prior discussion whatever with Britain's leaders. Learning of the action from the press, the British looked upon it as a conscious affront. Having invested $25,000,000,000 in Lend-Lease to Britain, America virtually threw away all the resultant good will, not by terminating Lend-Lease, but by doing it abruptly and tactlessly.

Next, the Congress managed to turn a new act of generosity toward Britain into an instrument for winning ill will. It voted to cancel Britain's $25,000,000,000 Lend-Lease debt and to extend $3,757,000,000 in new credit. To some, this may have seemed overgenerous aid even to a nation that had stood alone in thwarting the Axis in that long period before America was an active, effective combatant. Yet, by publicly treating Britain like an indolent relief client, we strangely managed to get more ill will than good out of the generosity. Over strenuous objections from more far-sighted members, a majority in Congress imposed impossible conditions on the loan, so impossible that the same Congress struck out the conditions the next year. More important, the public debates in Congress reflected so much hostility and misguided contempt for the British that Americans appeared to the world to be throwing coins at a despised beggar.

The Soviet Union, meanwhile, had started a concerted campaign to widen every small crevice between the United States and other free nations. Americans grudgingly gave aid to others, Soviet propaganda said, only to stave off the inevitable collapse of the U. S. economy. It added that Americans were determined to remake other nations in the image of themselves, then turn them into American economic colonies; it was all part of a "Wall Street plan" to exploit workers around the world. Soviet propaganda, which had earlier concentrated its fire on Britain and then Germany, had turned full blast on the United States. For two years America inadvertently helped out.

EFFECTIVE international persuasion has two main components: (1) A continuing awareness of the likely reactions of others—to be borne in mind when deciding on action, and (2) an organization and mechanism equipped to explain actions fairly, to combat the lies and misunderstandings of others, and to persuade foreign peoples that the United States deserves their cooperation. Washington in 1946-47 hadn't yet recognized that both components are essential if America is not to waste billions of dollars and perhaps thousands of lives.

Even while American leaders seemed to be forgetting the "decent respect to the opinions of mankind" of the Declaration of Independence, they were having trouble deciding whether any mechanism of persuasion was needed at all.

Benton, who had done some work with Nelson Rockefeller,

had had to take time at the outset to learn more about the complex field of international persuasion. He and his aides presently evolved a plan for setting up a permanent Office of International Information and Cultural Affairs, taking in what was left of the wartime information operations, plus the State Department's small cultural relations activities.

The new office would handle the exchange of students, scholars, technicians, and specialists, work which had proved eminently worthwhile in the eyes of many. It would handle the maintenance and servicing of libraries overseas. It would supply missions abroad with a daily, abbreviated wireless news bulletin; background features and photos; exhibit material, plus filmstrips; and a few documentary films adapted and translated from movies commercially made in the U. S. It would maintain public affairs offices abroad to run the modest program and to do contact work with editors and commentators in those countries. It would continue to publish *Amerika* magazine for Russia. And, finally, it would handle the sharply reduced Voice of America.

With Department approval of the plan, Benton found that he personally had to sell it to Congress if it was going to be sold. He soon discovered that many Congressmen, particularly in the House, didn't want to provide any money for the agency unless it was authorized by some permanent law. But he also found many of them extremely reluctant to put through any permanent law. Meanwhile, his operation was showing signs of disintegration, with some of the ablest men and women, discouraged, returning to private business. When Congress had finished, however, the operation emerged with some $19,000,-000 and no permanent legislation.

While Benton was battling with inordinate vigor to save the program, somebody down the line, without his immediate knowledge, assembled an art exhibit. It was to be shipped abroad for the commendable purpose of showing foreign audiences that Americans were something more than uncouth money-grabbers. The paintings consisted of avant-garde items. Their quality was debatable even among art connoisseurs. It was sheer poison to those members of Congress whose taste had not gone beyond "Whistler's Mother." And it was a dubious operation to many others. The exhibit cost only a few thousand dollars (and private bids for it later exceeded this cost) but it almost cost the government its entire information operation. When Benton came up for his next appropriation, the House knocked out all funds for overseas information. The Senate, after vigorous intervention by the President and by Secretary of State Marshall, voted a total of $13,800,000, of which $1,430,000 was for liquidating various functions.

Meanwhile, Benton and his colleagues had a battle royal trying to get permanent authorization for the program. They finally won out in the Republican-controlled Eightieth Congress because they had converted two GOP stalwarts, Senator H. Alexander Smith of New Jersey and Representative Karl Mundt of North Dakota, to sponsor the authorizing legislation. Despite large-scale resistance in the House and the opposition of Senator Taft and a few others in the Senate, they won valiant support from Senators Vandenberg and Hatch. Between them, these champions finally converted large numbers of their colleagues and pushed the authorizing legislation through.

Senator Smith and Representative Mundt, working with Assistant Secretary Benton, conceived and carried out a brilliant idea: They embodied in their Public Law 402 a provision that there should be two advisory commissions appointed by the President and confirmed by the Senate. One, the U. S. Advisory Commission on International Information, would study and make periodic recommendations on the radio, press, film, and publications work of the U. S. Information Service around the world. The second, the U. S. Advisory Commission on Educational Exchange, would work similarly in the whole "cultural" field. ("Educational Exchange" had been adopted as a euphemism for cultural relations, because of a fear that voters who might sneer at "culture" could scarcely oppose "education.") It was to study and recommend on the exchanges of students, professors, specialists, editors, and others; on the maintenance of U. S. libraries and information centers overseas; and on any other activities in so-called cultural fields.

The President appointed first-rate men to the two commissions.* Ever since, both commissions have studied the program here and abroad with great care. With the perspective of informed "outsiders" they have continually made recommendations which have generally been followed. They have unquestionably increased the effectiveness of the entire program. The great problem of both commissions has been to get overworked members of the Congress to read the semi-annual reports that Congress itself ordered the commissions to make.

ALL THE TIME he struggled for Congressional support, the energetic Bill Benton also waged a continuing campaign outside Congress. He made scores of speeches before influential groups, explaining why an international information and educational exchange program was necessary. He went before the hostile American Society of Newspaper Editors and ultimately persuaded the society to name a committee of three to study the whole international information problem. A committee was named, held long hearings, and took a trip around the world. It reported, first, that there was a genuine need for a

* *U. S. Advisory Commission on Information:*
  Mark Ethridge, publisher, Louisville *Courier-Journal* (later succeeded by Ben Hibbs, editor, *Saturday Evening Post*); Mark A. May, director, Institute of Human Relations, Yale University; Philip D. Reed, chairman of the board, General Electric Company; Erwin D. Canham, editor, *Christian Science Monitor*; Judge Justin Miller, chairman of the board, National Association of Radio and Television Broadcasters.
  U. S. Advisory Commission on Educational Exchange:
  Dr. Harvie Branscomb, chancellor, Vanderbilt University (later succeeded by Dr. J. L. Morrill, president, University of Minnesota); Dr. Edwin B. Fred, president, University of Wisconsin; Dr. Harold W. Dodds, president, Princeton University; Mr. Mark Starr, educational director, International Ladies Garment Workers Union, New York; Dr. Martin R. P. McGuire, professor, Catholic University, Washington, D. C.

government information operation and, second, that Benton's State Department organization wasn't flawless but was generally effective.

Benton also waged a major battle to get the Associated Press and United Press to supply their news services to the Voice of America. They had reluctantly done so (under extreme pressure, in the case of the A.P.) in wartime, but had terminated the service immediately after the war. Having battled against the British Reuters and French Havas in selling news around the world and having charged both with being under the thumb of their governments, they shied away from even cooperating with the Voice of America. A minority of the controlling voices in both organizations thought they were wrong, particularly since the A.P. continued to furnish news to the Soviets' own Tass agency under an exchange arrangement. Nonetheless, Benton failed in this fight. The International News Service, under direction of Seymour Berkson, provided news to the Voice. The A.P. and U.P. stuck obdurately to their positions. Today they are so deeply committed to that position that they doubtless feel compelled to stick to it until more time passes.

UNDER the leadership of Senator William Fulbright of Arkansas, Congress took in 1947 one noteworthy and enlightened step in the field of international educational exchange. It had specified that millions of dollars in foreign currencies, owed to the U. S. by other nations which had bought surplus U. S. property overseas, should be used to finance the international exchange of students and teachers. Few today question the enormous good-will value of that program.

In addition, Congress in 1946 took the step of authorizing full United States participation in the United Nations Educational Scientific and Cultural Organization, with the purpose of fostering better understanding through interchanges in those broad fields.

The United States had come a long way. For the first tim
in history, the government had a legal international information program, recognizing Americans' obligation to themselves
and to the world to present a "full and fair picture of America, to make clear our aims and our policies."

Abraham Lincoln, while President, had said:

> When the conduct of man is designed to be influenced, persuasion,
> kind, unassuming persuasion, should ever be adopted. . . . If you would
> win a man to your cause, first convince him that you are his sincere
> friend. . . . Assume to dictate to his judgment, or to command his
> action, or to mark him as one to be shunned and despised, and he will
> retreat within himself, close all the avenues to his head and his heart.
> . . . Such is man, and so must be understood by those who would
> lead him, even to his own best interest.

The United States of America, more than eighty years later,
had at last begun to heed Lincoln's advice. Thrust into the
role of leader among free nations, it finally had provided itself
with a modest mechanism for international persuasion. And it
had begun to learn that one doesn't win allies among those one
seems to despise.

A major factor, without question, was the fact that American Congressmen had begun to see the world. Approximately
half the members of Congress in 1946 and 1947 went abroad
on official trips, some of them serious business and some sheer
junkets. Two or three of the travelers were not impressed; one
said he found "nobody hungry in Europe" and nobody needing
help. A majority, however, obviously came back with broader
horizons. Exposed to the Soviets' systematic campaign of
misrepresentation and confronted with wide-spread misinformation about America, they began to see the need for a systematic, continuing program of information and persuasion.
More than any other factor, the exposure of Congressmen to
conditions beyond their borders accounted for the fact that by
1948 America was able to start rebuilding an overseas information program. The stiffest opposition thereafter came

largely from those Congressmen who had never traveled abroad, plus a few who had suffered mental atrophy before doing so.

THE BROADENING of Congressional horizons paved the way for other belated moves in foreign affairs. A new generation of enterprising younger men had begun to take over from the more traditional veterans of the State Department. Under the supervision of Secretary George Marshall, whose sense of broad strategy made up partly for his lack of diplomatic experience, they had begun thinking imaginatively of the problems presented by Kremlin recalcitrance. And they had found a Congress more amenable to bold strokes in foreign affairs than ever before.

The early results in broad foreign policy were not flawless. In order to thrust back Communist pressure on Greece and Turkey, a Presidential announcement declared, "It must be the policy of the United States to support free peoples who are resisting attempts at subjugation by armed minorities or by outside pressures." That statement of policy became known promptly as the "Truman Doctrine," and the Congress quickly voted funds to assist Greece and Turkey. With that assistance and bolstered by their own determination, the two nations succeeded. Nonetheless the Truman Doctrine, well-meant but drafted without enough awareness of foreign reactions, backfired in many parts of the world.

Since the then Greek Government had a reputation for corruption and oppression, America seemed to many to be underwriting the forces of reaction. Since, in his announcement, the President had said American officials would supervise the use of U. S. dollars in Greece, he seemed to underscore the theme that America was hell-bent on economic imperialism. More important still, it indicated to some that America had embarked on a program of using troubled small nations as pawns in a gigantic contest with the U.S.S.R. By early 1947, the State

Department crew was ready to try again. In prolonged evening discussions, it had evolved a new plan without these drawbacks. Secretary of Commerce Harriman and others contributed to the plan. Dean Acheson, then Marshall's Under Secretary, tried it out in an obscure speech in Cleveland, Mississippi, on May 8. He trial-ballooned a program inviting European countries to get together and draft a plan for their own recovery, indicating that the United States would help them to carry it out. The Soviet and its satellites could come in on the plan if they really wanted to. The plan also avoided any idea of American interference in the internal affairs of other nations.

Tipped off to the speech, two or three imaginative news writers commented favorably. After that reaction, Secretary Marshall himself officially and more specifically proposed the plan in a commencement speech at Harvard University on June 5. Backing away from the "Truman Plan" and its picture of direct Soviet-American conflict, he proposed a policy which "is directed, not against any country or doctrine, but against hunger, poverty, desperation, and chaos."

Curiously, Marshall and his aides didn't recognize the power of the idea. They did not fanfare it. The speech got routine coverage by campus correspondents. It was the British Foreign Office that grasped the full potential of the proposal. After quiet inquiry to Washington to make sure Marshall was serious, Foreign Secretary Ernest Bevin publicly hailed the Marshall proposal as a great new plan. It was then that the world, including the United States, became excited about the program.

The United States at last had an idea that fired the imaginations around the world. Sixteen European nations soon met in Paris to draw up a program of the sort called for by the "Marshall Plan." The Soviet Union, in one of its more inept moves, not only declined to cooperate, but crudely denounced the

Marshall Plan as a trick of American imperialism. It abruptly rebuked Poland and Czechoslovakia when they indicated they would like to cooperate. The Kremlin instigated strikes and sabotage against the workings of the Marshall Plan.

The whole business, reported by the press and exploited by the reinvigorated U. S. Information Service, turned into a psychological victory for America. By public statements, by press, and by radio, the contrast between the U. S. and the U.S.S.R. attitudes was emphasized. America had offered hope, hope for all nations that were willing to take initiative and meet us half-way. The Kremlin seemed to have set out to prevent the recovery of Europe, and to prolong the agony which would make Europe ripe for Communism. Signs abounded that millions who had at least listened to Soviet propaganda now began to get a new picture of the world conflict.

With support not only from the Administration but also from such broad-gaged Republicans as Senator Arthur Vandenberg, Congress finally adopted the Marshall Plan. In so doing, it showed its distrust of the State Department, akin to distrust of foreign offices around the world, and set up a special administration—ECA—to handle the program. At the same time, however, the Congress gave new recognition to the potent force of opinion, here and abroad. It authorized, indeed instructed, the ECA to publicize its activities abroad and to see that the American people got "full information" on its performance. This sort of recognition of the opinion factor was novel in Congressional history. True, the Congress was intent on seeing that America got "credit" and "gratitude" from the nations abroad, forgetting that simple gratitude usually breeds envy and jealousy. What was really wanted was a spirit of mutual self-help. In this, it is now clear, the U. S. made a mistake; some ECA efforts at winning "gratitude" boomeranged. But in its broad recognition of the importance of world opinion, Congress reached a new high mark.

DURING the entire 1946-50 period Congress had difficulty making up its mind on many problems in the strange new field of international persuasion. At one time it demanded that the Voice of America broadcasts should be carried out by private companies under contract to the Department of State, with the Department exercising "broad supervision and control." By 1948 the small band of critics of the program had dug out and periodically waved on the floor of Congress a minor procession of scripts that they labeled as "silly," "useless," or "misrepresentations." Their first major assault was built around a collection of scripts on various parts of the United States—a collection actually based on material from John Gunther's *Inside U.S.A.* (and occasionally from various W.P.A. state guidebooks of the 1930's) but distasteful in some ways to the elected representatives of those states. The critics exhibited such scripts as documentary evidence that a government propaganda service was undesirable, that the work should be left to private enterprise. Congressional defenders smilingly pointed out that the sins had been committed by private enterprise—as required by Congress. Congress ended up by demanding that the State Department take over again the actual production of the Voice's radio programs. The issue had gone the full circuit.

THE IDEAL propaganda, of course, is the propaganda of action, action taken and then fully publicized by an alert, aggressive information campaign. It was in the winter of 1948-49 that the British and Americans stirred men around the world with one of the most spectacular cases of "action propaganda" in many years, the magnificent performance of the Berlin airlift.

As the Soviet Union blockaded West Berlin and as American and British planes kept the city free with air-borne supplies, the demonstration of Anglo-American determination put new spunk into frightened free peoples. The U.S.I.S. wisely went all out in publicizing the story. The Voice of America put on special broadcasts describing the endless landings and take-offs of supply-filled planes. Films running into thousands of feet were made and spliced into newsreels around the world. The incident of American pilots dropping candy to hungry German kids near the Berlin air drome was reported in words and pictures. Reams of statements and interviews and hundreds of photos were distributed.

The impact was greater than that of any single event since the end of the war. What better demonstration could there be that the great free nations were determined not to let down beleaguered free peoples anywhere? What better reflection could there be of the potential might of free nations? And what better demonstration could there be of the inhumane, short-sighted tactics of the Kremlin rulers?

When Ambassador Philip Jessup at the U.N. and Ambassador Bedell Smith in Moscow finally cornered Soviet representatives and showed them the wisdom of ending their futile blockade, the story was complete. Through films, press material, and radio, added to the full reporting of the free press itself, the U.S.I.S. strove to drive home the point: that Soviet rulers can be, and will be, thwarted when the free nations show calm and determined resistance. The end of the blockade left the free peoples of Berlin with a spirit of determination unequaled anywhere in Europe. It left millions of free peoples elsewhere with new hope and new confidence.

GEORGE V. ALLEN, an able career diplomat and former ambassador who succeeded Benton in early 1948, found the going easier, due in part to the national election, which had retired a number of the more parochial-minded members of Congress. Benton had fought for the baby, got it legalized by Congress, and had begun at least to get its nominal parents in the State Department to pay a little attention to it. Now George Allen, coming onto the scene in 1948 and wearing the old school tie of the career Foreign Service officer, had the job of getting the child christened and recognized as a full-fledged member of the family. Far more alert to the role of mass persuasion in the twentieth century world than most of his colleagues, he studied the operation and quickly became impressed with its importance. He performed valiant missionary work in "selling" the strategy of persuasion to the Foreign Service.

During the next two years the program maintained a fairly steady pace. It still faced substantial pot-shotting in Congress but usually managed to get $30,000,000 or so a year for its operations in all the eighty-odd nations of the world.

The bulk of the output was still devoted to presenting a "full and fair picture" of America to the world. Most of the operations were still geared to the concept of the sort of sound "international public relations" required in a peaceful world. Only in radio and a few minor activities was there recognition that the U. S. faced an all-out ideological war with a ruthless enemy. In radio in 1947, Bill Benton's regime had inaugurated broadcasts to Russia—which the Soviet Government did not welcome. The programs totaled only an hour a day but were gradually increased in the three following years. A Benton proposal for a semi-public foundation to take over radio broadcasting had gone into the overcrowded Congressional pigeonhole, but long-standing proposals for a stronger Voice of America began to get at least some action in the late 1940's. Recognizing that the Voice could deliver a really strong signal abroad only if relayed by booster stations overseas, the Benton organization had included proposals for such stations in its 1948 budget. They disappeared with the drastic Congressional cuts. In the budget for 1949 and 1950 they reappeared, and Allen finally induced Congress to provide $11,320,000 so that the Government could at least start building such a system.

THE "PEACETIME" MISSION

Throughout the years 1946-50, the whole international information and educational exchange program of the government was basically a "peacetime" program. It had been laboriously hammered out to meet what all hoped would be postwar conditions. Accordingly, it was not quickly changed to meet the Communist menace.

With the end of the war in Europe, O.W.I. had faced the problem of intensifying Sykewar in the Pacific and of beginning "peacetime operations" in Europe. After many long sessions while I was O.W.I. Overseas Director, I had summed up in an official staff order what the peacetime job was to be:

> We cannot say that O.W.I.'s operations in Europe are to be exclusively either "information" or "propaganda." Our primary task is to present the United States itself and the United States Government's war and peace policies as convincingly as possible in order to win respect for this country and support for its policies and aims. In the best sense of the word, we are primarily *active propagandists* for the United States.

> However, we can be *effective* propagandists only if we can make foreign audiences pay attention to our output and trust what we say. Hence our output must be presented in an interesting context. And it must be presented as part of a general service which is known to be reliable and above distortion or suppression. An example: We may and should go out of our way to see that American policies are fully and convincingly explained in all of our media, but we may not suppress important American criticism of these same policies.

> For practical as well as idealistic reasons, O.W.I. continues to stick to the truth—to abjure distortion or suppression. At the same time, O.W.I. puts primary emphasis on honest material which seeks to win support for the policies and aims of the U. S. Government.

That still left the question of how we presented the U. S. to the rest of the world. In that same staff order the guiding principles were laid down in these terms:

In our so-called Projection of America, we are not trying to "sell America." We are trying:

1. To bring about a fuller understanding of America, its life, its government and its ideals—including faults as well as virtues—because we are convinced that America stands up well under examination and that knowledge of this nation fosters respect for it and confidence in it. We try to present a really balanced picture of America.

2. To present the case for democracy not by argument but by example. The U. S. believes that democracy is the best form of government yet devised and that the country which adopts a democratic form of government is far less likely than any other to plunge the world into war. However, we do not help the cause of democracy by bluntly telling non-democratic countries that their forms of government are inferior. We should illustrate how democracy works here and let our audiences reach their own conclusions.

For all practical purposes, those were the aims of the United States information program for the succeeding four years. Workers in the program had no doubt about its worth. They knew American diplomacy had often been thwarted by misunderstandings abroad. They suspected that thousands of Americans died in the Pacific because the Japanese believed them to be too money-hungry, too soft, and too cowardly to fight with valor and tenacity. Some said there might never have been a World War II had Hitler, Hirohito, and their henchmen recognized the strength, determination, and moral fiber of America.

Bill Benton and later George Allen fought to see that such a situation should not arise again. They repeatedly summed up the tasks of the program in roughly these words:

The United States Government can no longer be indifferent to the ways in which our nation is portrayed in other countries, but is obliged to give a full and fair picture of the

United States abroad. This follows since foreign relations are no longer relations between personal sovereigns or sovereign governments, but are more than ever before relations between peoples. Governments are being increasingly influenced in their conduct of foreign relations by the peoples of the world. Therefore many governments have organized information programs as established arms for conducting foreign relations. These programs are not merely indiscriminate good-will operations, but must be closely coordinated with foreign policy. Since the bulk of communications between peoples has been non-governmental in character, the role of government should be facilitative and supplementary. It should facilitate the operations of private international communicators and travelers; it should supplement them where necessary to see to it that peoples abroad get the full and fair picture of the United States required to promote the understanding on which peace is based.

Peace through understanding is the basic foundation of broad policy for the information operation. Since our present dominant economic and military power creates fear and distrust of us abroad, we need an information program to offset them in some measure. Another information objective is to promote correct understanding of our foreign policy, "cooperative, open, proclaimed, popularly arrived at." Finally, information programs can foster international trade, and programs for exchange of persons and skills can protect our prosperity by raising standards of living abroad.

THE ACTIONS of the Congress in 1948-49 had brought the U. S. Government a long way. At the war's end, America had all but abandoned the idea of international information. It had sometimes behaved as if the opinions of other peoples made little difference even in the modern world. But from that low point it had started over again. It had begun to conduct itself in a way that showed some respect for the opinions of mankind and had provided, as a continuing part of government, an organization that would help explain America, its aims and its policies, to the peoples on whose support America increasingly depended. The government had hardly yet recognized persuasion as an aggressive weapon in the cold war, but at least it had resurrected international information as an instrument of national policy.

6

Launching the Campaign of Truth

IN THE late winter of 1950, four months before the invasion of South Korea, a case of jitters ran through the ranks of informed officials in Washington. A stream of intelligence items led the State and Defense Departments to suspect that the Kremlin was about to "start something." Standing alone, no single item of intelligence was conclusive. Together they added up to a disturbing array of portents. The preponderant guess was that the Kremlin would not launch World War III, but would probably start an offensive in some limited area, with a satellite doing the actual fighting. The guessers usually pointed to Iran, Yugoslavia, Indo-China, and Formosa as possible targets. Sometimes they mentioned Korea.

The National Security Council, as the top cold war planning group, was just finishing its mammoth study of Soviet capabilities and intentions. As a result, the Council was pulling together the preliminary figures for a vast program of rearmament. Already Council members had begun to see that a parallel psychological offensive would be needed, an offensive much larger and more aggressive than anything tried since the war. My own findings, resulting from an intensive study made immediately upon taking office in February, 1950, supported the same conclusion.

President Truman decided to call for such a psychological offensive in a speech before the American Society of Newspaper Editors in Washington on April twentieth. A message from the White House summoned me to come over and review a draft which Mr. Truman's aids had prepared. As is usual with official speeches, it had to be a rush job; the speech was to be "frozen" and prepared for press release within a few hours. I found it was a fairly impressive draft, pointing out the great headway made by the Soviets' Big Lie and calling for an American counter-offensive. There was one major thing wrong with the speech: it was sure to cause headlines such as "Truman Declares Propaganda War." Happily, a new phrase came to mind. The American offensive was naturally to be based upon truth. Therefore, I suggested that the President call for "a Campaign of Truth."

We sprinkled that phrase through the text. As we had hoped, it led to such headlines around the world as "Truman Calls For Campaign of Truth," or variations of the same thought. The text of the speech featured these words:

We must make ourselves known as we really are—not as Communist propaganda pictures us. We must pool our efforts with those of the other free peoples in a sustained, intensified program to promote the cause of freedom against the propaganda of slavery. We must make ourselves heard round the world in a great campaign of truth.

This task is not separate and distinct from other elements of our foreign policy. It is a necessary part of all we are doing to build a peaceful world. It is as important as armed strength or economic aid. The Marshall Plan, military aid, Point IV—these and other programs depend for their success on the understanding and support of our own citizens and those of other countries.

We have tremendous advantages in the struggle for men's minds and loyalties. We have truth and freedom on our side. The appeal of free institutions and self-government springs from the deepest and noblest aspirations of mankind. It is based on every man's desire for liberty and opportunity. It is based on every man's wish to be self-reliant and to shape his own destiny.

As we go forward with our campaign of truth, we will make lasting progress toward the kind of world we seek—a world in which men and nations live not as enemies but as brothers.

With that kick-off, my State Department colleagues and I intensified the blueprinting and budgeting of a greatly expanded program. In night and day sessions, with cables flying back and forth between Washington and the various embassies, the program took shape. After prolonged hearings, the Bureau of the Budget and the White House approved a greatly expanded budget and sent it to Congress. There, it seemed certain to run into stalwart opposition, for neither the Congress nor the public then shared the sense of urgency felt by top officialdom. Joseph Stalin, however, soon changed all that by launching the war in Korea.

FROM the end of the war until the start of 1950, I had no connection with the U. S. Government's international information efforts, beyond an occasional talk with Bill Benton or George Allen. Just before Christmas of 1949, while I was Editorial Director of *Newsweek,* Under Secretary James Webb and Secretary Acheson asked me to come to Washington for a talk. When I arrived I found that they had laid on what I later came to know as "the full treatment." They had had a vacancy on their hands ever since George V. Allen had been moved from the post of Assistant Secretary of State for Public Affairs to that of Ambassador to Yugoslavia two months earlier, and they intended to fill that vacancy. They asked me to take on the job, which included supervision of the Voice of America and all other international information and educational exchange operations, plus many responsibilities having to do with information to the American public, the United Nations Educational, Scientific and Cultural Organization (UNESCO), and other activities. Acheson, whom I had not previously known, emphasized the "vital importance" of the assignment. Neither he nor Webb showed concern when I pointed out I was not a "good Democrat" but rather a "mugwump" who had consistently voted split tickets.

Then to my surprise Messrs. Acheson and Webb took me to the White House for an "off the record visit." (This simply involved going through a side entrance, not covered by the press, and up through a basement elevator to the President's office.) In a fifteen-minute talk, the President spoke in some detail of the importance of the assignment, ending up, "I think you should take it, and I hope you will take it."

The matter really was settled then, for I had had no experience in turning down invitations from the President of the United States. However, I asked for two days to think it over. The two days were used for trying to square matters with my associates at *Newsweek* and with my wife, neither of whom had shown much eagerness for the idea.

As an incidental observation, the talk with President Truman left me with a curious reaction. Here was a man with the simplicity and friendliness of, say, the corner merchant. I felt none of the deep impressions that I had experienced on the two occasions when I had had brief talks with Franklin Roosevelt in that office. Yet here was a man who clearly understood the problem of international information work far better than Roosevelt ever had. He obviously had "done his homework" on such problems and had a good grasp of broad international issues.

AFTER being confirmed by the Senate, I took office in February, 1950. I spent the next few weeks learning my way around, participating in top-level policy meetings in the Department and appraising the whole international information program. A few able men from the editorial and advertising fields agreed, at some sacrifice to themselves, to join me in government. They worked with me in appraising the existing operations and the future course that should be followed.

Within some six weeks, all of the study and appraising produced six basic conclusions. They were:

1. The Voice of America and the whole International Information and Educational Exchange Program of the Department were staffed, with certain exceptions, by surprisingly able, conscientious, and hard-working individuals. They came from all parts of the country and from many professions, a large number of them from the newspaper and radio fields. They had a sort of missionary zeal that contrasted sharply with the average man's idea of a government bureaucrat. Voluntary work after hours and on week-ends was more the rule than the exception. Moreover, every individual in the program had been subjected to a full field investigation by the F.B.I., the strictest security system existing in any normal government agency.

- The program, however, suffered from continuing inability to recruit enough first-rate executives and radio engineers. This, I later confirmed, resulted from a fear of being slandered by irresponsibles and from the program's low pay. Doing at least twice as much broadcasting as N.B.C., the Voice of America had less than one one-hundredth as many well-paid jobs as N.B.C. In fact, it had no job paying as much as $11,000 a year. In the months ahead, I succeeded with only about one out of every twenty first-grade men I sought to recruit.

2. Most, but not all, of the informational work being carried on abroad impressed careful investigators as effective. The man-to-man contacts of public affairs officers overseas with leading editors, commentators, and others, straightening out misconceptions about the United States, were clearly worthwhile. American libraries and information centers in major cities abroad had proved their value. One had only to look at the lists of leaders of thought—editors, professors, and political leaders—who were using those libraries to realize their worth. The showing of American documentary films to some ten

million foreign citizens a month was unquestionably helpful. Under the exchange-of-persons program, lecturers, doctors, specialists, writers, editors, and labor leaders from abroad were being brought to this country to see at first-hand how American democracy operates. Their writings and speeches after they returned left no doubt that their trips did a great deal toward making the U. S. and its aspirations understood abroad.

3. The Voice of America radio operation was still smaller than that of the British or the Russians, but it was generally proving its worth. It was operating around the clock, with a total of seventy daily programs in twenty-four languages. The response from abroad was encouraging. A survey showed that eighteen percent of the people of France listened to the Voice of America. Letters received from abroad by the Voice had gone from ten thousand a month to more than twenty thousand a month in a year. In the satellite areas, embassies reported the Voice had substantial and devoted followings, but that efforts to "jam out" the American radio were increasing. It was clear that the Voice should be strengthened—particularly to the Iron Curtain areas, where it was most important.

4. The whole overseas information program was not, by and large, getting down far enough among the people—into the masses where the raw material for Communism is so often found. It was not getting out enough beyond the major cities. It was still too heavily concentrated on the upper crust. This was defensible in a few nations where an élite group dominated everything. Certainly it was understandable, since the world-wide information and exchange-of-persons program, including the Voice of America, was costing less than General Motors alone spends on its public relations and its advertising. But the fact remained that the program was not penetrating deep enough, nor reaching out far enough into the provinces of most countries.

5. Because of the subtleties of the work and the ever-changing moods of peoples abroad, the program needed less master-

minding in Washington and more tactical planning by good propagandists on the scene abroad.

6. The program had done a good, modest public relations job overseas, but, given the critical world picture, this was not sufficient. It was not enough just to have the U. S., its motives and aspirations, understood. The time had come to take the psychological offensive, with a bolder, more aggressive campaign.

What did "taking the psychological offensive" really mean? Standing alone, it sounded like one of those pat phrases like "being more affirmative" that political orators love to mouth. In a "Campaign of Truth," much more precision was needed. Obviously, it was desirable to produce a restatement of American propaganda objectives, a statement going far beyond the old "full and fair picture of America" concept. My colleagues and I set to work on that, with much help from Wallace Carroll, one of the ablest of wartime propagandists whom I had borrowed from the editorship of the Winston-Salem *Journal* and Twin-Cities *Sentinel,* and from Joseph B. Phillips, former *Newsweek* Foreign Affairs Director.

When the draft was finished, I discussed it at length with Mr. Acheson, with Foster Dulles (then special consultant to the Secretary), with the State Department's top command, and with a subcommittee of the Senate Committee on Foreign Relations. Modified slightly, it became the program's guiding document. Some parts of the plan cannot be publicized even now. However, a summary, made in 1950 for interested members of Congress, at least sketched the broad outline:

The new psychological offensive is aimed at achieving four objectives.

"The *first* is to establish a healthy international community. This, in a way, is our most important basic objective. It involves creating a climate of confidence in the free world; confidence as opposed to scares and name-calling and saber-rattling; confidence that we and the free world are doing with determination all that can be done to create a peaceful world. It involves encouraging a spirit not of gratitude (which breeds envy) but of self-help and self-reliance in the other free nations. It involves stimulating in every way the spirit of international cooperation by giving others a chance to participate in the great design of peace, freedom, and recovery.

Our second objective is basically that of presenting America fairly and countering all the misconceptions and misrepresentations about us around the world—of so demonstrating the decency and the moral and physical strength of America that we make other peoples *desire* to cooperate with us.

Our *third* objective is that of deterring the Soviets from further encroachments. This means frustrating their psychological preparations for war by showing the Soviet and satellite peoples that we are friendly toward them and that their government is a war government. It means demonstrating to the Communist élite, in Russia and abroad, that they have underestimated the strength of present-day capitalism. It means convincing Soviet and satellite leaders that if they do bring on war, it will prove ruinous to them.

Our *fourth* objective is that of helping to roll back Soviet influence, not by arms, of course, but by all means short of force. This means making the captive peoples realize that we feel that they still belong with us. This means weakening the will of Red Army officers and Red officials at home and abroad. It means keeping the Soviet bear so busy scratching his own fleas that he has little time for molesting others. On this side of the Iron Curtain, it means encouraging and strengthening non-Communist forces, including non-Communist trade unions.

After careful study we are convinced that most, if not all, of these objectives can be achieved with the correct deployment of America's psychological resources."

THAT jawbreaking phrase "correct deployment of America's phychological resources" proved to be a whopping problem. My colleagues and I had to spend much of the following two years battling to get Congress to support such "correct deployment." Indeed, one of my chief regrets is that I, like my predecessors, was forced to spend more effort on this struggle than on the contest with Soviet propagandists.

When I took office, a "normal" international information budget request for some $35,000,000 was already part way through Congress. With no more than the mildly rough treatment that government officials had come to expect from some of the appropriations subcommittees of Congress, the program emerged with some $31,000,000—about what each of several American corporations spends annually on public relations and advertising. Only two months later, I found myself going to Congress to urge a virtual tripling of operations, plus a $41,000,000 expenditure for gigantic new transmitters. The proposed expansion did not approach that advocated by some (including *Fortune* magazine, which urged spending $500,000,000 a year on exchange of persons alone), yet it was a vast increase, which, as I told Congressional committees, I would not advocate except under crisis conditions.

The outlook for Congressional approval was gloomy. Most Congress members simply did not share the sense of urgency the Executive Branch felt. Suddenly, however, Joseph Stalin took care of that. He pulled the trigger for the Korean invasion and flooded the world with propaganda to the effect that the United States had started it all. A frightened and angry Congress was, for once, in a mood to support substantial international persuasion by the United States Government.

The House voted a major part of the money requested. In the Senate, an unusual thing happened. Through a quirk of legislative procedure, my colleagues and I went before the full twenty-one-member Senate Appropriations Committee instead of the usual small subcommittee that was addicted to sharp slashing. Moreover, the Committee's aging chairman, Kenneth McKellar of Tennessee, set the stage with a flattering introduction of me as the new Assistant Secretary. He probably did so because two of my old friends in Tennessee had assured him I was neither a criminal nor a Communist.* For the one and

* The hilarious opening of that hearing led the *New Yorker* to print the following:

SOFT, GENTLE SOUTHERN BREEZES OVER CAPITOL HILL
(*From a hearing of the Senate Appropriations Committee*)

CHAIRMAN McKELLAR. All right, gentlemen, are there any other questions? At this point I want to ask a question or two. I do not do it very often, but sometimes I do.

You were born in Alabama; were you not, Mr. Barrett?

MR. BARRETT. Yes, sir; I was.

CHAIRMAN McKELLAR. In what part of Alabama?

MR. BARRETT, Birmingham, Alabama.

TELEGRAM OF COMMENDATION OF MR. EDWARD BARRETT

SENATOR McKELLAR, I happen to have been born a hundred or so miles from there. Let me just read a telegram that I got from an old friend in Tennessee, concerning you, Mr. Barrett. It is from Nashville, Tenna., addressed to me, as follows:

I UNDERSTAND THAT THE ASSISTANT SECRETARY OF STATE EDWARD BARRETT IS TO APPEAR BEFORE YOUR APPROPRIATIONS COMMITTEE TOMORROW. I COMMEND HIM TO YOU AS DESERVING THE UTMOST CONFIDENCE. BORN IN BIRMINGHAM, ALA., HE IS THE SON OF THE LATE EDWARD BARRETT, PUBLISHER OF THE BIRMINGHAM AGE HERALD, AND IS THE TYPE OF SOUTHERN AMERICAN WE LIKE TO SEE IN OUR STATE DEPARTMENT.

The telegram is signed by William E. Beard, editor emeritus of the Nashville *Banner*. I have known him a long time, and while I have not known Mr. Barrett, I will say I am glad to put this commendation of him in the record from an old friend. I can say that the Birmingham *Age Herald* is one of the leading papers of our southern country. I feel that it is my duty to state to you that he is an American and is working for America.

MR. BARRETT. Thank you, Mr. Chairman.

SENATOR HILL. Mr. Chairman, may I associate myself with you in that statement?

CHAIRMAN McKELLAR. I will be delighted to have you do so.

SENATOR HILL. Having known Mr. Barrett since the time he was in swaddling clothes, and having known his distinguished father and his charming mother, I will say he is of the stuff of which we are proud.

MR. BARRETT. Thank you, sir.

SENATOR McCARRAN. Mr. Chairman, I do not want to be left out of this.

CHAIRMAN McKELLAR. We would be delighted to have you join us.

SENATOR McCARRAN. I am of southern lineage myself.

CHAIRMAN McKELLAR. I always knew there was something mighty fine about you.

SENATOR McCARRAN. Mr. Barrett came from south of the Mason-Dixon line, and my folks came from the south of Ireland. So we are related.

MR. BARRETT. I guess the Barretts were there, too, at one time.

SENATOR WHERRY. May I ask a question, Mr. Chairman?

CHAIRMAN McKELLAR. Yes, sir.

only time in my government career, my colleagues and I were permitted to give an organized presentation of a budget before an appropriations committee, without interruptions and tangential discussions. After some two hours of that and two hours of questions, the committee voted every dime requested. The figures were later compromised in a House-Senate conference, but the great bulk of the appropriations was granted.

The opportunity to give a connected presentation had helped. But the Kremlin had done most of the job. By launching the Korean war it had proved to have more influence on the Congress of the United States than could the President, who had resoundingly endorsed the Campaign of Truth budget request. Not only that budget but budgets for military expansion and economic aid sailed through.

The honeymoon ended there. By the time the next Campaign of Truth budget went to Congress, the picture had changed. Americans were growing weary of the Korean war; Stalin was making "peace" gestures; and the Congressional sense of urgency had vanished. From then on, every dime extracted from Congress was paid for in anguish, toil, and bloody brows.

In supporting one large request, my colleagues and I not only gained no opportunity to make a connected presentation but were unable to persuade either of the busy appropriations subcommittees to listen to a single broadcast, visit a single installation, view a single film, or witness a laboriously prepared chart presentation. We suffered a deep, if temporary, budget cut.

In a continuing series of private conversations, I helped persuade perhaps two hundred members of Congress that the

---

SENATOR WHERRY. Could a fellow whose ancestors came from South Wales get into this, too?
CHAIRMAN McKELLAR. Yes, sir. We would be delighted to have you.
SENATOR SALTONSTALL. Mr. Chairman, is this one occasion when you would let New England participate with the South?
CHAIRMAN McKELLAR. We will be delighted to.

program was needed and was being reasonably well conducted. Many fine men in Congress gave the operation valiant support. The program—and I—continued, however, to have some twenty vehement enemies in Congress, and unfortunately four of these had membership on the all-important appropriations committees.

Sometimes irate or petty actions by a few such individuals jeopardized the entire program. In one case, for example, a Congressman whose seniority gave him vast power over appropriations privately "suggested" I remove from the program a key executive, about whom he had heard slanderous tales, and a desk chief, who had once offended powerful constituents. I declined to do so, explaining why. Whether for that reason or not, the Congressman showed a type of hostility I had never seen when the next Campaign of Truth budget came before him. Again, Senator McKellar, whose memory was rapidly failing, forgot his effusions of a year before and opened a hearing by asking me, "Are you a Communist?" He carried on in that amiable vein.

One Senator with great power on appropriations used to have his aide phone on the eve of hearings and urge the immediate hiring of two or three constituents. Failing to scrap required procedures in order to oblige, we encountered new hostility in hearings. The same Senator once announced publicly that he was going to show that the Voice of America was shot through with "Communist sympathizers and fellow travelers," then staged closed-door hearings to prove his point. For hours the committee heard a procession of disappointed job hunters ("they didn't hire me because I was too anti-communist"), embittered ex-scriptwriters ("I guess my scripts weren't Leftist enough"), and long-known ultra-nationalist cranks. The hearings disintegrated when no Senators remained to hear the witnesses, one of the members terming the sessions "a farce" as he left the room. No more was heard of that subject, but the responsible Senator unfortunately made no amendment to his original public statement.

Once the whole Campaign of Truth was nearly decimated at the urging of a powerful subcommittee chairman. This Senator used as his main argument the fact that the U. S. Information Service had regularly sent to some of its one-hundred-odd libraries around the world the *Reporter,* a left-of-center but vehemently anti-Communist magazine, which had published a sizzling article about the Senator himself. Incredible though it sounds, he persuaded the Senate Appropriations Committee to cut the budget nearly in half in retaliation for this "insult to a fellow Senator." When the question reached the floor of the Senate on August 24, 1951, he put forth the same argument.

This time the friends of the information operation were ready. A number of responsible Senators who really knew the program, ranging from the Democrat Brien McMahon of Connecticut to Republican Karl Mundt of South Dakota, cut loose. They cited the widespread distribution to U.S.I.S. libraries of the *Saturday Evening Post,* which frequently blistered President Truman himself, and of *Life* magazine, which habitually berated the information services' boss, Dean Acheson. They pointed out that the U.S.I.S. could scarcely "project America" honestly through its overseas libraries if it eliminated every item critical of any important American. They talked of "misguided efforts at censorship." They told of effective work being done by the agency. After three hours of this, the Senate finally voted to defeat the proposed slash by 52 to 16, the largest margin by which an appropriations committee recommendation had been defeated in fifty years. The affronted Senator never spoke to me civilly after that. Yet, more important, he thereafter showed an increasing appreciation for the importance of international information work and for the job being done by U.S.I.S. workers.

The difficulties, it should be added, were not solely the fault of a few members of Congress. Two old-line State Department hands, embittered over past rough treatment by a key Campaign of Truth official, had systematically spread poison about him among a few appropriations committee members, whose confidence the two then had. One frustrated group within the U.S.I.S. organization continually sent to committee members letters, generally anonymous, indicating that the whole organization was coming apart at the seams. Committee members couldn't confirm or disprove such generalizations without extensive investigating. In addition, committees that were accustomed to voting funds for 3,237 miles of roads and 23 new post offices, found this business of propaganda vague and nebulous. No one could prove last year's funds had been well spent by producing a cage filled with 7,000 Russians who had deserted Communism. The committee could see and touch new post offices; it could not see ten million Indians or Britons who had been made a little less suspicious of America than they were a year earlier.

Finally, my colleagues and I could scarcely be credited with flawless conduct. There were occasional slips in the vast operation. In the period of forced-draft expansion, construction of radio facilities fell well behind schedule—due largely to metal shortages, difficulties in getting engineering help in competition with private industry, and hitches in negotiating for overseas bases. Under pressure from the National Security Council, we had rushed one large appropriations request for further radio transmitters to the Congress without the months of delay required to spell out every detail. The Congressional committee, not sharing the Council's sense of urgency, turned it down indignantly but asked that it be spelled out in greater detail and resubmitted later.

In the end, the U.S.I.S. managed each year to get most of the funds needed to keep it going at roughly three times the rate existing before the Campaign of Truth was launched. Before I returned to private life, a full-scale investigation by committee members traveling abroad, plus five months of digging by its staff investigators, convinced the House Appropriations Subcommittee that the operation was reasonably sound. Only one member, who had declined to travel and investigate, remained hostile.

Throughout the whole two years, however, the U.S.I.S. program was repeatedly in jeopardy. The danger came not from the great number of responsible, conscientious members of Congress but, usually, from vindictive or uninformed action by a few individuals. If their cases are not discussed in detail here, it is because the influence they wielded was only a symptom of more basic difficulties.

The fact is that the so-called Voice of America program will always make easy pickings for a few strategically located Congressmen any time one of them has what he considers a legitimate complaint or simply wants a headline. The elementary reason is that the program has no militant organized supporters. Unlike most projects that come before the Congress, it has no strong lobby behind it. Moreover, some theories and techniques of international persuasion will always be subject to legitimate differences, which the irresponsible can label as "sabotage" or "helping the enemy." Finally, while propaganda appears superficially to be simple business, it proves upon study to be extraordinarily complex, and few members of Congress have found the time to study its complexities. On every one of the rare occasions from 1942 to 1952 when responsible Congressional groups studied the problem with thoroughness, they became convinced that a large U. S. Information Service was needed and that the work was being done not perfectly but far more effectively than was generally realized. Sound, intelligent, and consistent handling of the problem will come when, and only when, some broad-gaged Congressional committee exercises the responsibility of mastering the propaganda subject, of helping to guide the program, and of taking issue with uninformed or mischievous attacks when they bob up in Congress.

AMID Congressional skirmishes, the more important battle against Communist propaganda continued at an intensified rate, and the Kremlin masters began to show sensitiveness to it. Through *Pravda,* through Tass, and through Soviet domestic broadcasts, they began more and more to answer "the lies told by the Voice of America." They also began increasingly to reply through the satellite press and radio. It has long been an axiom of international propaganda to ignore the other side's output unless it is causing damage. Hence, the hard-working Voice of America crew took heart when public answers to the Voice by the Soviet and its satellites increased from 45 in three months of 1949 to 125 in the corresponding months of 1951.

The Soviet rulers showed other signs of sensitiveness. One by one, they forced the U.S.I.S. to close down information centers in satellite areas. When one of the last of them closed in Budapest, Hungarians, who had visited the centers at the rate of 8,000 a month, massed in such numbers for a farewell visit that police were called out to clear the streets in front of the building.

The Kremlin meanwhile imposed increasing obstacles to the distribution of the U.S.I.S.'s Russian-language magazine *Amerika* in the Soviet Union. Originally started during the temporary "era of Russo-American good feeling" toward the end of the war, *Amerika* contained material that was cleared with Russian censors before it was printed and distributed in 50,000 copies a month. Nominally selling for 10 rubles (legally $1.25) an issue, it long was in such demand that single pages resold on the black market for as much as 25 cents, 50 cents, and even $1.00.

Amerika was a handsomely printed magazine that, despite Soviet censorship, managed to refute some of the most blatant Soviet propaganda about the outside world. One effective article, for example, simply told, with charts and pictures, the factual story of the average American worker and how long he had to work to earn enough to buy a shirt, a ham, or a pair of shoes. To Soviet readers who had been told of the downtrodden, exploited American laborer and yet had to work ten times as long to buy the same items, that was dynamite. By 1950, the Kremlin increasingly prevented the Russian distributors from putting the issues on newsstands. The U.S.I.S. thereupon started building its documentary case history and finally in July, 1952, suspended the magazine. In an official announcement, it told the world how Soviet fear of truth had caused the action.

The difficult task of expanding the Campaign of Truth meanwhile proceeded. A veteran government administrator named Charles Hulten, drafted from his job of managing State Department operations around the world, had taken over as general manager of the program. He instituted improved recruiting methods, new administrative procedures, systematic blueprinting of operations, and management controls. When Hulten was switched to a long-promised overseas assignment late in 1951, a crack advertising executive with wide international experience, Thurman L. Barnard, agreed to take over temporarily. He continued instituting management improvements of a sort that have been too rare in large-scale government operations. Like any organization functioning in several score countries with a shortage of first-class executives, the information program continued to have administrative headaches, growing pains, and occasional flubs. Nonetheless, the private management engineering firm of Booz, Allen and Hamilton studied a major segment of the operation, made recommendations, and concluded in 1951, "The program today is in a sounder position, conceptually and management-wise, than at any time since the Department of State took it over."

By mid-1951, when indiscriminate pot-shotting had begun to affect morale, I summed up in a staff memo the achievements of which the Campaign of Truth team could be proud.

Chiefly to reflect the range of operations, it seems worth quoting:

MID 4751

TO ALL MEMBERS OF THE STAFF OF THE U.S. INTERNATIONAL INFORMATION AND EDUCATIONAL EXCHANGE PROGRAM

Just a year ago, the President and other top national authorities requested urgent expansion of the U.S.I.E. program into a great new Campaign of Truth. That campaign was painstakingly developed, country by country, target group by target group, with the closest collaboration of our embassies and legations abroad. Then, after extensive Congressional hearings, the major part of the funds requested was made available just six months ago. In effect, you were ordered to triple the scale of these complex operations in nine months, meanwhile sharpening the objectives and content into a much more militant campaign. And you were ordered to do this under quite proper but severe restrictions, which made is impossible to add new personnel without prolonged security investigations, evaluations, and clearances requiring an average of at least three months per person.

All this, in effect, meant that you and your colleagues had to carry not only the already heavy operating burden, but had also to carry the enormous load of multiplying the scale of operations at the same time that you recruited added manpower.

Despite the burdens and strains involved, you can look with pride on a record of having:

1. Completed work on major improvements to three radio installations abroad and started work on four others, in addition to effecting important changes to installations in the United States—with the result that we are now overriding the immense Russian jamming at least 100% more effectively than eighteen months ago.

2. Increased the Voice of America's daily program hours by one-third; added seven additional languages to its programs, with a planned total of forty-five languages by June 30, and increased its daily transmitting hours by 50%.

3. So sharpened the content of our programs that reports from competent authorities (specifically, ambassadors) refer to the Voice of America as the "most effective single weapon the free world has behind the Iron Curtain."

4. Completed, with the active assistance of a score of the nation's top scientists, a bold and imaginative technical plan for converting the

Voice into the most powerful radio network the world has ever known.

5. Systematically recruited by aggressive campaigns in 32 states, over 2,700 additional qualified workers, many of them outstanding writers, editors, technicians, and foreign-language specialists. Among these are two of the nation's ablest advertising men, a dozen well-known newspaper correspondents, an outstanding radio executive, etc. We now have 6,318 persons at work, and 1,741 are in the investigative pipeline.

6. Inaugurated overseas a vast program of enlisting the active cooperation of hundreds of local, native organizations abroad, with the result that we have worked with them in effecting the production and distribution, under their auspices, of nearly 500,000,000 booklets, leaflets and posters exposing Communist imperialism and supporting the cause of the free world.

7. Increased by some 50%, through the private enterprise unit, the active participation by private American organizations in the Campaign of Truth.

8. Opened 6 additional U. S. information centers to serve as arsenals of ideas in particularly critical areas—and moved far along toward the opening of 29 others, to make a total of 133 in operation by June 30, 1951.

9. Carried out the most ruthless sort of reevaluation of operations in area after area, resulting in drastic sharpening up of media and operating techniques.

10. Shifted the emphasis of the exchange-of-persons program to increase by over 30% the proportion of leadership types who are able to influence large numbers of their fellow citizens immediately upon their return home; and increased the U.S.I.E. exchange program to where the rate at the end of this year will involve the exchange of more than 3,700 persons a year between this country and foreign lands.

11. Increased the translation program so that more than 2,000,000 translated copies of 277 different American books and documents will be issued this year in 23 foreign languages, with local publishers carrying the main burden of cost.

12. Stepped up the rate of film production and acquisition by almost 300%, including such spectacularly effective films as *Korea, In Defense of Peace,* and *Dwight D. Eisenhower.*

13. Effected arrangements under which the total film audience we reach abroad will, by the year's end, be tripled to a rate of 400,000,000 persons a year.

14. Increased the publications program more than tenfold, even though, under the new plans, each publication is cleared in advance by the embassy concerned.

15. Effected under the general management plan such administrative improvements as systematic, country-by-country evaluation, establishment of program priorities, revision of field reporting procedures, improved liaison with ECA, organizational streamlining, tightened budget management, improved orientation procedures, the educational exchange manual, etc.

16. Perfected a system of preparing, clearing, and periodically revising basic psychological plans for each of the key target countries.

17. Effected the important innovation of having Campaign of Truth representatives participate in top policy-making in the whole foreign relations field.

18. Activated an interdepartmental psychological strategy board, an organization to insure coordination of the total Government information effort abroad.

For all of this, you have earned the praise of the two conscientious watchdog commissions of distinguished private citizens, set up by the Congress. In the words of the Advisory Commission on Information, "The program is being efficiently administered. . . . The expansion authorized by the Eighty-first Congress as the 'Campaign of Truth' is being effectively carried forward."

In the words of the Advisory Commission on Educational Exchange, "the job (of expanding the educational exchange program) has been well done."

However unfair the current sniping may seem, keep up the good work—well aware that your efforts, added to those of loyal public servants in other fields, may well mean the difference between peace and war.

THE U.S.I.S. had early recognized that posters and pamphlets exposing the phoniness of Communist imperialism were most effective when distributed abroad by natives of the country concerned. It found that effective arguments for the free-world cause were somehow less effective if they had a U. S. flag figuratively stamped all over them. So officers of the program went to work to persuade native groups abroad to cooperate in exposing Kremlin intentions and supporting the security program of the free world. There was nothing tricky about this.

Such organizations saw the world conflict as Americans saw it and could properly cooperate in joint enterprises. The going was slow at first, but by late 1951 progress was substantial. More than four hundred such organizations began working with the U.S.I.S. They ranged from a veterans' organization, a labor union, and a church group in Country A of Europe, to a religious society, a teachers' association, and a merchants' club in Country T in Asia. The U.S.I.S. would usually provide raw material, ideas, and consultation. Sometimes it would do the printing; sometimes the local group would.

One such local group, which the U.S.I.S. had stirred into action and systematically assisted, became particularly effective. Later one of the more voluble and least informed American commentators told his audience of the organization and how much more effective it was than the "inept U. S. Information Service." U.S.I.S. officials could only smile.

Information Service editors worked with one of the great religious groups of the world in preparing a booklet about the Communist war on religion. U.S.I.S. helped with the printing. Tens of thousands of copies in six languages went out to the religious leaders in small communities. Bearing the imprint of the organization concerned, it told why Communism was the mortal enemy of that religion. Orders and reorders for the booklet came in.

U.S.I.S. helped with the original copy for millions of handbills which were edited in their final form and ultimately distributed by an anti-Communist union in Italy. As one evidence of the campaign's effectiveness, I later saw a stack of 500-odd membership cards of the rival Communist union. They had been turned in by members converted to the new union.

U. S. film specialists worked with foreign newsreel organizations, providing them with sequences on the growing might of the free world, on the U.N. debates about Korea, on organized protests against slave labor in the Soviet Union, on Point IV projects, and on church protests against Soviet persecution of priests and ministers. All were factual and accurate; none bore the U.S.I.S. label.

In the field of radio, U.S.I.S. found that cooperative arrangements also paid dividends. In twenty-seven free countries, the agency induced national networks to relay to their own audiences special Voice of America programs from New York. The broadcasts were tailored to meet the networks' needs, but they always emphasized the basic themes of a united battle against tyranny, of U. S. peaceful aims, and of international decency. Even more important, U.S.I.S. ultimately reached the point where it provided the skills and talent for producing more than one hundred broadcasts a week over the networks of nations abroad. These ranged all the way from straight news presentations to local versions of the American soap opera. The latter were basically true-to-life presentations, with a Communist villain and a democratic hero. The U.S.I.S. did not boast of its participation in such programs, but neither did it go to extremes to hide the fact. In Country Y of South America the system produced mild embarrassment. There a U.S.I.S. radio specialist won that nation's equivalent of the American Peabody Award for his regular radio commentaries.

Simultaneously, the U.S.I.S. developed and expanded its Private Enterprise Cooperation Unit in the United States. This became a unit of about a dozen individuals with offices in Washington, New York, Chicago, and San Francisco. It cooperated with private organizations that had cooked up effective international projects. It also developed projects that could best be carried out by private American groups, persuaded these groups to undertake them, and then moved on to the next project. Its undertakings included letter-writing campaigns, in which Americans of foreign descent wrote to relatives abroad by the tens of thousands; collections of magazines and cultural material to be provided to schools and institutions abroad; distribution of selected materials by American business offices abroad; donations by American organizations of community receiving sets as gifts to groups abroad; privately sponsored traveling exhibits to illustrate American cultural and industrial progress; and tours by American concert artists to refute the Communist line that Americans were cultural illiterates. In the first six months of 1952 some six hundred such projects were under way. None alone could be decisive. Taken together, they played an important role in the Campaign of Truth.

THE OUTBREAK of war in Korea had given new meaning to the Campaign of Truth. Few realize that the U. S.–U.N. decision to resist in Korea was, broadly speaking, a propaganda decision. On world military maps Korea was not strategically important; indeed, the United States could not hope to hold it in the early days of a world conflict. Economically and politically, it was less vital to America than other areas. What was important and what all hands recognized was that a U. S.–U.N. failure to resist unprovoked aggression in Korea would be interpreted world-wide as a sign of weakness, as a sign that other areas could not count on U.N.–U. S. help in defending themselves. It would be an invitation to neutralism, or to Communism.

As expected, the quick decision to defend Korea had an electrifying effect throughout the free world. In Asia, millions took it as the first sign that the U.N. and U. S. meant business, that they could be counted on for help in an emergency, and that resistance to Communism was hence worthwhile.

With the Korean outbreak, the Secretary of State activated an inter-departmental committee on international information, which I chaired, and turned it into a psychological strategy board. One of its first joint actions was to make all U.S.I.S. personnel in Korea immediately available to General MacArthur. That was the beginning of the psychological warfare campaign which, by the end of 1952, had helped persuade over 100,000 North Koreans and Chinese to surrender.

One major event in the Korean war, incidentally, confirmed an important lesson of modern psychological warfare. That lesson is that close study of an enemy nation's broadcasts to its own people can sometimes provide a clear tip-off as to that nation's intentions.

After General MacArthur's magnificently conceived landings at Inchon, he started his march toward the Yalu. He did so despite the fears of some of his colleagues that U.N. forces would not be strong enough to carry the march through. Those of us in the State Department who were studying propaganda trends also raised warnings. We had begun to note an ominous tone in Chinese home-front propaganda.

In a campaign that crescendoed, the Peiping Government noisily sought to convince Chinese citizens that they had a great stake in the Korean war, that they had real cause to hate the white forces of the U.N., and that they had an obligation to enlist en masse for the Chinese "Volunteer Army." This seemed to old propaganda hands to presage the throwing of masses of Chinese troops into the North Korean battle lines. My colleagues and I raised these warnings with the Secretary of State and his associates. They, in turn, raised them with the Pentagon. General MacArthur's headquarters, however, did not credit the warnings—not until the Chinese forces suddenly swarmed into the war, split the U.N. armies dangerously, and forced them back far below the 38th Parallel.

WHILE the Voice of America and the U.S.I.S. worked away, allied U. S. services in Japan, Germany, and Austria cooperated with national authorities of those countries in carrying out pro-democratic programs. And from Berlin and Vienna they managed to reach large audiences under Soviet control. The enterprising RIAS (Radio in American Sector), for example, performed spectacular work. It gave the residents of

East Germany a steady diet of news, tipped them off about Communist informers in their midst, emphasized developments suppressed by the Communists, and provided perhaps the best entertainment in Germany. I have seen East Germans sneak into RIAS headquarters at the rate of seventy a day to provide news for broadcasts into the Soviet Zone.

Meanwhile, an important private ally had entered the propaganda battle. The Committee for a Free Europe had been formed by Joseph Grew, the late DeWitt Poole, and a list of distinguished citizens. Originally, the committee had the mission of helping important exiles from Iron Curtain countries, exiles who might some day play a role in the restitution of freedom to those nations. Some one got the idea of starting radio broadcasts to provide a voice for those exiles. The programs at first were ineffective little items sent out over a weak transmitter. Later, however, the Committee for a Free Europe set up a powerful standard transmitter in Munich, Germany, and later added a short-wave station in Portugal—all aimed at satellite audiences. There were bumbles and slips, as in every new propaganda operation I ever knew, but by 1951, Radio Free Europe, then under C. D. Jackson and Robert Lang, was clearly having an impact. Its full schedule of Munich broadcasts to Czechoslovakia, defectors reported, drew a large audience in that restive nation. The Committee for a Free Europe and other organizations sent "Winds of Freedom" balloon-born leaflets into Czechoslovakia and Poland. While criticized by some as a flamboyant stunt, the leaflets made a hit with many Czechs and doubtless helped sustain their spirit of resistance. The Czech and Hungarian Governments officially protested against Radio Free Europe broadcasts.

Radio Free Europe did not overlap or conflict with the Voice; rather it supplemented government broadcasts. The Voice, a world-wide network broadcasting in forty-six languages, spoke for the American people, spreading the truth about democracy and the free nations and spiking Soviet lies.

Radio Free Europe, transmitting only to the satellite countries, provided a voice for free Poles or free Hungarians to speak to their captive fellow countrymen. It sent back messages from escapees and denounced informers within the Communist regimes.

As of this writing, the complementary Committee for Free Asia is still in the inevitable early stage of ineffectiveness. It should find itself later. Meanwhile, in a world-wide battle for men's minds, in which Communist expenditures well exceed $1,500,000,000 a year, Americans need every weapon, public and private, that can be put into service.

BY EARLY 1952, after I had completed the two years' service to which I had originally agreed, it was time to turn my responsibilities over to others. By then, I had helped put through a reorganization that should free the next Assistant Secretary of a mass of operating details and permit him to concentrate on working with the Department's top command on basic policies. The world-wide network of information operations would be set up in an International Information Administration, reporting to the Secretary of State but theoretically freed of a morass of Departmental red tape.

I therefore submitted my resignation. The President, on the Secretary's recommendation, appointed as Assistant Secretary of State my former deputy, Howland Sargeant, who had been a tower of strength, had mastered the intricacies of foreign policy, and had developed genuine astuteness in the business of international persuasion. His added distinction, which the press never forgot, was that of being the husband of Myrna Loy. To the post of I.I.A. Administrator, the President appointed Wilson Compton, one of the famous Compton brothers, a former business executive, later president of Washington State College, and a past member of delegations to international conferences.

As the Campaign of Truth moved into a new period, my

associates and I could look back on a mixed record of hits, runs, and errors. Errors included too-rapid expansion in two or three countries. There, new information operatives had shown up and begun to trip over each other before first-rate operating chiefs arrived and put them to work on systematic, effective, and not-too-visible assignments. Delays in construction of radio facilities, avoidable or not, made another black mark. Perhaps most important, I had failed to persuade the Administration authorities and Congress to allocate to the program the dozen or more "super-grade" jobs (paying more than $10,800 a year) that would be necessary in order to lure into the program the minimum number of first-rate executives so badly needed.

On the plus side, the program had unquestionably become more aggressive and was better tailored to each audience abroad. The Campaign of Truth had made progress toward allying itself with the powerful religious forces that can yet become Communism's greatest foe. The campaign at least had begun to put Soviet propagandists on the defensive. And the whole operation had attained a scale and scope much greater than ever before in peacetime—and more in keeping with the enormous job yet to be done.

Moreover, the Campaign of Truth had rounded up hundreds of Americans with some basic knowledge of foreign lands and languages and had added to them other hundreds of young men and women from press, radio, and movie fields. Then it had put all to work, at home and abroad, on jobs where they would learn more and more about the customs, traditions, and languages of other peoples. In a nation committed to world leadership, they are bound to become an important nucleus, a sorely needed reserve, for meeting world problems of the future.

Those outside the program who studied it closely came up with generally encouraging reports. The extensive world-wide investigation by a House subcommittee had shown the operation, in the words of the subcommittee's chairman, "pretty good"—glowing praise from him.

As for the press, Communist-front journals naturally berated the U.S.I.S. At the other pole, the Chicago *Tribune* group of ultra-nationalists never said anything favorable about any part of the activity. One columnist of that stripe published twelve important factual misstatements about the program in less than two weeks. By and large, however, the press had been objective, fair, and encouraging.

As early as mid-1950, *Time* magazine made a comprehensive study of the Voice of America, criticized it in some respects, and ended up with the finding that the Voice was "well worth the effort—and the taxpayers' money—that goes into it." The following year, the Kiplinger organization, after criticizing the Voice in its newsletter, authorized a study and ended up with a *Kiplinger* article saying, "The Voice thus continues to attack on all fronts, and by all signs, it is winning." The *Saturday Evening Post,* early in 1952, did a comprehensive survey and then published a laudatory report on the Voice as "The Hole in the Iron Curtain." Abroad, the Swiss weekly *Curieux,* late in 1951, published a full-page analysis of the Voice, and its editor wrote, "One has to conclude that the V.O.A. broadcasts are widely listened to behind the Iron Curtain and that they play a considerable role in the cold war between East and West."

The other less spectacular U.S.I.S. activities earned far more bouquets than brickbats from the non-Communist press at home and abroad.

Finally, the two distinguished advisory commissions set up by Congress to serve as its watchdogs reported that the program still had faults but had made commendable progress. The Advisory Commission on Educational Exchange noted the "excellent staff," "vigorous, forward-looking leadership," and "the devotion and enthusiasm" of the program's officers. While urging improved evaluation and other measures, it added that "on the whole the job has been well done" and later reported "continued improvement."

The Advisory Commission on International Information, similarly urging increased efforts to improve evaluation of effects, reported the program "efficiently administered" and its personnel "greatly improved." In fitting recognition of the men and women who carry on the work year after year, it added:

We are particularly gratified at the way in which the information program's personnel has been steadily improved. It takes a great deal of patriotic self-sacrifice for men and women who are highly skilled and highly paid professionals to leave their long-range posts and come into governmental service under conditions of uncertainty and often abuse which have prevailed in recent years. These people deserve the highest recognition and gratitude of their country. There are not a few of them. They have recognized the gravity of the world crisis and they have enlisted voluntarily in the war of ideas. . . .

But the greatest credit goes to those who have stuck by the battle through thick and thin—and sometimes it has been very thin, when complacency or unawareness spread over national thinking. Some of them have turned down very lucrative job opportunities—and this is particularly true in the radio field—just because they felt deeply and sacrificially that they were enlisted in a significant cause. . . . We have no hesitation in saying that many of those who have taken this program through its slimmest days possess skill and ability which compare very favorably with that to be found anywhere.

7

"The Voice of McCarthy"

IN LATE March of 1953, a Voice of America producer called upon the Voice's music library for a recording of "Song of India" to be broadcast in response to requests from Indian listeners. The record was no longer available, the librarian explained with a straight face. "You see," she added, "it's by Rimsky-Korsakov, and we're supposed not to use anything by Russians."

The ban, soon rescinded, was just one hysterical small incident in a strangely hysterical era. Under the prodding of Senator Joseph McCarthy and some unusual young aides, incredible things happened for a few weeks. A new command in the State Department rescinded a directive criticized by the Senator, issued a new one, and then rescinded that. Voice of America broadcasters competed with each other to sound so stridently anti-Communist that the Senator couldn't charge them with "softness." Proved public servants on the Voice installed recording machines in staff meetings to insure against being misquoted by informers planted in the organization. Old colleagues hesitated about talking with each other. Refugees from the Iron Curtain, now working in the Voice's various language programs, said conditions reminded them of their days of terror. Other employees recalled the police-state excesses in George Orwell's *1984*.

101

The international information program of the United States Government had simply had the misfortune to become the guinea pig for the first investigation by a Senate Permanent Investigating Committee under the junior Senator from Wisconsin. A nation not yet aware of his techniques was temporarily shocked by his "disclosures." The committee could well have uncovered certain administrative shortcomings, cases of extravagance arising from rapid expansion, and perhaps even a few dubious propaganda policies. But such matters are rarely spectacular. Ignoring some of the most important of the program's basic shortcomings, McCarthy focused on testimony about supposed subversion or sabotage. In the televised hearings, a procession of dissident personnel made a number of emphatic allegations. Those who testified constructively in private were seldom heard in later public sessions. Men with key responsibilities were rarely featured as witnesses. Private citizens on the "watchdog" committees set up by Congress itself were not even subpoenaed.

While the Communist press and radio gloated, the New York *Times* investigated the investigators. It then editorialized: "What harm this whole foolish episode has done to the prestige of the American propaganda effort is, of course, incalculable." Publications as diverse as the Washington *Post*, the Des Moines *Register*, and the Catholic magazines *America* and the *Commonweal* deplored the hearings' methods. The last-named, contending that McCarthy "poisons whatever he touches," observed, "The voice of a Joseph McCarthy must never become, in fact, the voice of America, but the danger that it may is both clear and present now."

INTERESTINGLY, two parallel Congressional investigations in this strange spring of 1953 provided a case study of the right way and the wrong way to go about such matters. In the summer of 1952, the Senate of the Eighty-second Congress had established a special Foreign Relations subcommittee to investigate the entire international information and educational exchange program with an eye to effecting improvements. Starting out under the chairmanship of Senator William Fulbright of Arkansas, it set about the work conscientiously and constructively. Later, when the Republicans gained control of the Eighty-third Congress, Senator Bourke Hickenlooper of Iowa assumed the chairmanship and carried on in the same spirit.

Feeling that the proof of the pudding was in the eating, the committee and its staff made a study of the impact of the Campaign of Truth in other countries. Members and staffers visited nations abroad to gather first-hand information. Back in Washington, they summoned for formal hearings responsible executives of the program. Then they summoned well-known private citizens belonging to the two advisory commissions which Congress had set up to study, evaluate, and criticize the program.

The Hickenlooper committee engaged the services of a staff who prepared extraordinarily thorough studies of the immense Soviet propaganda mechanism, of British operations, and of American activities. The committee called distinguished Americans who might be expected to have sound judgment in the field.

The committee, winning justified praise from the responsible press, concentrated on the program's real flaws and their main causes. Those root causes, much testimony seemed to indicate, numbered five: (1) The great difficulty of developing sound evaluation techniques for measuring the persuasiveness of various parts of the program, (2) the continuing inability to recruit enough first-rate executives (because of low pay and fear of being slandered), (3) the excessive red tape, budgetary rigidity, and bureaucratic rivalries that are perennial but not altogether incurable problems in the government, (4) the fact that responsible executives in the program had always had to spend more time combatting irresponsible charges of nonexistent faults than they could devote to correcting real and basic faults, and (5) the tendency to overrate the Voice of America, as opposed to less spectacular operations in free areas.

The Hickenlooper committee seemed to feel the new Administration, which had appointed the well-regarded Dr. Robert L. Johnson to head the program, should be given a chance to solve its own internal management problems.

IT WAS while this responsible inquiry was going on that the junior Senator from Wisconsin soared off on his own investigation amid a roar of allegations that he had found "sabotage." Two months later he had failed to prove a single such case, but he had treated the nation to its first sampling of the 1953 Model of Joseph R. McCarthy. In that, he had the invaluable assistance of an eager young (26) counsel named Roy Cohn, whose techniques rivaled McCarthy's own. Together, they well surpassed the excesses of some of the most lop-sided inquiries of the 1930's. A few instances illustrate the technique:

§   A young woman who had been discharged by the Voice was put on the stand before television cameras to give well-rehearsed attacks on veteran public servants as being pro-Communist. Only after more than a week of hers and other allegations did the criticized staff members get an opportunity to appear in rebuttal. They did so to the apparent satisfaction of other Senators. Their answers were not televised.

§   One employee of a news desk testified darkly that editors had substituted the word "democratic" for "anti-Communist" in one of his stories in order to "soften" it. He added, under prodding, that he could not recall a single instance when the word "anti-Communist" had been permitted by his editors.

The chairman avoided quoting the full "subversive" item as finally broadcast. It read: "In Guatemala City, citizens paraded before the United States Embassy celebrating the inauguration of Dwight Eisenhower as President of the United States. Last night, leaders of *democratic* organizations, speak-

ing at a mass meeting of their followers, hailed Mr. Eisenhower's inauguration as 'another blow against world Communism.'"

The counsel and his investigators, to whom all files were
made available, failed to mention that there had been repeated use of the word "anti-Communist" and that, for example, two days before the disputed story, the word was used
fourteen times in copy approved by the desk in question. Some
who volunteered to testify on such matters were not called
upon by Cohn. No one, of course, mentioned that the effectiveness of a broadcast is not necessarily to be measured by the
number of times the word "anti-Communist" is used.

§ Once McCarthy put Earl Browder, ex-chief of the U. S.
Communist Party, on the stand for a long quizzing, presumably on the sound premise that one can always make himself a
hero by publicly squaring off against a known Communist.
The excuse for the televised hearing was that the State Department had "used the taxpayer's money" for putting Earl
Browder's books in its libraries "around the world." McCarthy
and Cohn failed to tell the public that available "evidence"
showed that exactly three Browder volumes were among the
2,000,000-odd books owned by the State Department library
system, that there was no record that the Department had pur-
chased any of the three (which presumably were parts of collections donated to the libraries) and that there was no evidence that any of the three books was then actually on the
open shelves of a single library.

Young Cohn once even questioned the inclusion in U.S.I.S.
libraries of the prize-winning poems of Archibald MacLeish.
It seems MacLeish, one-time Librarian of Congress, was known
as a "liberal." When Dan Lacy, capable recent chief of the
library system, explained the entire book-selecting system logically in an executive session, he was not put on the stand publicly. The Senator apparently was not significantly interested
in Mr. Lacy's view that the overseas libraries under the law

are designed to present a rounded, honest view of every field of American endeavor, not simply a propaganda picture; or in his view that it is not consistent with the dignity of the United States Government to use suppression, mendacity, or guile in its library system.

(Actually, of course, the average U.S.I.S. library contains books as diverse as Sherwood's *Roosevelt and Hopkins* and Beard's *Roosevelt and the Coming of the War,* Taft's *A Foreign Policy for Americans,* Chambers' *Witness,* Biddle's *Fear of Freedom,* and Hoover's *Memoirs.* The system contains 18,000 volumes that are on the American Legion's approved anti-Communist list. But, at least up to the spring of 1953, there had been no thought that every book must suit the personal taste of any one individual, even a Senator. Some suspect that when other free peoples begin to question the freedom of American thought and conscience, America will then have lost its struggle for the minds of men.)

§   An ex-engineer of the Voice made publicized charges that two giant transmitters had been willfully mislocated. Under prodding from Senator McCarthy, he indicated he suspected sabotage. McCarthy and Cohn did not make public a thick file of official correspondence and documents showing the full story of how the transmitter locations had been recommended and rerecommended by a team of M.I.T. scientists after studying the findings of the Radio Corporation of America, the Bureau of Standards, and the Army Signal Corps. Nor did the Senator put on the stand some nationally known engineers and scientists who waited in Washington for two days to testify on the reasons for the location.

The fact was that competent engineers had belatedly come to differ as to whether the sites were the best conceivable, but no responsible man among them had even hinted at sabotage.

§   One junior official produced headlines across the country by testifying, under careful questioning, that the Voice had spent $65,000 on a mobile studio, had found it no good, and had to have it rebuilt—at a total cost to the taxpayers of "about $100,000." He later rechecked this allegation and wrote Cohn and McCarthy that he had been in error, that the total cost to the Voice had been $41,000, that the contractor (R.C.A.) had paid for necessary alterations, and that he wanted to retract his testimony. Weeks later the letter had not been made public.

§ At one point the Security Division of the Department of State transferred one minor employee who had given the committee testimony which even his new superiors apparently considered misleading. McCarthy immediately demanded his reinstatement. The State Department complied. Thereafter numerous insecure Voice employees whose competence had been questioned by superiors lined up to testify.

§ One witness, Reed Harris, stated the affirmative case forcefully and publicly, at the cost of being grilled at length on some silly writing he had done as a college youth twenty-one years earlier. His resignation was accepted a month later by his newly appointed boss, Dr. Robert Johnson—who, however, braved the Senator's displeasure by praising Harris' record.

§ The investigators once singled out as an example of "sabotage" a State Department directive saying that Soviet-endorsed authors like Howard Fast could be quoted by the Voice and other media to refute the Communists' own arguments. The new administration of the Department of State, still not sure of itself, hastily rescinded the directive. It then rushed out a new one forbidding quotation of "Communists, fellow-travelers, et cetera, under any circumstances." The Department soon had to concede that, even if it could identify an et cetera, the directive made little sense, because a cardinal principle of effective persuasion is to quote the opposition against itself. Secretary Dulles, after several weeks of Departmental drafting and redrafting, issued a new directive in effect rescinding the last one.

§ A few subordinates in the Voice, who had been eager to

indulge in more international name-calling than the embassies abroad considered wise, dissected in televised hearings the various instructions they had received. McCarthy implied that there must have been subversion behind any effort to substitute temperate persuasion for shrill denunciation. In the course of it all, the world public was treated to detailed discussions of confidential matters involving American policy toward India, Iran, and Russia. One Russian desk employee was induced to make televised statements which could have landed him in jail if he had been caught saying the same things to a private citizen.

A tentative decision reached in 1952 to suspend certain Hebrew broadcasts—on grounds of economy—was portrayed in the hearings as part of a pattern of supposed sabotage. A few weeks after this testimony, the Eisenhower Administration also decided to suspend the Hebrew broadcasts—again on grounds of economy.

§ In numerous bits of testimony, any official who had discouraged shrilly aggressive propaganda became by implication a part of a "pattern" of subversion. In the Voice, as in any propaganda organization, there are those who favor the subtle approach and those who favor more strident tactics. Many able Voice employees from Eastern Europe, for example, understandably yearn for the liberation of their countries and, hence, will be satisfied by nothing short of war. These men have always had to be held in check by their superiors, since official U. S. policy has never condoned their brand of fire-eating provocation. In the McCarthy inquiries, any U. S. official or ambassador who discouraged such provocation was made to seem part of "a subversive pattern."

§ On the day when Stalin's death offered great propaganda possibilities, the head of the Voice's Russian desk and a number of other Voice specialists were not on the job. They were cooling their heels outside the Senator's chamber, waiting their turn to be commended or pilloried in proportion to their willingness to demean themselves by giving the kind of testimony desired. Those who made even vague allusions to some "pattern" generally came off unscathed. Those who gave constructive testimony generally did not—if they ever got a public hearing.

Behind the strange procession of testimony was an unusual group of investigators, all appointed by McCarthy. The original investigator, at first operating unofficially, appeared to be Howard Rushmore, once a sub-editor of the Communist *Daily Worker*. He said he had left the Communist organ when reprimanded by his *Daily Worker* superiors in late 1939—some months after the Nazi-Soviet Pact had driven most "recognized" ex-Communists out of the Party. Rushmore early got in touch with Cohn, helped him, and ultimately joined his staff. Cohn himself was a 26-year-old lawyer, who worked for the Truman Administration until the 1952 election and then performed the dexterous feat of leaping to the McCarthy bandwagon. Teamed with these two was one Donald Surine, who had once been fired by the F.B.I. and about whom a Senate Subcommittee on Privileges and Elections had officially reported in 1951: "The testimony of Surine before this subcommittee contains an apparent willful and knowing misstatement of a material fact. . . . The subcommittee is of the opinion that this testimony . . . should be transmitted to the Department of Justice for such action as it deems appropriate." Another investigator was one G. David Schine, also 26. His qualifications seemed to consist of having once written essays on Communism and having helped his father run the Schine resort hotels.

It was this group of investigators, aided by some assistants with the same approach, who blueprinted the hearings. Other Senators on McCarthy's committee, obviously not informed of all the staff's activities, appeared unhappy, but not so much as actually to tangle with the chairman.

Cohn and Schine, subsequent to the first series of hearings, evoked wide ridicule abroad by publicly professing to investigate the personnel and efficiency of the overseas operation on a 18-day April trip through six European countries. The distinguished advisory commissions—whose testimony was not sought —had spent many months, over a period of five years, on the same assignment.

In his syndicated radio column, John Crosby, a frequent critic of the Voice of America, wrote on March 13, 1953: "The Voice, for all its faults, is taken seriously enough by the Communists so that they spend millions of dollars trying to jam its broadcasts to keep them from being heard on the other side of the Iron Curtain." He also observed: "The whole intent of the McCarthy investigation seems to be not to investigate but to do the utmost damage to the Voice."

No evidence had come to light to support the theory of some that the hand of the Kremlin was somehow behind the inquiry, without any Senator's knowledge. The whole episode, however, underscored the danger that someday the Kremlin could easily resort to one of the oldest devices of international intrigue: planting an agent, having him profess loudly that he has turned anti-Communist, and then having him point accusingly at agencies or individuals whom the Kremlin desires to undermine.

I HAVE NEVER been one of those who believes that the blame for so-called "McCarthyism" rests solely with the junior Senator from Wisconsin. I have long felt and repeatedly said that the government in Washington in the postwar years did not publicly show enough profound concern over the possibilities of Communist infiltration. There are reasons for believing that we Americans have sometimes overestimated Soviet military strength and underestimated the degree of possible penetration by Soviet agents into free-world institutions. The Truman Administration, while taking more drastic steps than those taken by any previous administration to thwart penetration by foreign agents, probably did not go far enough. Nor, in its early days, has the Eisenhower Administration. To date, neither has revealed to the public even the amount of serious concern that has been shown internally.

If the Truman Administration had early taken the initiative and publicly embarked on a wholesale and convincing review of its own loyalty and security system, many of the excesses of McCarthyism might have been avoided. Certainly the public would have been less swayed by the Senator's hyperbole.

For the sake of perspective, it should also be emphasized that the junior Senator from Wisconsin was far from the originator of guilt by association, sweeping allegations without proof, and so-called smear tactics. Some of the same attributes, in milder form, showed up in Washington investigations of business organizations in the early 1930's. A famous political publicist indulged in milder "smear" tactics when he systematically fed certain Congressmen an array of material that had the effect of slandering the Hoover Administration. As far back as the 1890's, similar tactics were involved in the then-current wave of anti-Catholic hysteria in America.

In the late 1930's, many of America's less judicious liberals used guilt-by-association techniques in attacking such early anti-Communists as Eugene Lyons, Frederick Woltman, and Lawrence Spivak. Any of these men seen talking with a Father Coughlin or a Gerald L. K. Smith, even if simply seeking information, had the point used against them as evidence of their being "pro-fascist." One of the key-hole columnists who is loudest today in denouncing various liberals was then in the van of those who habitually labeled anti-Communists as "pro-fascist." It was for this reason that many of the old anti-Communists, still bitter, rushed to McCarthy's assistance when he started cutting loose with exaggerated charges. They supplied him with facts, charges, and—most of all—suspicions by the carload.

The basic fault, obviously, is the tendency of us Americans to oversimplify. Millions today still say: "McCarthy is against Communism. I am against Communism. Therefore, I am for McCarthy." Few stop to remember that there is one threat almost as dangerous to American society as Communism itself. That, of course, is disregard of the principles of fair play, elemental decency, and innocent-until-proved-guilty, for which the fathers of America fought. Such disregard was not justified in the 1930's; it cannot be justified now; it is peculiarly dangerous in the world of today.

PERSONAL NOTE: Watching what I considered the gross miscarriage of common decency in the McCarthy hearings, I wrote an article for the New York *Herald Tribune,* of February 25, 1953. It was reprinted in a dozen other newspapers. In it I pointed out the Voice's known faults, then added:

In the nation's interest, the whole business should be taken out of the carnival tent and subjected to intensive but impartial investigation under a chairman who has a reputation for being more interested in making progress than in making headlines. . . . International persuasion is inordinately complex business, requiring long, patient study. Its effectiveness is not to be glibly judged by the number of times the word "anti-Communist" is used in scripts.

Friends have urged me not to "get mixed up in this mess," not to answer inquiries about it. They said that, by so doing, I would only subject myself to concerted attacks and distortions by the inquisitor and his journalistic satellites. Thus far I have heeded their advice. I have hoped that Senators Mundt, Symington, and Jackson could force the current hearings into channels of objective inquiry. They have been unable to do so. Unfortunately, officials of the Voice have been instructed to keep silent, to say nothing unless the current inquiry unexpectedly offers a hearing to the other side of the story. So some one who knows the complex field of international persuasion has to speak up.

Subsequently, when requested to testify before the Hickenlooper committee, I repeated some of the same thoughts in different words. I pointed out that international propaganda was intricate business for conscientious adults, and could not be solved by "childish" and one-sided inquisitions.

"Getting mixed up in this mess" soon proved an accurate prediction. Two days after that testimony was reported in the press, a U. S. marshal in New York served a subpoena on me late in the afternoon to appear next morning before Senator McCarthy. Obviously nettled by my use of the word "childish," McCarthy's young counsel, Roy Cohn, said to me on the telephone, "We want to show you how the children can do." He and McCarthy did just that, questioning me for two hours, in effect, on why I had chosen to criticize their proceedings. Other members of the committee were restrained and fair. I supplied all the answers as forthrightly as I could, in executive session. Unlike destructive witnesses, I was not thereafter scheduled for any immediate public hearing.

IRONICALLY, the whole strange performance was gumming up the nation's propaganda mechanism at just the time when important constructive developments were taking place. President Eisenhower had a capable, conscientious team of advisers, headed by William H. Jackson, making a commendable study of all operations and strategy in the so-called "psychological" field (including matters going far beyond simple, overt persuasions). In the White House, C. D. Jackson, Emmet Hughes, and others were working with the President on broad psychological strategy—including the President's superb April 16 speech telling the Kremlin what it could do if it really wished to prove peaceful intentions. And Robert Johnson was seeking systematically to bring about further improvements in the international information and educational exchange organization.

It was in the midst of all this that the public was led to confuse dissent with disloyalty. The result was to shatter the morale of decent public servants and to drive trained propagandists into returning to private life. The always difficult job of executive recruitment became more difficult.

McCARTHY's curious "investigation" provided bases for these conclusions:

1. Unless the Congress adopts a code of ethics and fairness for investigations (like the code proposed by Representative Keating of New York), it will always be possible for certain types of chairmen and counsel to abuse the investigating power. By agile tactics and by concentrating on testimony from malcontents, they can make any agency or private business seem disgraceful.

2. The intangible qualities and experimental nature of international persuasion will always make the field easy prey for headline-hunting inquisitors. This would be true even if propaganda operations were far more efficient than any developed to date.

3. America can never conduct an effective operation in international persuasion if the whole plant is to be pulled up by the roots and publicly dissected every few months by men who have not conscientiously studied the intricacies of the work.

4. If, on the other hand, the Congress will concentrate its propaganda responsibilities in one permanent, mature, and well-staffed joint committee (as spelled out in chapter 20), then real progress can be made and will be made.

8

The Electro-Magnetic War

"*YOU KNOW*, the best brains in the country haven't yet been focused on finding all possible ways of getting the truth through the Iron Curtain."

Justin Miller, then president of the National Association of Broadcasters, made that remark at a small dinner he gave just after I became Assistant Secretary of State early in 1950. It wasn't clear whether Miller's remark impressed the few Congressmen present or his fellow members of the U. S. Advisory Commission on International Information. It made a deep impression on me and set me digging, as one of my first official efforts, into the whole maze of international communications. From that research, one fact quickly emerged: *Like it or not, the United States was in the midst of a full-scale electro-magnetic war with the Soviet Union.*

The first shots in that war were fired in February, 1948. U. S. Government monitors then noted raucous noises interfering with Voice of America Russian-language transmissions beamed to Asiatic Russia from West Coast, Honolulu, and Manila transmitters. Engineers readily spotted the noises as systematic jamming. Such technical procedures as triangulation indicated that the jammers were located in the Soviet Union.

The Soviet technique was not new. It amounted just to

broadcasting various noises to disrupt any communications on the same wavelength. In World War II all major powers had early used such jamming as a tactical weapon against enemy *military* communications. Then Germany, Italy, and Japan began jamming in an effort to block Allied broadcasts to the Axis peoples. The Allies never jammed normal broadcasting. With the end of the war, peace returned to the air waves and was interrupted only by some reciprocal jamming by Spain and Russia in 1946.

In early 1947, when the U. S. Government found the Kremlin systematically misrepresenting this country to the Russian people, the Voice of America started a short (one-hour) daily broadcast to the Soviet Union in Russian. Even then the Kremlin did not begin jamming the Voice. Within a year, however, the American Embassy in Moscow detected many signs that Russians were listening to the Voice. It was then, in February, 1948, that the Soviet began its first weak attempts to drown out the Voice's trans-Pacific broadcasts. In March and April, jamming began against Voice Russian programs relayed from Munich and Tangier. In August, the Russians started jamming B.B.C. transmitters which relayed the Voice's Russian programs. British and U. S. locating equipment confirmed that the interference was coming from about twenty-five transmitters in the Soviet Union.

On August 12, 1948, a woman in New York started a chain of events that really set the Russian electronic defense into high gear. A Russian school teacher, Mrs. Anna Kasenkina, escaped from her Soviet captors by jumping from a window of the U.S.S.R. Consulate in New York. The Kremlin suppressed the news entirely within Russia and the satellites. The Voice of America carried it full blast. Within a few hours, embassy employees of the U. S. and other nations found the jump was being talked about in elevators, restaurants, and buses all over Moscow. Twenty-four hours later, Soviet official organs felt forced to admit the episode, but their distorted versions evoked snickers. "It may have been the Kasenkina affair," says General Walter Bedell Smith, then Ambassador to Moscow, "that caused the Kremlin to decide to eliminate this source of truthfulness"—by all-out jamming of the Voice of America.

At that time, according to many indications, the U.S.S.R. started construction work on a far more elaborate new jamming network, even while intensifying its more routine interference. On April 24, 1949, the new jamming set-up went into operation with a vengeance. On every frequency used by the Voice for Russian broadcasts from the United States, the Far East, and Europe, multiple squawks appeared. Russian broadcasts from the B.B.C. and the Vatican radio ran into a din. The air waves were filled with beeps, squawks, and siren-like howls. Meticulous tests by agencies of the United States and other governments indicated the U.S.S.R. was now using at least 100 sky-wave (long distance) jammers and 250 ground-wave (local) jammers. Clearly the Kremlin had embarked on a major campaign to blot out anything in the Russian language from the outside world.

The whole jamming business violated at least two international telecommunications conventions, to which the U.S.S.R. had subscribed, but by that time Soviet violation of agreements had become routine procedure. Brushing aside protests within the U.N. and outside, the Kremlin kept intensifying its campaign. By early 1950 the local ground-wave jammers had increased to 500. The coordinated actions of the jammers made it evident that all were linked by a complex teletype network.

In April, 1950, the Soviet went beyond the jamming of Russian-language programs and began trying to jam the Voice in Polish, Czech, Hungarian, Rumanian, Slovene, and Serbian. The blockage of those satellite-language programs was far from complete but research indicated that only about five percent of Voice transmissions in the Russian language were getting through to Moscow.

Clearly the Kremlin intended to go much further. Its extraordinary campaign and elaborate mechanism even then made two things clear: (1) the Soviet Government deeply fears the truth from the outside world, and (2) the Voice would have to employ most unusual measures in order to get its programs continually heard in the U.S.S.R.

VOICE OF AMERICA engineers, headed by a veteran of international radio named George Herrick, had already done much research into counter-jamming measures. With help from the Bureau of Standards and others, they had devised new techniques that showed promise. However, they talked in a kind of engineering gobbledygook that was about as clear to my non-technical colleagues and me as Urdu slang. To double-check and to be sure no bets were being missed, we decided in mid-1950 to heed Justin Miller's suggestion: to have a team of outstanding American scientific brains review the whole radio counter-offensive and its work for possible new measures.

With the enthusiastic cooperation of Secretary Acheson, Under Secretary James Webb and I asked President Robert Killian of the Massachusetts Institute of Technology to have M.I.T. round up a team of outstanding scientists to tackle the whole problem. M.I.T. did so with astounding thoroughness.

The group that was soon assembled and cleared for security included such scientists as Edward Purcell, the world-renowned expert on radiation who later won a Nobel prize; Merle Tuve, who was widely credited with developing the proximity fuse; Jerome Wiesner, chief of M.I.T.'s Research Laboratory of Electronics; John R. Pierce of the Bell Telephone Laboratories; Lloyd Berkner, brilliant all-around scientist and former executive secretary of the Pentagon's Research and Development Board; and Dana K. Bailey, radio propagation expert from the U. S. Bureau of Standards.

To keep the project from becoming too narrowly technical,

M.I.T. put it under Dean John E. Burchard, a social science specialist experienced in administering large special projects. A few others like Clyde Kluckhohn, eminent Harvard anthropologist, and John A. Morrison, the University of Maryland geography specialist on Eastern Europe, were added. In all, the group comprised thirty top-flight American minds. I had meanwhile enlisted Davidson Taylor, former vice president of the Columbia Broadcasting System, to represent the Department of State in coordinating the work. We dubbed the enterprise "Project Troy," for the wooden horse behind hostile walls.

With night sessions and day sessions extending over many months, the team labored away. We emptied the State Department's "brainwave files" of extreme ideas submitted by outsiders and staff members and passed them to Project Troy team members to study. They looked into the entire lot: transmitting messages via migratory birds or seals (impractical), floating messages downstream (most rivers run the wrong way), and bouncing signals off the moon (potentially feasible but long-range). They found possibilities in distributing leaflets by balloon, which had been tried as early as World War I.

Most important were their verifications and findings in the radio field. Many are still classified, but some can be mentioned.

Project Troy early examined the super-duper of all the schemes devised by Herrick and his Voice of America crew: the "Ring Plan." This imaginative—and expensive—program called for stringing a necklace of fourteen powerful short-wave, medium-wave, and long-wave transmitters around the periphery of the Soviet-dominated land mass. The units were to be linked by multiple relay circuits, so that the most effective link could be selected in times of bad atmospherics. After studying the plan, for which the Congress had already appropriated some funds, the Troy group found it "an ambitious step, boldly conceived and, in our opinion, basically sound."

The group similarly studied and endorsed "Operation Clipper," another plan already adopted by Herrick and his crew. By attaching an electronic device to each Voice transmitter, this system increased about tenfold the strength of the signal at the point of reception, thereby permitting the Voice to override much jamming.

Another technique already in force was known by the cozy name of "cuddling." Under this, Voice engineers simply put a few Voice of America transmitters on frequencies so close to those used by the U.S.S.R. domestically that the Russians couldn't jam the Voice transmitters without jamming many of their own. For a while, cuddling apparently stumped the Moscow strategists. Ultimately, they decided that even their own programs weren't worth letting outside voices through. They started jamming the cuddle frequencies—and themselves—with some regularity.

In 1950, the engineers of the Voice of America developed new "brute force" techniques. These involved massing a vast array of transmissions in an effort to swamp Soviet jammers. First, the Voice used all its available transmitters to broadcast Russian-language programs simultaneously. The engineers even threw baby transmitters in Munich into the array, because they found that each, little larger than an upright piano, tied up two or more Soviet jammers. Later, arrangements were made for western nations—including Britain's B.B.C., Italy's Radio Rome, and the Vatican Radio—to join in the simultaneous transmissions. Soon a total of more than seventy free-world transmitters were broadcasting to the Soviet in Russian for a half-hour each evening.

By the time the Troy team got deep into the electro-magnetic war, such ingenuity by the Voice's engineers was beginning to pay dividends. From a low of about five percent, the Voice had come back to where some twenty percent of its broadcasts were getting through to Moscow, and sixty to seventy percent to smaller cities and rural areas. Tests showed a large majority of Voice broadcasts to be audible in satellite areas. The showing was all the more remarkable because the Kremlin, in its now-frantic jamming drive, had again doubled its jamming network. By late 1950, it had some two hundred long-range or sky-wave jammers and at least one thousand local or ground-wave jammers in operation. Rough guesstimates by Troy team members indicated the Soviet probably employed as many as ten thousand scarce technicians in its jamming operations—more than all U. S. information workers around the world.

The Troy group highly commended the work of the Voice's engineers. They reviewed and helped improve new projects just aborning. And they added others that are still highly classified. In collaboration with Voice engineers, they even figured out on paper ways to combine new super-powered transmitters together and to focus their power so sharply that they could light an electric light bulb fifty miles away and deliver an unprecedented signal a thousand or more miles away. They devised and started testing a new relay technique that may yet revolutionize communications and ultimately simplify transoceanic television. For more than a year, initial experiments carried on between the states of Iowa and Virginia have proved largely successful. For the Voice, the new technique should immensely improve the standard of its signals reaching relay bases overseas.

Most important of all, the Troy scientists studied the whole electro-magnetic war and reached a surprising conclusion: For every expenditure made in increasing the Voice's power, the Soviet must spend at least five times as much in manpower and equipment to combat the increased strength. If certain large-scale electronic measures were adopted, the ratio could go far above five-to-one. Moreover, the true cost to the Soviet would be still greater. Since its electronic industry is more limited than America's, diversions for jamming Voice broadcasts would impede U.S.S.R. developments of radar, communications, and other military electronic gear.

Finally, if, as now planned, the Voice's added strength is largely in the field of medium wave (like standard broadcasting in the United States) instead of short wave, the Soviet's added jamming power cannot be used against western military communications (all short wave) in event of war.

Thus radio warfare, aside from the influence it has on listeners, can become economic warfare of the first magnitude. In no other field, except preemptive buying of a very few scarce materials, can the U. S. deter the U.S.S.R. so effectively for so few dollars.

DESPITE all this, Voice of America technicians have never had smooth sailing. First-rate engineers and electronic experts, scarcer than good cooks, could draw far better pay in industry than in government. So Voice technical ranks have never been filled, and the small staff has been perennially overworked. Each overseas relay base had to be located on another nation's land; that required months and sometimes years of negotiation. Most nations didn't even want to negotiate unless the Voice could guarantee that it had the money allotted and was ready to proceed with installation. Congress, on the other hand, never wanted to appropriate for a transmitter until the site was all set. So the poor old Voice always faced a chicken-and-egg problem.

Other complications perennially plagued the Voice. Its technical bosses had sometimes bruised Congressional feelings in picking domestic transmitter sites and in dealing roughly with some semicompetent employee who would then run bleating to his Congressional patrons. More important, Herrick and his colleagues had the occupational failing of many top radio engineers: incurable optimism. They would give Congressional committees optimistic but "sound" forecasts of when a new super-transmitter could be completed; they would finally win an appropriation on that basis but three months behind schedule; then they would run smack into new metals priorities, unforeseen diplomatic hitches over relay sites, and still tighter shortages of engineers. The next year some Congressional subcommittee chairman, informed that Transmitter A was far behind schedule, would soar like a two-stage rocket. When he landed, he was rarely in a mood to listen impartially to a plea for four more super-transmitters, no matter what it would cost the Soviet in relation to America's costs.

It took me many months to learn that, in international radio, all "sound engineering estimates" concerning likely construction time should be precisely doubled. International broadcasting, I learned, wasn't normal radio; it involved too many delayed appropriations, intricate diplomatic maneuvers, intragovernment tangles, and shortages of skilled personnel. Doubling the estimates proved just about right, but that didn't become apparent until one major appropriation request for added transmitters had received a drubbing from a key Congressional committee.

GEORGE HERRICK provided a case history of why it is hard to keep good professionals in government for long terms. He impressed his colleagues as a splendid, if incurably optimistic, public servant—hard-working, imaginative, and widely respected in the radio industry. Unable to complete college, where he studied engineering, he had acquired much of his knowledge the hard way. After a short term as engineer for a small network of stations, he had given more than ten years of his life to the Voice of America, working his way up through the ranks. He had built the largest control board in the world and had won wide-spread plaudits for his speedy erection of the Voice's mammoth transmitter in Munich. Offered more than double his salary to become chief engineer for a national network, he had been patriotic enough to remain with the Voice.

In view of that record, I was shocked to find George Herrick being slam-banged around on more than one occasion. True, some of his transmitters fell well behind his optimistic schedule, because of the Korean war and resulting metals shortages, loss of personnel to private industry, loyalty-clearance delays on new manpower, and related difficulties. But on one occasion members of one subcommittee went far beyond that, questioning his integrity and publicly wondering why "a man with so little experience in private industry should be entrusted with so important a job." Part of the subcommittee even publicly charged "mismanagement and maladministration" of the Voice's radio facilities.

With Secretary Acheson's concurrence, I promptly asked Justin Miller, as head of the National Association of Broadcasters and as a member of the U. S. Advisory Commission on International Information, to appoint a special committee from the radio field to investigate the charges impartially. He named three recognized radio specialists.* They studied the situation for weeks, examined documents, heard witnesses, and came up with a detailed report. In it they found "no significant evidence of mismanagement," made a series of helpful recommendations of a detailed nature, and urged "speedy completion of the facilities expansion plan" as "vital to the interests of the United States."

Shortly thereafter, the Awards Committee of the Department of State singled out George Herrick for special honors. The citation read in part, "George Q. Herrick for superior service, loyalty and devotion to duty—and especially for his outstanding contribution to the development of the clipper amplifier which has made possible a vast increase in the effectiveness of each domestic and overseas transmitter."

In 1953, long after I had left government, the cycle started

* The three were William A. Fay, manager of WHAM, Rochester, New York; Donley F. Fedderson, chairman of Northwestern University's Department of Radio and Television; and Theodore C. Streibert, president of WOR, New York, and Director of the Mutual Broadcasting System.

over again. Senator Joseph McCarthy made the same sort of charges against Herrick, emphasizing that he did not have a formal college degree in engineering. Well-known experts had come to differ over the location of two transmitters, which many of them had endorsed in the first place. So, on the basis of a statement from one unhappy ex-employee of the Voice, the Senator publicly implied Herrick had been guilty of "sabotage." A first-rate engineer on Herrick's staff committed suicide, leaving a letter complaining of harassment and insisting that, if there was anything wrong with the location of transmitters, the error was made in good faith and on the advice of well-known experts. In the midst of the tragedy, George Herrick must have wondered why he had passed up fat outside salaries to stay in government.

HAPPILY, all developments were not adverse in Congress. Needed operating funds were regularly voted. In alternate years, roughly speaking, the Congress appropriated large funds for strengthening broadcast facilities. It voted $11,320,000 in facilities funds for the fiscal year 1950, $41,288,000 for 1951, and $9,533,939 for 1952. With those funds, many improvements have been made. The power of the Munich transmitter has been doubled. New relay bases have been constructed at Tangier, North Africa, and Salonika, Greece. Construction started on three unprecedentedly powerful transmitters overseas. Other large-scale improvements are under way. A new-type directional antenna, sharply focusing its signals, should give these focused signals four thousand times the power of those of any major station in America! The power should not only immensely improve the signal reaching relay points abroad, but should blast powerful broadcasts directly to the Iron Curtain zones.

Two of these new-type transmitters in this country ran into widely misinterpreted snarls when the dispute, mentioned earlier, broke out in 1953 among competent experts regarding their location. They were to have the power of 1,000 kilowatts each—twenty times the strength of any transmitter in this country—and were to be located, on the advice of some of the Project Troy experts and others, at points where they would have maximum signal strength at peak hours. Later some experts came to feel the transmitters could better be located further south, where, they said, the signal would be more consistent, though weaker at peak hours. While the world heard from Senator McCarthy only that the transmitters had been flagrantly "mislocated," the State Department suspended construction of the two.

Presumably, they will finally be constructed and will effectively replace much weaker and obsolescent transmitters now leased from private companies.

Voice officials have always recognized one potential threat. The Soviet theoretically could make the radio weapon impotent by confiscating all domestic receivers. Those now capable of hearing one or more Voice transmissions appear to total above 3,000,000 in Russia, 2,000,000 in Czechoslovakia, and smaller numbers in other satellites. But for such confiscation, the Kremlin would pay a heavy price. It would immensely increase home-front grumbling. It would impair the Soviet system for spreading its own gospel, in which it relies heavily on both short-wave and standard broadcasting. And "wired radio" throughout the vast area would be astronomically expensive.

Nonetheless, the outside possibility has always existed. For that reason, the Voice, with help from scientific organizations and major radio manufacturers, has focused much research on small, long-life receivers that might be infiltrated into key areas in large numbers. It had to abandon an earlier project because the sets proved too expensive, too bulky, and too short-lived in terms of battery power. With the help of transisters (minute ersatz tubes requiring only infinitesimal power) and other new developments, the use of such receivers is now nearer reality.

Meanwhile, another radio development of basic significance has taken place. In late 1950, the Voice embarked on one of the most fascinating undertakings of all—Project Vagabond, a floating radio station of great power. This had been a pet brainwave of mine for years, and I was happy to find, upon taking office, that Voice of America engineers had at least toyed with such a plan. It wasn't entirely novel. Late in the Mediterranean campaign of the last war, I had helped sell such an idea to the Eisenhower headquarters and had finally helped persuade the Anglo-American naval command to provide an ancient Italian freighter for the purpose. Electronically, it proved a success; navigationally, a flop. Just as the floating transmitter attained full working order, the war in Europe ended. Then the S.S. *Phoenix,* as we informally christened her, set out for the Pacific, waddling across the Atlantic at the handsome gait of five knots. Ultimately, she and her motley civilian crew cleared the Panama Canal and were about to set out across the Pacific when—Japan surrendered! The good ship *Phoenix* was never able to catch up with the war, but her transmitters worked and proved that sea-going broadcast stations were feasible.

This time, after some difficulty, my colleagues and I persuaded the appropriate Congressional committees to go along with a project for a new sea-going transmitter. Voice engineers could evoke little enthusiasm from the Navy but finally induced the Maritime Commission to ante up a small but fast freighter, then mothballed. The U. S. Coast Guard agreed to staff her, and Project Vagabond was under way. After interminable red tape and countless financing and construction problems, the Vagabond (officially christened U.S.S. *Courier*) was commissioned at Hoboken, New Jersey, in March, 1952, and dedicated by the President and assorted dignitaries in Washington in April.

As of this writing, the U.S.S. *Courier* is tied up off the Greek coast, generating her own power (enough to light a small city), picking up broadcasts from New York, and boosting them on their way with two potent short-wave transmitters and one standard transmitter that is three times as powerful as any in the United States. Even with a balloon-supported antenna, serving in place of a highly directional antenna on shore, the *Courier* is hitting certain Iron Curtain zones with a potency unexcelled by any other non-Communist transmitter. Should the scene of conflict—cold or hot—shift, the *Courier* can hoist anchor and move to the contested area at the respectable speed of seventeen knots. And, unlike land-based transmitters abroad, she could more readily avoid capture in the event of enemy advances in an all-out war. All old propaganda hands hope for Congressional approval of more Vagabonds with the greater power now known to be practicable.

In the aggregate, the Vagabonds, the Ring Plan, the Cuddles, the Clippers, and the still-unmentionables prove one thing conclusively: It is possible, at relatively small expense to put Malenkov and the Kremlin crowd on the defensive on the one front where they and we are in open conflict—the radio front. The Voice of America can hit them increasingly with the one weapon they fear more than any other—the weapon of truth. And if they are to counter that weapon effectively (without the desperate step of wrecking their own radio), they must spend at a rate many times our own and at a sharp cost to the military mechanism that now threatens the world. As David Sarnoff, Board Chairman of R.C.A. has said, "International broadcasting is a major weapon which can pay for itself many times over."

9

Truth Pays Off

> *"It is always the best policy to speak the truth, unless you are an exceptionally good liar."*—JEROME K. JEROME.

D E M O C R A C I E S have proved exceptionally poor liars. Because they must operate in a goldfish bowl, always visible for public inspection, they can seldom get away with untruths.

Totalitarian states, of course, have proved more successful —in the short run. The Big Lie will be believed, said Hitler, if it is repeated often enough. Sometimes, however, even the oft-repeated Big Lie can backfire. That happened when the war broke out in Korea.

After the North Korean forces swept into South Korea on June 25, 1950, the Soviet and its satellites launched a mammoth campaign to accuse the United States and the forces of South Korea of starting the war. By international broadcasts, by official statements, by the Communist-world press, and by every other medium, they pointed the accusing finger at the Americans and South Koreans. This time, however, facts were too strong for them.

A United Nations commission was in Korea at the time of the outbreak. It was chaired by an Indian, had representatives from six other nations, and contained no United States repre-

sentative. The Commission officially reported the clear facts
that the North Korean Communists had launched the offensive. The United Nations Security Council, often regarded
as a propaganda forum for Soviet spokesmen, this time became
an effective sounding board for the truth. As the full facts were
revealed before the United Nations, one after another of the
neutrals and neo-neutrals became convinced. The U.N. reports and speeches appeared in the press everywhere outside
Soviet-dominated areas. Radio carried it behind the curtain.
With fifty-three nations, from India to Norway, agreeing that
Communists had launched the aggression, even the most slavish swallowers of Kremlin propaganda began to have doubts.
Ironically, the U. S.–U.N. setbacks helped convince them.
Around the world the U. S. Information Service quoted from
editorials to the effect that if the U. S. had planned and started
the aggression, it at least would have been well prepared for
the action. The U. S. reported fully and frankly on the early
trouncing being administered to Republic of Korea, U. S., and
U.N. forces. Obviously no nations would launch an aggression
without enough preparations to prevent such immediate setbacks.

Samplings of opinion in a dozen countries confirmed that
the Kremlin this time had gone too far. Its mammoth campaign pinning the guilty label on non-Communists had proved
so patently false that few believed it. Moreover, it raised
doubts about all Communist propaganda in the minds of millions who had not doubted before.

FALSE PROPAGANDA had boomeranged on totalitarian states in
other ways. In 1941 and 1942, German propaganda invented
sensational reports of U-boat victories to make up for Nazi
military reverses in Russia. The reports ultimately found their
way back into the Nazi bureaucracy. Postwar study of German documents shows that the German intelligence service
in November, 1942, was convinced that the Allies then lacked

the shipping to put an army into North Africa. The Nazis failed effectively to resist the North African landings because they had been fooled by reports originated by their own propaganda service!

Today Soviet propaganda about the imminent collapse of capitalism has fooled no one more than the men in the Kremlin. It is a simple story: following Stalin's lead, Malenkov and his colleagues make statements about the weakness of American capitalism; Soviet newsmen and agents in America go on a search for items that will please the bosses at home; they wire them back to Moscow; and the Kremlin becomes convinced it is right by the flow of "new evidence." There are indications that the Kremlin may be similarly misled by such "new evidence" supporting its claims that America has aggressive intentions.

"ONE THING is clear: This cold war is dirty business. We've got to learn that we can't be too squeamish about always sticking to the truth."

A distinguished American publisher made that statement before an audience of some two thousand persons in a panel discussion in 1951. It was seconded, in effect, by another distinguished speaker. As a member of the panel, I objected strenuously. I argued that truth and truth alone should be America's weapon in official propaganda. The typical American audience agreed overwhelmingly.

Those of us who argue for sticking to the truth are not motivated solely by ethics. We are convinced that truth offers not only the moral course but the cold, practical, effective course.

When General "Vinegar Joe" Stilwell came out of Burma in 1943, he announced bluntly, "We took a hell of a beating." Over considerable opposition, the O.W.I.'s Voice of America broadcast Stilwell's frank admission around the world, even to Axis countries. The Voice even repeated it several times.

When the war was over, the Allies learned that this had been a singularly happy decision. Germans, Italians, and Japanese testified that they had come really to believe the Voice of America first when they heard it carry Stilwell's statement. "We felt that if the Americans made such admissions to the world," said one, "they must be telling the truth."

Advocates of the devious school of propaganda argue that truth is a strait-jacket. At least, it is a jacket that wears well.

It was in perhaps the most successful propaganda campaign that the Soviets have carried out in recent years that they demonstrated the short-term success of chicanery. The Kremlin propagandists cynically singled out "peace" as the most effective argument they could employ, whether justified or not. Their obvious aim was to undermine popular support for rearming by the Western nations. Unimpeded by facts, they launched their campaign with a vengeance. They labeled American, British, and French war leaders as warmongers. They made Picasso's dove their emblem in many countries. They induced both Communists and innocents by the millions to sign "peace petitions," calling on all peoples to demand "the outlawing of atomic weapons." The petition was a preposterous fraud, for the Soviet Union had blocked the U.N.'s atomic-control plan, supported by forty-eight nations. Yet the Communists claimed to have 600,000,000 signatures on their petition.

International Communist gatherings, where imperialism masqueraded as anti-imperialism, were labeled "peace congresses." From extensive public opinion samplings, the U. S. Government found that millions in Western Europe and lesser numbers in Asia and Africa were beginning to swallow the Soviet theme: the Communists wanted peace; the Western leaders were aiming for war!

The Soviet campaign proved a tough one to combat. The United States was embarking, to be sure, on a vast rearmament effort. The Americans were inducing other non-Communist nations to join in that effort. Sure, America knew the reason: a strong defense offered the best hope of achieving peace. As someone bluntly put it, "The best way to avoid war today is to prepare for war." But all this was less readily understood by coolies in Asian rice paddies, by peasants in French fields, or by workers in Italian factories. The Communist "peace offensive" planted seeds of doubt about American intentions and germs of the idea that maybe the Kremlin did want peace. No diplomat who had dealt with the Russian Communists in the United Nations was fooled, but millions of others began to wonder.

The U. S. soon found that it would take a large array of weapons, plus considerable time, to combat the phony peace campaign, particularly since the Kremlin was blatantly distorting history to make its case. In the free world's new counter-offensive, serious argument, humor, and irony played their part. The Picasso dove was cleverly caricatured as a disguised tank. Perhaps the best example was that done by Jean Paul David's *Paix et Liberté* movement—"The dove that goes boom." This the U.S.I.S. had reproduced in pamphlets, handbills, and newspaper engravings throughout the world. Carefully planned speeches by American diplomats and others in the United Nations emphasized the way the Soviet Union, while prating about peace, had vetoed one peaceful proposal after another on forty-seven occasions. The U.S.I.S. then disseminated these speeches or excerpts from them throughout the world by radio and by press wire. Public affairs officers overseas helped persuade newspapers of other nations to feature the speeches. Editor after editor began to refer to "the Soviet's phony peace campaign" or "the spurious peace campaign of the Kremlin."

Perhaps most important, the Allied counter-offensive received an enormous assist from the Kremlin's own propagandists dealing with the Korean war. Before long, as noted earlier, their expensive campaign to prove American guilt served rather to convince millions that the Kremlin's elaborate propaganda machine could be a lying mechanism.

Still other moves were needed, however. U. S. representatives abroad and representatives of the British and French Governments helped to persuade hundreds of reasonably prominent citizens that they had been duped into signing the original Communist peace appeal. When they renounced that appeal, Allied information services joined in publicizing the renunciations.

By the summer of 1951 the Communist label on the concept of peace was badly tarnished. However, the identification of the United States and its allies with peaceful aspirations was far from accepted around the world. There was need for some way to dramatize American aims, a way to state the peaceful desires of free governments in concrete, believable form and to put the Soviet Union on the spot. Fortunately, those in the U.N. and in the U. S. Government who were working on disarmament proposals came up with a plan that happened to meet the need admirably. As a result of long months of work in quest of some practicable program for balanced reduction of arms, there emerged a three-power disarmament proposal. In developing it, John Hickerson, Assistant Secretary of State for United Nations Affairs, took the lead under Secretary Dean Acheson's general direction.

NATURALLY, all hands doubted that the Soviet Union would buy any genuine disarmament program that provided safeguards. Hickerson and all others correctly insisted, however, that the United States had a moral obligation to put forth only a plan that it believed in and was willing to put into operation. A plan, presented for propaganda purposes alone, could be prepared in a matter of days. The preparation of a genuine American-British-French plan which could be offered in good faith required months of effort. There were seemingly inter-

minable meetings with the appropriate authorities in
Pentagon, from Secretary of Defense Lovett down. There w
endless meetings within the State Department itself, some
them running into the evening and extending into week-ends.
There were long discussions with the President's aides in the
White House and then with British and French officials. The
task was made all the more difficult by the need to preserve
absolute secrecy. If the Kremlin got wind of the plan, it would
probably try to "jump the gun" with some spurious proposal
of its own. At the very least, it would be set to combat the
proposal in some devious way. As if to disprove much of the
loose talk of disloyalty in the State Department, the secret
was superbly kept during all the months of preparation.

Finally, on November 7, 1951, the day that the United
Nations Assembly convened in Paris, the three Western powers
made their proposal. It recommended, in substance:

First, a continuing inventory of all armed forces and armaments in every country having substantial military power. The
inventory would be checked and verified by nationals of other
countries working as inspectors under the United Nations.
The inspectors would be given authority to find out the real
facts and to keep a constant eye on what each country was
doing in the way of armaments. In other words, all nations
would be required to lay their cards on the table, face up, and
to keep them there.

Second, a specific program for the reduction of armed
strength. The entire disarmament program might be developed before any part was put into effect, or it could start
with the continuing inventory and inspection system.

Third, a plan for the program to move forward step by step.
Each step, when completed, would build confidence for the
next. If at any time there were a breach of trust or an act of
bad faith, all participating nations would have immediate
notice and could act in time to protect themselves.

The President followed up that night in a twenty-minute speech. He stated frankly that this was a plan he doubted the Soviet Union would accept but that it was an honest plan, a fair plan, and a plan deserving the support of the people of the world. He added: "We are not making it [the proposal] in any sudden spirit of optimism. We are not making it as a last gesture of despair. We are making it because we share, with all the members of the United Nations, the responsibility of trying to bring about conditions which will assure international peace and security. The people of the world want peace. To work in every possible way for peace is a duty which we owe not only to ourselves, but to the whole human race."

If the Soviet propagandists had been as infallible as some consider them, they could have followed a foxy routine in blocking the plan. They could have said, in effect: "Why, this is fine. Of course, we'll go along with it if you can convince us that you really propose to start negotiating immediately." By such a move they could have convinced millions that they did have peaceful intentions after all. Then, of course, they could have quietly killed any hope for the plan by the devious and intricate negotiating methods at which they are so expert.

The Kremlin minions were not so smart. Andrei Vishinsky, then Soviet Foreign Minister serving as chief U.S.S.R. representative at the United Nations, rose in the General Assembly and told the world that he found the proposal laughable. He said: "I could hardly sleep all night after having read that Truman speech. I could not sleep because I kept laughing."

If the Soviet was going to reject the proposal, it couldn't have done so in a way that better illustrated its own cynicism and bad faith. Within seventy-two hours U. S. and allied information officers had plastered much of Western Europe with posters picturing Vishinsky laughing at the very concept of peace. Editorialists around the world emphasized that Vishinsky's behavior had belied the Soviet's peaceful protestations. The free-world radios stressed the same story.

Vishinsky, doubtless prompted by second guessers in Moscow, soon tried to change his line by attempting a more serious answer to the three-power proposal and ultimately by pretending to negotiate on it. By then, however, the damage had been done. By putting forth a sincere disarmament proposal, by truthfully publicizing it, and by having it promptly derided by the Soviet representative, the free nations had finally driven home the falseness of the Kremlin's "peace program." It all proved that the democracies had no choice but to rearm.

Any fatuous American proposal cooked up for propaganda purposes alone would never have achieved the result. It took a genuine plan that could be honestly publicized to show up the hypocrisy of the Kremlin. Again, a truthful policy had paid off.

Subsequent Soviet-sponsored peace petitions garnered only a fraction of the signatures of the original. Newspapers around the world gleefully reprinted U.S.I.S. cartoons by Herblock ridiculing the Soviet's peaceful pretensions. Moscow propagandists, of course, did not give up. Even though "peace" had become a tarnished watchword for them, they continued to stage periodic "peace congresses."

Soon after Stalin's death, the Kremlin elaborately demonstrated that it still valued "peace" as a propaganda device. While Malenkov was obviously bargaining with Beria and others and seeking to consolidate power on the home front, he embarked on a series of "friendly" overtures. The Soviet rulers talked of "peace," began inviting a few visitors into the Soviet Union, arranged a partial exchange of ill prisoners in Korea, and made other gestures. In brief, they did just what many had often thought Stalin would have been smart to do: they talked reassuringly at a time when crucial decisions were being made in NATO, in the Washington Administration, and in the U. S. Congress.

Some of the more warm-hearted and soft-headed in Europe and the United States hailed the gestures. Dwight D. Eisenhower and the U. S. Government, having learned the lessons of the past, were appropriately skeptical without closing the door to any real settlements.

After some weeks of drafting and redrafting, the President restated the American position in a speech that admirably embodied the best principles of international persuasion. Speaking for "a free world aroused," he said: "We welcome every honest act of peace. We care nothing for mere rhetoric."

The President then called for the "deeds" that would be welcomed: limitation of armaments with international inspection; a Korean settlement with an end to attacks on Malaya and Indo-China; a free, united Germany, under a freely elected government; a peace treaty with Austria; and "full independence" of the East European satellites.

He then clearly restated another American point, "This government is ready to ask its people to join with all nations in devoting a substantial percentage of the savings achieved by real disarmament . . . to develop the undeveloped areas of the world, to stimulate profitable and fair world trade, to assist all peoples. . . ."

By eschewing empty rhetoric, by truthfully restating clear principles of American foreign policy, the President had again put it up to the Kremlin to act. Convincing deeds were not forthcoming.

There will be other peaceful but empty gestures from Moscow, including "peace-loving" answers to questions periodically submitted by Western newspaper correspondents. If the Western democracies are alert, however, future Trojan doves of peace from the Kremlin should never again achieve the kind of mass deception they once achieved.

10

The Problem of Words

O N E   D A Y in 1950 an able but weary public affairs officer, who had just completed the long flight in from his post in Southeast Asia, showed up at a Washington meeting. It was one of those "skull sessions" that are an essential part of propaganda planning. When asked to comment on then current American propaganda efforts, he was in no mood for the amenities. He blurted out:

"Just two things. First, tell the big shots of both parties in Washington to quit just slapping down Soviet proposals. Sure, we Americans know the proposals are phonies, but a lot of leaders out in the Far East don't. The way we've been acting, we make the Commies seem like reasonable people and ourselves unreasonable.

"Second, you Washington people, from Truman on down, ought to quit prattling so much about 'liberty'—at least so far as my area is concerned. What does it mean to the mass of people out my way? Not a blooming thing. They are hungry. While we talk about liberty and freedom, some Commie agitator comes along and says: 'Under Communism you'll have plenty to eat. You'll own the land you now farm for somebody else.' The poor little native brightens up and says: 'Oh, so that's Communism. Well, I'm a Communist.'

"It's just as simple as that."

139

In a few blunt words that weary officer from the field had pointed up two basic lessons in international persuasion: (1) There are persuasive ways and ineffective ways to say the same thing, and (2) To persuade effectively, choose terms that are meaningful and persuasive to the particular audience. Both points underscored the intricate nature of the tools with which the international propagandist works—the words that must be chosen with far greater precision than the average American would suppose.

Experience has long since shown that empty propaganda—words not supported by demonstrable facts and actions—can rarely have any lasting effect, except a bad one. When the actions or facts exist, the way they are explained, the precise words used, and the manner of presentation become vital.

Wartime events proved how "honorable capitulation" could persuade an enemy who would never be influenced by "prompt surrender"; how the "Peace Movement" in Germany made respectable what was unthinkable as "a plot against Hitler." Later, "campaign of truth" proved far superior to "propaganda offensive." "Captive peoples" meant far more than "Soviet allies" or even "satellites." "Mutual security," while not ideal, was infinitely better than "U. S. foreign aid."

In domestic politics, the majority party speaks of "efficient organization," while the minority speaks of "sprawling bureaucracy." One faction in a political convention paves the way for victory by successfully labeling its particular proposals "the fair-play amendment"; no one likes to oppose fair play. In international persuasion, the precise choice of phraseology assumes equal importance—and far greater intricacy.

In late 1949 and early 1950, the Soviet Union already had a practice of coming up periodically with "proposals" that were as spurious as three-dollar bills. Stalin would give out an "interview" suggesting atomic disarmament, even while spurning every workable atomic-control proposal worked out in the

U.N. Or, he would vaguely but loudly indicate a willingness to hold a four-power meeting at the very time when his representatives were thwarting diplomatic efforts to achieve a basis for such a meeting. The U. S. Government recognized such noisy statements as designed for propaganda purposes alone. So it would occasionally reject a spurious proposal flatly and explain the thoroughly logical reason why. To those who read the U. S. answers fully, they made complete sense. To the millions who didn't, however, America appeared to be negative and not interested in preserving the peace.

In the top policy councils of the Department of State, my propagandist-colleagues and I continually urged a modified technique, describing it in the words, "If you must say 'No,' say 'No' affirmatively." It was no more than the lesson that American management and labor representatives had gradually learned. If one side in a labor controversy wants to earn public support, it does not put itself in the position of seeming incessantly to "reject." Rather, it makes counter-proposals, or requests the other side "to be more specific."

In 1950, the Department of State began increasingly to say "No" affirmatively. If a Russian official made an obviously empty suggestion for a special conference, the U. S. would not just reject the idea and explain why. Rather, it would ask the Kremlin to be specific and particularly to indicate whether it was prepared to modify the positions it had previously taken. Instead of simply turning down another Kremlin proposal, Secretary Acheson found it better to make a counter-proposal, embodying thoroughly logical points that the Soviet Union had persistently spurned.

The technique led to such headlines as, "U. S. Again Urges 'Workable' Peace Measures," instead of, "U. S. Spurns Soviet 'Peace Bid.'" The technique was sound and clearly justified. The American position in such cases was a practical position, generally one that had earned support of the vast majority of the United Nations. By submitting or resubmitting a workable proposal each time the Soviet made some spurious suggestion, the U. S. Government put the Kremlin in the position of saying "No."

By the time of the early Korean armistice negotiations, Americans had learned the lesson well. The Communists were no longer able to get away with their old trick of blocking workable settlements and then making vague but high-sounding "proposals" which the U.N. would have to reject as meaningless. Instead, U.N.–U. S. negotiators kept making proposals and counter-proposals that were clearly practicable. The Soviet was forced to do the continual rejecting. Gradually, the procedure impressed average citizens around the world with what typical U.N. delegates had known all along: that it was the Soviet Union which was blocking an armistice.

As recently as Christmas, 1952, Dwight Eisenhower and John Foster Dulles, then President-elect and his Secretary-designate, admirably employed the same simple technique. Stalin had found the time appropriate for one of his periodic Russian lullabies. Picking out one of the sets of questions perennially submitted to him by newspaper correspondents, he had again issued propaganda answers saying that war was not "inevitable," that he regarded "favorably" the possibility of an Eisenhower-Stalin meeting, and that he would "cooperate" in seeking an end to the Korean war. With sound logic, Eisenhower and Dulles could have dismissed the Stalin words as "obvious propaganda" and as "words unsupported by deeds." If they had done so, as a few press pundits urged, the world's headline readers would have got the impression that "Eisenhower Spurns Stalin Overture." Instead, after conferring with Eisenhower, Dulles wisely stated:

I have read with interest the published account of Mr. Stalin's views. If these mean that Mr. Stalin has concrete proposals to make to the new Administration after it takes office, he can rest assured that they will be seriously and sympathetically received.

Diplomatic or United Nations channels of communication are always available for such purposes and for exchanges of views designed to find ways to promote peace and international good will.

That statement effectively said "No" affirmatively. It said, in effect, that the U. S. was not taken in by the Stalin words but that it would consider seriously any genuine proposal if Stalin should choose to make one through official channels. It earned such headlines as "Dulles Calls on Stalin to be 'Concrete.'" It put the onus on Moscow, not Washington. To a few irresponsibles and jingoists of the American press, Dulles' statement was "defensive" and "naïve." To millions around the world, yearning for some hope, it portrayed a United States that was mature, understandably skeptical, and firm, yet always open to reason.

In his first few weeks in office, Dulles committed some propaganda blunders (like his order that the Voice of America should never quote any Communist). But that first semi-official act was sage affirmative use of truth as a weapon.

The episode illustrated a simple working principle: In phrasing public statements, "think back from the headline." Recognize that the great mass of even literate populations never get beyond the headline or the brief radio bulletin. Then think of the headlines desired and phrase the statement to that end.

ONE ELDERLY GENTLEMAN in Congress has never got out of his head the notion that the Voice of America should simply have one set of English-language scripts, then mechanically translate these into all of its forty-six languages. Actually, the international broadcasters of the B.B.C. and the Voice of America early learned that such broadcasting could be close to sheer waste, that radio can persuade effectively only if it talks in terms that are meaningful and persuasive to each particular audience reached.

The problem recalls the tale about three men of differing

nationalities who were asked to write an essay about elephants. The Englishman titled his, "Hunting Elephants with Rod and Reel," the Frenchman produced a small illustrated booklet on, *"L'Elephant et Ses Amours,"* while the exiled Pole turned out a tract with the red-ink title, "The Elephant and the Polish Question!"

In World War II, the Roosevelt-Churchill Four Freedoms had appreciable appeal in most areas of the world. The reasons for that appeal, however, varied widely. To economically advanced areas of Europe, "Freedom of Thought" proved appealing. To underdeveloped areas of Latin America, "Freedom from Want" was particularly persuasive. To sections of Asia seriously threatened by the Japanese, "Freedom from Fear" was most influential. Today, "Freedom of Worship" has particular appeal in the Soviet satellite states.

Every experienced propagandist has learned that even while telling the same basic story world-wide, he can tell it most persuasively in each area by employing those terms that have the most meaning and appeal to the immediate audience. He soon learns that the word-concept "freedom," for example, has enormous appeal to a Filipino but is almost meaningless to a Japanese. To his amazement, he eventually learns that *there are no universally effective propaganda terms.*

So complex have the problems of semantics become to those operating in forty-six languages that one weary propaganda executive once broke up a meeting by rising, mopping his brow, and announcing, "I'm afraid I'm becoming anti-semantic." Nonetheless, because official announcements must necessarily deal in words, top information officers of the government have no choice but to search continually for those word-concepts with the greatest appeal to the greatest number of people. To aid in the search, I once prepared a list of 42 positive word-concepts—words like *peace, liberty, honor,* and *human dignity.* To this was added a list of 14 negative word-concepts—terms like *slavery, thought control,* and *foreign domination.* The State Department then sent the lists to its public affairs staffs in a total of 157 cities around the world. It asked the public affairs officers, who had systematically studied public opinion in their areas, to rate the terms, on a scale of 0 to 100, on the basis of their propaganda effectiveness in the immediate area.

The answers, finally compiled and analyzed in the winter of 1952-53, proved fascinating. No single key word was scored highly by all posts. *Peace* ranked highest in most of the Far East but lowest in Indonesia (where the accepted translation implies "peace at any price"). It ranked well down the line in Europe, Latin America, and the Near East—perhaps because of Soviet distortion of the term. *Liberty* stood high in many countries of Latin America and Europe but low in Japan, Hong Kong, and Indochina. *Independence* ranked second (just below *peace*) in the Far East but well down the list in Latin America.

Though there was not even near-unanimity on any word, the highest rated positive words for all areas, on the average, were *independence, freedom, education, prosperity, security, national culture, peace, liberty, justice, progress,* and *honor.* The lowest rated positive words on the average represented the concept of cooperation and mutuality: *mutual assistance, world friendship, neighborliness, brotherhood, democratic unity,* and *harmony.*

The most effective negative word, on the average, turned out to be *slave labor,* followed by *Soviet imperialism, slavery, foreign domination, Communism,* and *iron curtain.* There were wide variations, however. *Iron curtain* understandably rated high in Europe, low in the Far East. *Foreign domination* ranked first in the Far East, low in Latin America.

The precise ranking of key words by the U.S.I.S. missions in each area were as follows:

POSITIVE KEY WORDS
LISTED BY AVERAGE RANK SCORES AND REGIONS

Key Word	World Average	Europe	Latin America	Africa & Near East	Far East
Independence	74	67	62	83	88
Freedom	71	71	71	71	79
Education	71	67	71	76	83
Prosperity	67	71	62	64	76
Security	67	64	62	67	79
National culture	67	67	67	64	67
Peace	64	62	64	62	90
Liberty	64	62	71	64	71
Justice	64	64	64	67	60
Progress	64	57	67	74	60
Honor	64	60	69	67	55
Human dignity	62	62	67	64	45
Faith	62	55	62	71	45
Self-government	62	60	57	67	69
Democracy	60	57	64	57	57
National equality	57	55	57	57	69
Cooperation	57	57	60	57	43
Human rights	57	52	55	62	52
Truth	57	60	57	57	45
Free world	57	64	55	55	48
Racial equality	55	50	43	57	76
Common good	55	52	50	40	45
Technical assistance	55	48	57	60	52
Freedom of thought	55	57	57	50	45
Anti-colonialism	52	33	45	67	69
Integrity	52	57	52	50	55
Welfare	50	60	48	40	48
Decency	50	55	57	43	43
Mutual defense	50	52	45	48	48
Well-being	48	52	48	48	45
Mutual assistance	48	48	43	55	40
Humanity	45	52	43	40	38
Godliness	45	38	43	57	36
World friendship	45	48	43	45	45
Anti-slavery	43	45	40	45	38
Democratic strength	43	50	38	38	36

Neighborliness	40	45	38	36	40
Brotherhood	40	38	33	45	43
Individualism	38	45	33	40	19
Democratic unity	38	36	40	33	38
Harmony	33	33	33	31	31
Welfare state	26	36	33	29	19

NEGATIVE KEY WORDS
LISTED BY AVERAGE RANK SCORES AND REGIONS

Key Word	World Average	Europe	Latin America	Africa & Near East	Far East
Slave labor	79	79	79	79	71
Slavery	71	57	79	79	64
Communism	71	71	79	71	71
Soviet imperialism	71	71	71	79	50
Foreign domination	71	71	64	86	86
Iron curtain	71	79	79	64	57
Police state	64	71	50	64	57
Kremlin puppets	57	64	57	57	64
Totalitarianism	57	64	57	57	50
(New) Colonialism	43	43	36	57	50
Big lie	43	43	50	50	29
Thought control	43	43	50	43	43
Indoctrination	36	43	29	43	36
Statism	29	29	21	29	21

That little study of word-concepts, plus the accompanying remarks submitted by public affairs officers, illustrated many points: the extraordinary persuasiveness of the phrase *slave labor* in describing conditions in Soviet-dominated countries, the unusual appeal of *education* in many areas, and the need to use simple terms, instead of cosmic concepts, in talking to simple people with limited horizons.

Most of all, it illustrated again the need for carefully tailoring international information materials in accordance with the local tastes, customs, and concepts in each nation. That means that published material should be translated and edited in final form, not in Washington, but on the scene abroad. Even Voice of America broadcasts from the United States, if they are to be effective, must be subjected to continuing detailed criticism, guidance, and (where possible) editing by persons as close to the target audience as they can possibly be.

Any bureaucrat who thinks, as an occasional one does, that he can sit isolated in Washington and produce in final form the ideal item to persuade Indonesians, Chileans, or Finns ought to be isolated indeed—in a padded cell.

FOOTNOTES ON HEADLINES

Countless incidents, trivial and significant, have sidelighted the continuing struggle for an effective campaign of international persuasion. A few such incidents appear worth reporting.

NOWHERE in Europe is humor more effective as a propaganda weapon than in Czechoslovakia. Experience has shown that the Czechs delight in Voice of America output that ridicules the Communist puppets in Prague.

Once the Communist secret police stationed a number of secret agents outside the American Embassy in Prague. The Voice promptly called attention to these supposedly secret operatives, described their clothing, and suggested that the Czechs come around to have a look at them. The next day a steady procession of citizens filed through the streets, looking the agents over carefully, smiling at them slyly, and walking on.

The agents by the next day shifted to a car parked across from the Embassy. The Voice reported this and the fact that the agents cluttered the street with debris from their lunches. No more debris appeared on the streets. Still streams of citizens walked by, paused, ogled the agents with twinkling eyes, then walked on.

In 1951 the Moscow radio and other Kremlin-dominated propaganda channels tried to throw a scare into the Czechs by accusing American planes of dropping potato bugs over Czechoslovakia to ruin the current crop. Some five days after this, the Voice reported back to the Czechs a gag line that had begun making the rounds in Prague: "Have you heard what the Americans are doing now? They are dropping potatoes in order to keep their potato bugs alive."

* * *

ONE DAY about half-way through the war, we in O.W.I. headquarters in Washington received a message from our British office requesting help in finding a particular kind of typewriter for Prime Minister Churchill. It seemed that the Prime Minister had been fascinated by the clean, even typing of a thank-you letter he had received from General Joseph T. McNarney in the Pentagon. He had asked Sir Norman Scorgie, the

149

head of His Majesty's Stationery Office, to get him such a typewriter. Scorgie, unable to find one, requested O.W.I.'s help. We called McNarney's office, only to find that the typing had been done on a new electric typewriter then produced experimentally in upstate New York.

In no time two full colonels were assigned to the project. Meanwhile, a War Department official had mentioned it to the President. Next day a Europe-bound military plane made a special stop in Rochester to pick up a duplicate typewriter and rush it to London with the President's compliments.

The typewriter arrived at 10 Downing Street on Sunday, June 4, 1944, just two days before the invasion of the continent. Sir Norman received a frantic phone call from a Churchill secretary, who urged that typewriter mechanics be sent immediately. The secretary added: "Please hurry them. The P.M. is at work on the crate with a hammer and cold-chisel; he may break something."

Sir Norman somehow rounded up the mechanics on a Sunday and rushed them to Number 10, where they assembled and connected the typewriter. That evening a Cabinet Minister arrived, expecting to find the Prime Minister up to his neck in planning for the invasion that was just two days off. Instead, he found Winston Churchill, at his new typewriter, pecking out with two fingers: "Dear Mr. President . . ."

* . * *

A BASIC TRUTH, sometimes a sad truth, is that politicians live on publicity. If they fail to keep their names before the voters, the votes may fail to appear beside their names.

Axiom Number 1 for many Congressmen is that attack makes headlines; praise rarely does. When Senator Connally praised General Marshall on the Senate floor, scarcely a word of it was repeated in the metropolitan press. When Senator McCarthy next day attacked Marshall, it made headlines on most front pages.

One day in 1951, I got word that an irrepressible western Senator, now happily retired by the voters, was about to deliver a stem-winding speech attacking the Voice of America and the whole international information program. I had long known him personally, but it took me four days to arrange an appointment. Finally, I got into his office and persuaded him to tell me what was on his mind. I found that his whole criticism was based on false reports. I gave him the straight facts and offered to send him official papers proving those facts. The conversation ended jovially. As I shook hands upon leaving, he smiled wryly and said: "Goddam it, Ed, I knew I shouldn't have seen you. You've just ruined a swell speech."

WHEN the British and Americans opened a powerful new broadcasting station in North Africa in 1943, as previously mentioned, they boldly named it "The United Nations Radio." The experience provided a useful pointer on dealing with the Soviet.

Technically, we in charge of the project had no business using that name unless the project had the approval, not only of the British and American governments, but of other United Nations governments, particularly the Soviet. We should have sought the Russian's approval of the project. However, we had early learned that Soviet diplomatic officials, like those stationed in Algiers, dared not stick out their necks by any such positive action. So we simply notified them that we were inaugurating the United Nations Radio and invited them to sit in on a policy-planning board for the station. That gave them the opportunity to object. But, as anticipated, even the act of objecting would mean some Russian taking a risk. Hence, they did nothing and only went through the formality of having a representative sit with the board once or twice. Moral: Whenever possible, avoid asking the Soviet representatives' approval of a project. Instead, notify them of the project, giving them the opportunity to object, but recognizing that no Communist official likes to take such definite action without interminable consultation with Moscow.

O.W.I. amusingly confirmed this in 1945 after the Soviet had taken over control of Rumania and Hungary. The U.S. Information Service wanted to acquire one movie house in Budapest and one in Bucharest to show U.S. documentaries, for which the populations were eager. Our officials made the mistake of asking the concurrence of the Soviet representatives in Hungary. There followed such lengthy delays that the movie house was never opened. In Rumania, our people simply rented a theater and sent the local Soviet hierarchy handsomely engraved invitations to the opening. The Communists never took the formal step of objecting, and the theater operated for months.

* * *

ON THE DAY of the Allied landings in Sicily, Eisenhower's Psychological Warfare Branch carefully prepared a recorded message from the Supreme Commander to the people of Sicily. In order to ease the job of the landing forces, Eisenhower himself did the English recording for it, and one of the best United Nations Radio announcers recorded the Italian translation. It was a big day for psychological warfare, which had been assigned important status in the campaign. Top military brass came to the studios in Algiers to hear the propaganda kick-off. All was set. Italian listeners were alerted. An ominous voice told them that they were about to receive an announcement of great importance from the Supreme Commander of the Allied Forces. After a brief pause, there then came a torrent of tones sounding precisely like Donald Duck in a tantrum. An engineer, it developed, had put the 33 r.p.m. recording on a 78 r.p.m. turntable.

* * *

IT WAS in 1944 that I found O.W.I.'s alert film division was routinely going about the business of producing a documentary film on the mysteries of the atom and the possibilities of releasing incredible power from it. The film division, which had already produced a series of widely praised shorts, had got together a fascinating script about the cyclotrons and related projects in American universities. After Elmer Davis, as chief of O.W.I., had talked with top security people, it became my lot to kill the project—without in any way indicating to our own executives that the U. S. Government was engaged in a mammoth project in the field.

Robert Riskin, the able chief of O.W.I. films who had earlier won a Hollywood Oscar, was away. I arranged to talk with Philip Dunn, his talented writer in charge of the atom project. I could think of only one way to handle it: I got the script, read it carefully, then told Dunn and his colleagues that the whole subject was "just too dull and uninteresting" to justify spending U. S. dollars on it. When they protested, I was adamant. Knowing they had a Grade-A script, they left muttering dark words about the stupidity of their boss.

A full year later, when the first atomic bomb exploded over Hiroshima, I got a call from Phil Dunn, "I just want to say you're much less stupid than I thought—but a much better liar than I thought."

* * *

ONE of the most difficult problems, even in a free country, is to get the true facts into the hands of Communists and Communist sympathizers and induce them to read those facts. This requires extraordinary ingenuity, ingenuity of a sort that American Campaign of Truth representatives have happily shown on many occasions. In Italy, for example, Lloyd Free, United States information chief, and his colleagues repeatedly used artful negotiations to get films about American labor unions and American factory conditions shown before members of pro-Communist unions.

One of Free's successful maneuvers, in late 1951, concerned a small handbill, *Per Una Pace Stabile* ("For a Lasting Peace"). Skilfully designed to look precisely like conventional Communist output, the handbill bore the sub-heading, "25 Years of Soviet Efforts Toward Lasting Peace." The text recited, with straight face, thirty agreements that the

Soviet Union had signed, then recounted how the Soviet had vetoed, scrapped, or ignored each of these. The complete text (in English) was as follows:

---

25 YEARS OF SOVIET EFFORTS TOWARD LASTING PEACE

Year	Pledge	Result
1925	Turkish-Soviet Non-aggression Pact.	The U.S.S.R. denounced this Pact in 1945.
1926	Afghan-Soviet Non-aggression Pact.	In 1940 the U.S.S.R. forced Afghanistan to cede frontier territories.
1926	Lithuanian-Soviet Non-aggression Pact.	The U.S.S.R. annexed Lithuania in 1940.
1927	Iranian-Soviet Neutrality Pact.	The U.S.S.R. refused to withdraw her troops from Iran after World War II.
1928	The U.S.S.R. signed the Kellogg-Briand Pact repudiating war as a means of settling international disputes.	In 1929 the U.S.S.R. invaded Manchuria in order to regain possession of the Chinese Eastern Railway.
1929	The U.S.S.R. solemnly renounced war, signing a protocol to that effect with Estonia, Latvia, Poland, and Rumania.	The U.S.S.R. attacked Eastern Poland in 1939, and in 1940 seized Estonia and Latvia.
1932	Finnish-Soviet Non-aggression Pact.	The U.S.S.R. invaded Finland in 1939.
1932	Estonian-Soviet Non-aggression Pact.	The U.S.S.R. annexed Estonia in 1940.
1932	Latvian-Soviet Non-aggression Pact.	The U.S.S.R. annexed Latvia in 1940.
1932	Polish-Soviet Non-aggression Pact.	The U.S.S.R. seized Eastern Poland in 1939.
1933	The U.S.S.R. signed a Convention repudiating aggression with Finland, Yugoslavia, and Turkey.	The U.S.S.R. invaded Finland in 1939, broke off diplomatic relations with Yugoslavia in 1941, and denounced her Non-aggression Pact with Turkey in 1945.

Year	Pledge	Result
1935	Franco-Czech-Soviet Alliance.	The U.S.S.R. would not aid Czechoslovakia against Hitler in 1939.
1936	Alliance between the U.S.S.R. and Outer Mongolia.	The Soviets used this Alliance as a means to infiltrate Outer Mongolia. By 1945, Outer Mongolia had completely lost its autonomy.
1936	The U.S.S.R. became a member of the Committee for Non-intervention in the Spanish Civil War.	In the same year the U.S.S.R. sent weapons and war materiel to the Spanish Communists.
1937	Chinese-Soviet Non-aggression Pact.	In 1945 the Soviets plundered the industries of Manchuria.
1939	Estonian-Soviet Alliance.	The U.S.S.R. annexed Estonia in 1940.
1939	Latvian-Soviet Alliance.	The U.S.S.R. annexed Latvia in 1940.
1939	Lithuanian-Soviet Alliance.	The U.S.S.R. annexed Lithuania in 1940.
1941	Yugoslav-Soviet Non-aggression Pact.	The U.S.S.R. broke off diplomatic relations with Yugoslavia one month after signing the Pact.
1942	Anglo-Soviet Alliance.	The Alliance is still in effect, formally. But the U.S.S.R. has violated it repeatedly with such acts as the blockade of Berlin in 1948–49.
1942	Alliance between the U.S.S.R. and the Polish Government in London.	The U.S.S.R. broke the Alliance in 1943 by supporting the puppet Lublin Government.
1942	Anglo-Iranian-Soviet Alliance.	The U.S.S.R. violated this Alliance by refusing to withdraw Soviet troops from Iran after World War II.
1943	The U.S.S.R. announced the dissolution of the Comintern.	In 1947 the U.S.S.R. promoted the establishment of the Cominform.

Year	Pledge	Result
1943	Czech-Soviet Alliance.	In 1948 a coup d'état supported by the Soviet Union reduced Czechoslovakia to a puppet of the U.S.S.R.
1944	Franco-Soviet Alliance.	Although this Alliance is still in force officially, the U.S.S.R. has violated the spirit of the pact by supporting subversive organizations which seek to overthrow the French Government by violence.
1945	Chinese-Soviet Alliance.	At the same time they made this Alliance with the National Government of China, the Soviets were arming the Chinese Communists.
1945	Yugoslav-Soviet Alliance.	The U.S.S.R. denounced this Alliance in 1949.
1945	Polish-Soviet Alliance.	In 1947 the Communists seized power in Poland, transforming that country into a Soviet puppet.
1948	Finnish-Soviet Alliance.	Bitter attacks against Finland appear periodically in the Soviet press.
1946–1950	The U.S.S.R. repeatedly proclaimed her peaceful intentions in the U.N., through such spokesmen as Vishinsky, Gromyko, and Malik.	The U.S.S.R. blockaded the Western sections of Berlin and supported, even through diplomatic channels, aggression by Greek, Chinese, Indochinese, and North Korean Communists.

The Soviet Union has violated or denounced 10 non-aggression or neutrality pacts in 16 years. The Soviet Union has violated 14 military alliances in 13 years. When the Soviet Union talks about peace, remember these facts!

THIS IS THE WAY THE SOVIET UNION WORKS FOR A LASTING PEACE

In addition to distributing a million of these handbills through normal labor channels, Lloyd Free and his colleagues tried a novel maneuver. They simply had bulk shipments of the handbills delivered to a major Communist Party mailing room in northern Italy. The well-disciplined oafs staffing the room automatically proceeded to send out more than 20,000 to the Party membership list!

The horror of the Communist hierarchy at this was extreme. Party officials issued a memorandum to all Communist officials. U.S.I.S. people promptly obtained a copy. It read:

It is necessary for comrades to avoid falling into the provocatory propaganda tricks of the enemies of Peace. It has recently happened that some sincere Partisans of Peace received and distributed, in the course of a popular festival, a leaflet which is published and circulated by U.S.I.S., entitled *Per Una Pace Stabile*. The above leaflet carried on a red cover a reproduction of Picasso's dove. It would have sufficed if our comrades had glanced through the text for them to have seen that this leaflet was a tangible proof of the defamatory American policy towards the U.S.S.R. . . . Equally ingenuous (are) those comrades who, especially in Genoa and Florence, used an atlas put out by the Information Division of the Marshall Plan, to teach geography to their children, without apparently realizing that every page contained shameless adulation of American imperialism. Some comrades even cut out and pinned up on the walls of their homes many pages of that atlas.

* * *

THE WAYS of diplomacy can be so wondrous that it is easy for one to get out on a limb if he is not in immediate touch with developments. At least, it was easy for me. I had just flown to California for two speeches, when the Korean war broke out. Naturally, I was besieged by Pacific Coast reporters seeking comment. They particularly asked whether I thought the Kremlin had any connection with the attack by the North Korean Reds. Thinking I was being appropriately diplomatic, I replied, "Can you imagine Donald Duck going on a rampage without Walt Disney knowing about it?"

When this was picked up by the wire services, I received a rush message from Washington to pipe down on statements about the Kremlin. Since the Soviet Union was not openly involved, it seemed, desperate efforts were then being made, on the advice of all old Russian hands, to pressure the Kremlin into calling off the conflict. This theoretically might still be done if the U. S. did not publicly involve the Soviet in the attack.

I did pipe down and, upon returning to Washington, I dropped in to apologize to Secretary Acheson. He told me to forget it, that the idea of pressuring the Soviet to stop the war was a long shot at best, and that events had proved I had done no harm.

* * *

WHENEVER high-powered experts in molding opinion first come into the international information field, they are tempted to start off with super-duper productions designed to sway millions the world over. Oftentimes the idea involves a flamboyant film or an elaborate booklet. Sometimes it involves a great radio program that would simply be translated into multiple languages and sent out over Voice of America transmitters. Only after such experts have worked in the field some months do they generally recognize that very few items, however superior, have universal appeal. Often the most effective work is the modest job done on the scene by workers thoroughly familiar with local conditions, attitudes and prejudices.

One simple example concerns the work in Korea performed by William Ridgeway, a youthful information officer (and not related to the general). On instructions from the home office, Ridgeway in 1950 went to work on a Korean newsreel for Korean audiences. With South Korea badly demoralized, its citizens were puzzled, confused, and unwilling or unable to read extensive press reports. Both army and civilian authorities recognized the need for simple ways to put across the fact that there was an orderly program for rehabilitating Korea, that Koreans and their Western allies were working hand in hand, and that there was hope for the future. Special Korean films offered enormous possibilities. So young Ridgeway went to work.

On a high priority basis, he quickly obtained three newsreel cameras from the State Department in Washington. Setting up shop in an abandoned restaurant near Pusan, he took local Korean photographers and trained them. He got his hands on thousands of feet of captured Russian raw film, and he went to work.

Within a few weeks Ridgeway's films were being shown in theaters throughout South Korea, in meeting halls, and even on street corners. In addition, U.S.I.S. mobile units showed such films to at least 20,000 persons daily.

A typical film would show Generals Ridgway and Van Fleet in company with Korean generals and civilian authorities mapping plans for the future. It would show the United States Ambassador decorating Korean heroes. It would picture hospitals and hospital ships staffed by Swedes, Americans, Koreans, and Filipinos. It would then picture the latest progress of the fighting and why it was necessary to keep roads open for convoys. It would add scenes, provided by U.S.I.S. in Washington, of the U.N. meetings on the Korean War, of Canadian destroyers, and of U. S. planes taking off for Korea.

Within a short time, young Ridgeway's improvised film industry had won him praise from U.N. civil and military authorities, plus a decoration from the Republic of Korea Government.

Part II

THE FOES WE FACE

11

Soviet Strategy

"*THERE ARE* two famous 'last words,'" says Charles (Chip) Bohlen, a veteran Russian expert in the State Department and Ambassador to the U.S.S.R. "One is 'alcohol doesn't affect me'; and the other is 'I understand the Russians.'" The jest is at least partly justified. Yet, if Americans are to defend themselves effectively, they have no choice but to try to understand the tortured reasoning, planning, and maneuvering of the little group of party leaders who ruthlessly dominate Russia and international Communism.

The United States and the other free nations today face many foes and many obstacles. These would endanger the achievement of a peaceful, orderly world if Stalin's heirs and their Communist apparatus did not exist. Hunger and destitution in poverty-smirched areas, of course, always make men easy prey for international Hitlers and Stalins or for home-grown Huey Longs. Parochial ignorance of other peoples can nourish spite and bitterness that threaten stability. And every country contains demagogues ready to foster international havoc in order to achieve local power.

These continuing problems, however, attain immediate, pressing urgency because of the existence of the central, aggressive foe—the little group of masters of the Soviet Union.

161

It is this small group, not "the Russians," that systematically generates hatreds and converts unhappiness into the enmities that threaten the world.

The distinction is important. The Russian people, or more properly the various peoples within the U.S.S.R., are not the root of the trouble. With all their inordinate love of their land, they have shown themselves to be courageous, moral, peace-loving peoples. Twenty years of ruthless anti-religious measures left them still at a point where seventy percent declared they believed in God (in a 1937 official census that Soviet authorities tried to suppress). And now, after two years of intense "Hate-America" propaganda, the citizens of Russia impress visiting foreigners as having been surprisingly little infected by the virus.

The self-styled enemy is the Soviet Presidium, with Malenkov and Stalin's wraith at its head. Replacing the old Politburo and dominated by the same group, the Presidium makes the decisions that are slavishly followed by the small and fanatical Soviet Communist Party and by disciplined Communist Party members throughout the world. It is the foe that must be understood as clearly as possible if peace is to be waged effectively. Those who don't at least strive to know what the opposition is like and how its mind works can scarcely deal with it intelligently.

WESTERN minds cannot easily fathom the thinking of the Soviet peoples, let alone the turgid dialectics of present-day Soviet Communists. Traditional Marxist dogma provides no blueprint, for the Stalinists can't lay claim to even the dubious respectability of pure Marxism. They have opportunistically modified Marx's tenets in the past when they found it expedient to do so. Professional Marxists are being liquidated regularly in Russia itself. Marx and Lenin are now valid guides only to the extent that Stalin has reaffirmed them.

Yet Stalin himself provided a surprisingly frank guide to present-day, revised Soviet Communism in his book *Problems of Leninism*. Its current edition, still accepted as the unquestioned guidebook of Communist functionaries, has become to the Party roughly what Hitler's *Mein Kampf* was to Nazism—and, as was too long true with *Mein Kampf*, has been too generally overlooked by the outside world. Out of the complex argumentation of *Problems of Leninism* and related documents can be extracted certain basic points. At the risk of oversimplification, they can be distilled down to this:

There is no God or moral law. Religion is the opiate of the people.

The material world is primary. To promote this material development and "end the exploitation of man by man," all tools of production must be vested in the state and operated by it. The political party directs the Soviet State. To win the struggle on behalf of the "masses," the party leaders are given "unlimited power based on force and not on law." The resulting dictatorship has the obligation of "suppressing the resistance of its class enemies." Non-conformists must be ruthlessly cleaned out.

But the "dictatorship of the proletariat" cannot be safe if it operates only in a few countries. For safety, it must be victorious "in all countries or in the majority of countries." There must be "Socialist encirclement . . . instead of capitalist encirclement. . . . The existence of the Soviet Republic side by side with imperialist states for a long time is unthinkable. One or the other must triumph in the end." Since the United States and other imperialists will inevitably try to destroy Communism by war, the Communist Party must, in self-defense, take the initiative in overthrowing non-Communist governments.

In colonial areas this means producing revolution. In non-colonial areas, it means infiltrating disciplined Party members into key positions and, when opportune, employing political strikes, sabotage, terrorism, guerrilla warfare, and civil war. Ultimately, there comes the time for the "decisive blows" which will "smash entirely the bourgeois state machine and its old army" and produce the "single state union" of international Communism.

The Soviet military machine is primarily for "defense," while the party apparatus carries on the offense. But any means is justified to help the party achieve its world goals. Tactics may be varied as expediency dictates. "How to retreat properly" is just as important as how to attack. Concessions can be made by the Presidium to "buy off a powerful enemy and gain a respite." But broad strategy for achieving the "single state union" remains constant.

In a very compact nutshell, that remains the creed and "campaign plan" of Soviet Communism as of this writing. So far there is little basis for assuming that the "peace gestures" of 1953 will prove any more than tactical moves to gain time for consolidation on the Soviet home front.

At the Communist Party Congress of October, 1952, Stalin indicated mild shifts, not in this long-term strategy, but in short-run tactics. In effect, he said that the Soviet bloc, including China, would redouble efforts to build up its strength until it attained invincibility. Meanwhile, the Party apparatus would spare no effort to aggravate tensions among the Western democracies in order to weaken their unity, resolution, and material strength. No change in the basic creed was indicated. Even the early Malenkov "peace overtures" fitted this creed. The future may yet bring basic changes, for anything can happen in the long power-struggle set off by Stalin's death. The opportunists of the Kremlin are capable of switching even fundamental doctrine when it seems expedient. But until that time, *Problems of Leninism* provides good guides for judging plans, policies, and aims.

STILL MORE can be deduced from the body of speeches, declarations, actions, and intelligence reports that conscientious Russian experts in this country are continually studying. With minor exceptions, they tend to amplify, not alter, the strategy of *Problems of Leninism*.

They indicate that the Kremlin has thought it could talk about the *possibility* of "peaceful coexistence" with Western powers because the *preferred* method for overthrowing Western governments is internal class warfare, rather than armed attack. Moreover, Soviet spokesmen have left no doubt that they mean precisely coexistence, not friendship. Molotov, in a 1950 speech, frankly made clear that "peaceful coexistence" called for the opposition to stand with arms folded, in effect, while the Soviets wielded the bullwhip. In Lenin's earlier words to a domestic foe, "If you . . . are really anxious to maintain neighborly relations, then be good enough to perform the tasks we assign you."

I am no Russian expert. I have devoted a total of many months, not many years, to studying the ways of the Soviet regime. But I have quizzed every Russian expert I could lay hands on. From Soviet published dogma and actions and from many other sources, they have drawn certain deductions, on which there is remarkable agreement, if not unanimity. In condensed form, the deductions are:

1. *Stalinist doctrine, still in effective force under Malenkov, holds that there can be no peace, no friendship between the Soviet Union and the United States; the latter must be defeated.*

Periodic talk of "peaceful coexistence" being "possible" is largely a sham, meaning only that the Soviet Union might conceivably attain its ends without armed attack. The Soviet's open, admitted aim is the ultimate overthrow of free governments in the "most important capitalist countries," with international Communism gaining domination over Europe, Asia, and ultimately the world. There is yet no substantial basis for occasional talk to the effect that this doctrine is "now obsolete."

2. *Even if these aims should somehow change under the Malenkov-Molotov-Beria triumvirate, the very nature of the present Soviet thinking requires that there be—or be created— an external enemy. For the foreseeable future, Enemy Number 1 will be the United States.*

Theoretically, of course, the Communist state resorts to dictatorship only temporarily. To justify continuing dictatorship, "a state of emergency" has become a permanent necessity. A purely domestic "state of emergency" would imply defects in the Soviet system. Therefore, the emergency must arise from the real or imagined existence of serious external enemies.

Up to World War II, the Soviet rulers built up first Britain, then Japan and Germany, as prime enemies. They picked as Foe Number 1 each time the nation that seemed the biggest obstacle to Soviet aims. Since World War II, and especially since early 1951, with what appeared only a temporary let-up after Stalin's death, Soviet propaganda has centered on the United States as the chief foe. *All* Americans have been portrayed as bent on destruction of the Russian economy, home, and family. Any nation cooperating with America is, to that extent, also an enemy.

3. *The Soviet hierarchy, infected by its own line, seriously fears that America intends armed aggression—a fact which makes the continuing world crisis particularly explosive.*

Since the ultimate test of Party loyalty is undeviating adherence to Party doctrine, even the ablest Soviet diplomatic or intelligence officer is afraid to report facts conflicting with the "line." A Gromyko, knowing much of conditions in America, hesitates to speak his mind freely, having noted the oblivion to which a Litvinov was consigned after doing some objective reporting. The result is cumulative, and dangerous, "added evidence" of Wall Street imperialism and aggressive intentions.

Among the ninety-five percent or so of Soviet and satellite populations who are not official Party members, there are substantial doubts that America plans to attack. Those doubts, though not openly expressed, are sensed by the Kremlin and are a deterrent to a Soviet "defensive war." Hence, any American tactics that help nurture such doubts, without indicating weakness, can help prevent a holocaust.

4. *Approved Soviet doctrine holds that the Party must incessantly struggle for what it wants at home and abroad— through agitation, subversion, propaganda, and through ruthless elimination of dissenters.*

Triumph can come, preached Stalin, only if the faithful go out and force it. They may vary the tactics but must persistently keep up their pressures. At the same time, they must never tolerate the slightest deviations within the Communist countries. This ruthless repression is what has kept the total population in Russian concentration camps constant at more than 10,000,000.

5. *The Soviet regime prefers to achieve its aims without starting World War III, and probably still believes it might do so.*

Communist success in taking over some of the satellites through subversion, trickery, threats, and propaganda—with only token military moves—have encouraged this belief. Mao's success in China also fostered the hope, offsetting the shock of Tito's escape from the flock. The repelling of Communism in Greece, Turkey, and Iran were regarded as temporary setbacks. So were democratic gains in Italy and France. Korea provided a major surprise, since the Kremlin doubtless expected all the peninsula to be in Communist-puppet hands before the free nations could possibly make up their minds to resist. There are, indeed, signs that the United States is suspected of trickery in having implied it wouldn't defend Korea in the event of all-out war.

More important, the Kremlin still hopes and believes America is nearing the inevitable (and oddly delayed!) economic collapse. Since American power seems the only great obstacle to Communism's further spread, the collapse is seen as causing great areas to fall into Communist hands without the Red Army having to march.

The Kremlin also *prefers* to avoid a World War III. In the first place, it doesn't relish the thought of atomic bombs plummeting on Russia, and some would get through even the elaborate new anti-aircraft defense network. In addition, the Kremlin isn't eager to send hundreds of thousands of Russian troops on an offensive into other lands. It remembers that the same kind of Russian soldiers who were magnificent in defending Stalingrad proved incredible duds earlier in an aggressive war on Finland. And it is none too sure of satellite troops. Finally, it doesn't want masses of Russian soldiers seeing "imperialist" nations. Those who did so in the last war found conditions so far superior to what had been described to them that they came home skeptics and malcontents. They required elaborate and expensive "re-education."

6. *Nonetheless, the Soviet may, sooner or later, undertake a massive offensive, and it certainly will continue building its great fighting force.*

Soviet doctrine makes no clear distinction, as we do, between measures short of war and measures involving war. To it, any effective means is legitimate. As recently as 1952, a restatement of strategy propounded in the presence of Stalin and the full Politburo stated the need for unceasing struggle, including resort to "just wars" where necessary. Such a "just war" could conceivably be triggered by warped Soviet minds, either imagining an imminent attack from the outside or just deciding coldly that war could succeed where other means fail in the overthrow of capitalism. Again, war could be launched by the newer Kremlin rulers in their anxiety to strengthen their hold on the home front, whatever the risk.

At any rate, the Soviet will maintain and enlarge its military machine: first, because it may choose to use it, and, second, because military might is needed to generate in others the fear that is indispensable in Soviet strategy. The Red Army's existence, even if never used, is a mighty force for gaining Soviet ends. The army also serves the Kremlin's domestic purposes. It provides a means for mass indoctrination of citizens, bolsters nationalist fervor, and serves as a melting pot for helping further to blend the multiple nationality groups within the U.S.S.R. The Kremlin needs it.

7. *It is all but useless to try to predict far in advance a timetable by which the Soviet will assault various areas, overtly or covertly.*

Some now predict conquest of Southeast Asia as target Number 1, absorption of the whole German industrial area as target Number 2, and so on. Such predicting for the long run can be little more than speculation. The Soviet's strategy, both clearly stated and clearly practiced, has been to probe incessantly for weakness, to advance when it finds the going easy, to retreat when it encounters opposition. The precise methods are those found necessary at the time.

The free world's difficult task, therefore, must involve continually helping to convert areas of weakness into areas of strength. It must be prepared to meet armed assault, knowing that Soviet Communists are swayed by power in others and have only contempt for those who plead from weakness. Yet, to prepare only against armed attack would leave the way open for conquests by all the other techniques which the Soviet has learned to use.

8. *Before his demise, Stalin had clearly laid out the plans for delivering "decisive blows" against Western democracies when there is "a crisis condition" in those countries.*

More precisely, he stated that the crisis condition arrives

"when it is perfectly apparent that the Communist vanguard is prepared to fight to the end, the reserves are prepared to support this vanguard, and the maximum consternation reigns in the ranks of the enemy." The vanguard, he made clear, could be the Soviet Union itself, with its Red Army and its economic power. The direct reserves are the satellites, the "proletariat" everywhere, and revolutionaries, particularly colonial revolutionaries. He added to these forces "indirect reserves" —those engaged in various group conflicts in capitalist states and hence open to having their unrest exploited.

9. *Stalinists see as the main function of Soviet strategy the "manipulation," through propaganda and other means, of Communists and the "masses" everywhere to achieve the decisive blow at the proper moment.*

They envision "manipulation" as involving three steps: (a) to *convince* people that the Soviet position on pressing issues is the right position, (b) to *arouse* them through agitation, making them willing to act, and (c) to *direct* their actions along lines the Kremlin wants them to follow. Those who can't be influenced positively are to be "manipulated negatively"—by fanning their grievances, confusing them, and undermining their will to resist.

10. *The Soviet's periodic "peaceful" talk and isolated gestures can never be taken as a change in its fundamental policy.*

Any basic change is highly unlikely in the absence of a complete change of regime or irresistible outside pressure. Meanwhile, some revealing words that *Taegliche Rundschau*, the Red Army paper in East Germany, published in the midst of the "peace gestures" of early 1953, seem to tell the story. The paper told how Lenin once made peace with the Germans in order to give the Soviet a "chance of putting the economy in order, to take advantage of disputes within the imperialist camp. . . ."

"Thus," it explained, "Lenin taught that detours often are necessary if, at a given moment, the opponent is superior in strength; that one must withdraw temporarily in order to summon up new strength. Only thus will it be possible to prepare the new attack, to establish the basis for final victory. . . ."

THAT is the self-proclaimed foe we face. It is a foe that gives first importance to the "manipulation" of the minds and wills of men. It is a foe that has developed an incredibly elaborate mechanism for "psychological manipulation." And, perhaps happily, it is a foe that Stalin said cannot win victory if it fails in such "manipulation."

12

Big Lies and Small Tricks

HITLER did not invent organized international propaganda, nor even the Big Lie. Among others in the distant past, Genghis Khan used both, systematically terrifying his enemies by spreading reports about his "limitless hordes" of ferocious "wolf-eating" Tartars. Hitler simply employed international propaganda on the largest scale the world had ever seen.

Now, however, the Nazis' Big Lie has become the Small Untruth beside the Soviet Union's techniques and apparatus for "manipulating" men's minds. A careful analysis made by intelligence agencies of the United States Government indicates that the Soviet Union and its satellites today are spending a minimum of $1,500,000,000 annually on the most colossal propaganda effort the world has ever known. This figure, many times larger than peak American expenditures on all kinds of international information, includes propaganda behind the Iron Curtain but does not cover the millions spent by local Communist Parties and Communist-front organizations in the free world.

Under the Presidium (formerly Politburo) of the Communist Party's Central Committee, a special Section of "Propaganda and Agitation" (Agitprop) directs all propaganda, foreign and domestic. The scale of the enterprise is indicated by the constant enrolment of more than 325,000 persons in special schools for the training of professional propagandists. There are some 6,000 schools at the local level. Another 177 regional schools provide higher training. Finally, "graduate work" in propaganda can be done at three institutions: the Academy of Social Sciences, the Higher Party School, and the Correspondence Department. In these three, 6,900 students are reportedly enroled.

The training process involves not only the teaching of Russians, Czechs, Poles, Chinese, and other satellites for work within their own countries and abroad. It also includes the training of carefully screened Communists for other countries. They are brought from the United States, from Italy, from Brazil, from everywhere, to be trained and then sent back.

That is not all. Training extends far beyond the special propaganda schools. Institutions for teaching Red Army officers, school teachers, engineers, doctors, dentists, and skilled laborers have regular courses of instruction in agitation-propaganda techniques. Between lectures on mortars or membranes, the professional trainee learns about manipulating minds.

The Presidium and Stalin himself showed intense awareness of the importance of propaganda. Indications are that Stalin's heirs will follow his precedent and help personally to compose the propaganda lines that are parroted by the whole sprawling apparatus. Captured German documents reveal one good example of the procedure: In 1939, the Germans had advanced into Poland faster than expected. Under the Nazi-Soviet pact, the Russians were supposed, at that point, to move in and occupy the Zone assigned to them by the agreement. The German High Command sent pleas to the U.S.S.R. to hurry up. However, Molotov, speaking for Stalin, insisted this could not be done until the Soviet could establish a propaganda justification—"a plausible explanation" in his words. Stalin himself then directed the propaganda build-up and held back his troops until it was completed.

WITHIN the U.S.S.R. itself, Stalin, Malenkov, and Company have made their propaganda incredibly pervasive. The vast trade-union organization, with its thirty-odd million members, operates chiefly as a propaganda mechanism. In fact, its function is officially described as that of a "transmission belt" between Party and workers. Naturally, education is dominated by propaganda considerations. Art and literature admittedly must be manipulated to achieve propaganda ends. All youth organizations are, by official definition, propaganda organizations. The Russian Orthodox Church is allowed to exist only to the extent that it can be made to serve as an instrument of propaganda. Press, radio, and films are direct instruments of government.

The very size of the Kremlin's propaganda machinery provides some ground for Western confidence. Any one who has worked in a government bureaucracy can imagine the tangles, confusions, and problems of a propaganda apparatus employing hundreds of thousands of workers!

Defensively, of course, the Soviet goes to extreme lengths to prevent its people from being "corrupted" by outside ideas. As noted earlier, it apparently spends more money trying to drown out the foreign radio than is spent on the world-wide operation of the Voice of America. There are signs that the imprisonment of William Oatis, Associated Press correspondent in Czechoslovakia, was framed months in advance because the news he sent out was being broadcast back by the Western radios in a way that was "unhealthy."

The positive objectives of Kremlin propaganda, beyond those of teaching Party dogma, have varied from one period to another. In the late 1920's, for example, the central objective was to convince Russians that an ideal state would ultimately be achieved if only the people would work hard and faithfully. In the 1930's and early 1940's the Kremlin soft-pedaled conflict with democratic nations. When it needed Western help in the war, it even made motions toward tolerat-

Soviet Slip: *These caricatures of Acheson appeared in the first issue of the Soviet magazine* Krokodil, *Dec. 10, 1951. In later issues the germ-warfare canister was removed from his back by the red-faced Reds. The reason: it preceded by two months China's charges of germ warfare against the U.S.*

LA COLOMBE QUI FAIT BOUM

"The Dove that Goes Boom": *This most striking of the many cartoons ridiculing the Soviet dove of peace was distributed by* Paix et Liberté *in France and reprinted in many other countries.*

Discarded Cards: *Some of the hundreds of Communist trade union cards which were turned in by workers who joined the Free Trade Union in Padova (Padua), Italy.*

↑ *"For a Lasting Peace": U.S.I.S. handbill cover simulating Soviet type. Italian Communists were duped into distributing it. Text on page 153. Original is in a flaming red.*

← *Safe Conduct Pass: The most effective of leaflets used in Africa and Europe during World War II. Distributed by plane and leaflet shell.*

Seagoing Transmitters: *The U.S.S. Courier, launched in 1952 and later put in service in the eastern Mediterranean, is a relay base with elaborate reception equipment: two 35,000-watt short-wave transmitters and one 150,000-watt medium-wave transmitter.*

Curtain Antennas: *Ten elaborate directional antennas, long under construction in the U. S., have been designed to increase vastly the signal strength of Voice of America transmitters. The minute automobile, to the right of the tower of this scale model, gives an idea of the actual height.*

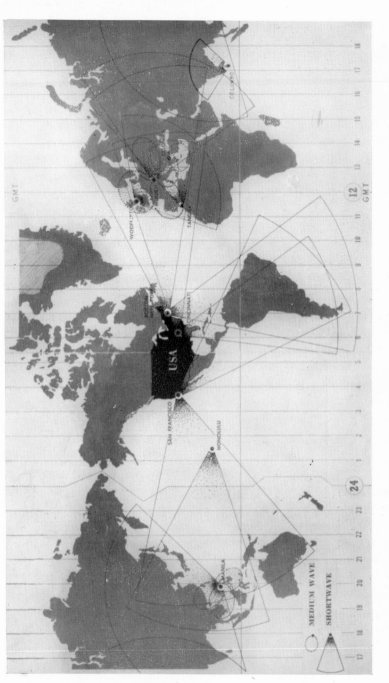

Global Network: This mercator projection map portrays the transmitters employed by the Voice of America. The medium-wave relay facilities in Manila, Munich, Salonika, and Tangier greatly enhanced the ability of the Voice to reach large target audiences.

ing religion. After World War II, the central theme abruptly shifted to the struggle between the Communist world and the non-Communist world, particularly the United States. In fact, the Soviet pictured that contest as entering its decisive phase, from which the Soviet Union was sure to emerge triumphant. Under this central theme, the propagandists played such sub-themes as that of "Russian superiority." Four years ago, this led to the clownish "Russians-were-first-in-everything" campaign, a line the Soviet carried to such absurd lengths that it became an easy target for ridicule in other countries.

At first, the anti-American theme was aimed only at the American system and the U. S. Government and its leaders. Secretary of State Acheson was the "lickspittle" and "agent" of Wall Street who was "implicated in dubious, dirty affairs of trans-Atlantic trusts." General Eisenhower "never won a battle," but "won a lot of decorations." "It took him twenty-five years before he became a major," and "Rockefeller gold created Ike the General." Even much lesser Americans drew epithets. The author of this book, for example, became "a stupid minion of Wall Street." All the time, the American people were just "dupes" and "victims" of their "Wall Street rulers."

Then on January 21, 1951, a chunky, near-sighted little man named Peter Pospelov, head of the Lenin Institute, rose before Stalin, Malenkov, Molotov, and the whole Politburo and formally launched a new phase of the "Hate-America" campaign. Suddenly the American people as a whole became the detested villains. "The hands of the American imperialists," rasped Pospelov, "are steeped in the blood of the Russian people." He cited an array of "documentary proof" of plots and crimes committed not by "Wall Street" but by ordinary American soldiers against Russians during the U. S. intervention after World War I.

That was the signal. It released a tidal wave of anti-American propaganda that had been laboriously built up for months.

In newspapers throughout Russia there suddenly appeared banks of photos showing Russians who had supposedly been killed, mutilated, and starved at the hands of Americans in 1919. With the photos appeared gory "eyewitness" accounts, statistics on supposed atrocities, enraged editorials and letters to the editor ("I Know Who Killed My Father.").

In Washington, propaganda analysts hustled into the research archives to find what in that intervention could afford any pretext for the campaign. They knew that some 14,000 troops had been sent into Russia briefly in 1918-19 to help guard a couple of railways and a supply depot threatened by the revolution. But these had been a small part of a much greater Allied force, and no one recalled any charges of atrocities on the part of the Americans. In stacks of books of all complexions reporting on the period, the researchers could find no mention of any such charges. The Soviet clearly had discovered the American atrocities as belatedly as it discovered some of its own inventions. No good Soviet editor, however, would permit himself to be cowed by facts. (The last one who did so hasn't been seen since.) *Pravda* set the tone for editorials, "We will never forget and never forgive what the Americans did." Twenty-four hours later, as usual, every little *Pravda* in Russia happened to editorialize, "We will never forget and never forgive what the Americans did." Each adapted the theme to its locality. In the Caucasus, it was crimes against the people of the Caucasus; in the Ukraine, the citizens of the Ukraine. More than half the "news" in some issues told of alleged American crimes that were thirty-two years old. To older Russians with good noses the age was doubtless apparent. But such oldsters had long since learned to keep their skepticism to themselves.

Even the spurious atrocity stories of World War I paled beside the belated inventions of Soviet propagandists. A typical item, repeated again and again in newspapers and broadcasts, reported:

In July, 1919, a large group of American soldiers broke into a village. A bestial orgy followed. The interventionists robbed and raped women and girls. . . . American soldiers arrested Mikhail Popov. . . . They gouged out his eyes, cut out his tongue, and drove nails under his finger nails. . . . In another village the American monsters took an expectant mother . . . cut off her breasts and pushed her tresses into her mouth and pulled them out of a hole cut in her throat.

Another, appearing originally in the Soviet Army's *Red Banner,* reported:

An American patrol detained a peasant woman who was expecting a child at any moment. While under arrest, she writhed in painful labor on the cold cement floor until she bore a child. Before the eyes of the inhabitants, an American soldier snatched the new-born infant by the feet and flung it into a bonfire. Then he pierced the unfortunate woman through the heart with a bayonet.

Through the Communist Party mechanism in each satellite, the Soviet issued directives on "How to Have a Hate Campaign." A smuggled copy of a Chinese directive included the following: "You must try during the rally to transfer the hate of the multitude upon the American imperialists. . . . Pointed remarks should be inserted. . . . In this way the minds of the multitude may be directed toward increased hatred for the American imperialists."

After more than a year of this, the Soviets ultimately found a way to bolster the hate program with new charges. They launched an ingenious new campaign on February 21, 1952 —thirteen months to the day after Pospelov fired the Hate-Americans salvo. The Chinese Communist news agency suddenly announced to the world that U.S. airplanes were dropping deadly bacteria on North Korea. Clearly, the theory was that, so long as American aviators flew over North Korea, the charge could not be conclusively disproved. It was like an individual trying to disprove rumors that he is "a little unbalanced."

Over the entire Soviet-controlled press-radio network, the

germ-warfare campaign crescendoed. Throughout Communist areas, there appeared photos of insects and of "disease germs" magnified by microscope. A common U. S. leaflet bomb, used to disperse Sykewar messages at the proper altitude, was pictured widely as an "American disease bomb." An alleged confession of an American flyer, telling of his long "germ-warfare training" in Japan, appeared throughout the Communist press.

Scientists in free countries soon debunked the germ pictures, demonstrating even that some of the insects pictured were known to be harmless. General Ridgway, Secretary Acheson, Secretary-General Lie, and many others issued strong denials of the whole germ-warfare canard. The "confessing" American flyer was proved not even to have been in Japan at the time he was supposed to have received his "instruction" there. These facts, of course, were not printed in Soviet areas. Only the Western radio reported them there. The Communists, undeterred, intensified their campaign, particularly behind the Iron and Bamboo Curtains.

In the United Nations Secretary Acheson challenged the Communists to submit their charges to an impartial investigation. In a resolution, he proposed that the investigating be done by a committee of the International Red Cross. The Soviet and its satellites easily blocked this and loosed a campaign to prove that the International Red Cross was an "American-dominated agency."

The campaign of hate continued. For bald dishonesty, it has been equaled only by another item of Soviet output. In mid-1952, after months of the hate campaigning, Moscow's English-language magazine *News* (intended for foreign consumption only) informed its readers with straight face, "There has not been a single instance of any Soviet leader or publication engaging in hate propaganda against the United States or the American people."

American specialists on Russia have differed as to what the

Kremlin's hate campaigners were up to. As of the spring of 1953, some feared that the Soviet was embarked on final psychological preparations for a general war—or at least for large-scale intervention in Korea. A majority doubted this. They considered the Communist campaign simply an all-out effort to intensify the building up of an "external enemy," to overcome the Soviet peoples' still-evident liking for Americans, and to prepare them for a long-drawn-out war of harrassment against the United States. Some thought the campaign sprang from genuine Kremlin jitters over the growing strength of the West. None knew the answer for sure. A partial let-up in the hate campaign in the spring of 1953 made the picture all the more confusing.

For non-Communist areas of the world, the Soviet Agitprop has developed an inordinately complex array of weapons. In America, the U. S. Congress is perennially and understandably disturbed over overlapping agencies of government. Should the Congress ever face a set-up like that in Soviet Union propaganda, the dome would blow off the Capitol. Soviet propaganda is carried out through Moscow Radio and the satellite radios, through an international film organization, through V.O.K.S. (the All-Union Society for Cultural Relations with Foreign Countries), through a network of Soviet Friendship Societies, through Tass (Telegraphic Agency of the Soviet Union), through Sovfoto (the U.S.S.R. photo monopoly), through the Moscow-guided World Peace Council, through the World Federation of Democratic Youth (W.F.D.Y.), through the International Union of Students (I.U.S.), through the Soviet Women's International Democratic Federation (W.I.D.F.), through the World Federation of Trade-Unions (W.F.T.U.), through "information staffs" in each Soviet Embassy, and through a host of other agencies directly or indirectly controlled from Moscow.

In radio, Lenin and Trotsky originated the techniques of

broadcasting to other peoples over the heads of their governments. In 1946, Stalin embarked on a great expansion of his international radio weapons. By 1950, the combined hours of international broadcasting by the Soviet Union and its satellites well exceeded the total of the United Kingdom and the United States. By early 1953, the Soviet Union was broadcasting a total of ninety-nine program hours a day in thirty-odd languages, over various transmitters beamed to other countries. The satellites, excluding China, were broadcasting another eighty-four hours daily. The British were doing eighty hours of such broadcasting, and the U. S., after doubling its output, was broadcasting forty-three program hours daily.

The Presidium and the international Cominform have seen to it that the Moscow transmitters serve an added useful purpose: to keep the Communist faithful up-to-the-minute on the latest Moscow propaganda lines. Wiseacres have said Earl Browder, ousted as head of the U. S. Communist Party for "deviationism," would still have his job if he hadn't lagged in replacing a tube in his radio set.

The Soviet has also converted "cultural exchange" into a weapon. Few Americans have realized the extent to which the Kremlin itself has lifted corners of the Iron Curtain to let through carefully screened and precisely directed travelers. Each has had a propaganda mission. In 1950, some 17,000 foreigners, all carefully screened, were brought into Russia, given a narrowly circumscribed view of "the Soviet way of life," subjected to intensive indoctrination, and sent home again. Most of these came as members of some 130 delegations to "congresses" of one sort or another. Some came from satellites, including China. A substantial but undetermined number came from the outside world. Some delegations numbered as many as 500. V.O.K.S. generally entertained them, showed them selected sights, and arranged for lectures. Many of the visitors were individuals selected for specific purposes. Some were non-Communists. Soviet representatives abroad occasionally picked out particular "do-gooders," those known for warm hearts and soft heads, and invited them for special visits. On occasion the Communists wined and dined "open-minded" professionals or businessmen at embassies in other countries. There a Soviet representative would sidle up to the guest, "confidentially" deplore some practices of the local Communist Party, and then invite the guest to make a guided trip into the Soviet Union itself. Often the device worked, converting the visitors into apologists for the U.S.S.R. In some cases it did not. Visitors from free countries dropped off in the early 1950's. Then in 1953 Stalin's heirs began trying the gambit again.

In 1950, the Soviet permitted some 39,000 of its own nationals to visit other countries. Many of them went to North Korea, China, and the satellites. Smaller numbers went to the non-Communist world. Most were selected because they had been so irretrievably indoctrinated that they could not be affected by what they saw. A few, mainly artists and athletes, were chaperoned carefully so that they had little chance to be "unindoctrinated." Some, like the writer Ilya Ehrenburg, served as two-way channels. In interviews and speeches abroad, they told glowingly of "the true Soviet way of life." Back home, they were used to "interpret" capitalist life for the Russian and satellite peoples. Typical of the interpretations was an article by Ehrenburg. He told of seeing American billboards, which depicted the Crucifixion scene along with this legend, "If Christ had been crucified today, He would have asked not for water, but for Coca-Cola."

Little noted by Americans, the Soviet began, in late 1950, an ambitious intensified "cultural offensive" through use of such unofficial emissaries. It became an offensive to prove conclusively that the West, particularly the war-minded U. S., was without culture, while the peace-loving Soviet Union was virtually becoming the Athens of the Twentieth Century.

At the International Music Contest in Brussels, three talented Russian musicians were entered and took first and second prizes. Two young Americans, unofficially representing the United States, trailed ninth and eleventh. At the International Music Festival in Florence, a skilled Russian ballet team made an enormous hit. America was not represented. In many other music, film, ballet, and theatrical festivals the same thing occurred. In most, the Russian performers were kept in complete seclusion, under close chaperonage, but performed outstandingly. The impression gained by many millions who witnessed the performances or heard them by radio was that any nation having such skilled musicians and such delightful ballet hardly seemed a warlike monster. And maybe there was truth, they thought, to the talk that the Americans were too preoccupied with war preparations to indulge in such pursuits.

The Soviet recognized what we Americans have been slow to learn: that there are many nations where "culture" isn't a politically abhorrent term and where intellectuals wield substantial political power (vastly more, it would seem, than American "egg-heads").

The Soviets directed their "culture-offensive" at Soviet-seized territories even before it was launching it in free zones. The case of North Korea illustrated the technique of culture campaigning. In 1945, some 3,700 North Koreans were enroled in one or another Soviet-oriented cultural society in Korea. By 1949, under Soviet control, the number had increased to more than 1,300,000. During 1946-48, 770,000 copies of 72 books by U.S.S.R. authors were published in North Korea. In 1949, there were distributed 537,000 copies of two books alone. Soviet "cultural representatives" gave almost 70,000 lectures and concerts in North Korea.

The new effort wasn't confined to the arts. In preparation for the 1952 Olympics, the Soviets staged an incredibly elaborate four-year program for selecting the U.S.S.R.'s best athletes and subjecting them to intensive training. The purpose was to impress the world with Russian manhood and with Soviet superiority in "peaceful pursuits." To a substantial degree, the effort succeeded. So did a parallel effort on the industrial front. From Italy to India, the Soviet impressed visitors at industrial fairs with sleek pilot models of farm machines, autos, and mechanical gadgets. The technique lost some of its glamour only when arrangements were made to have orders placed for the equipment, thus publicizing Soviet inability to make deliveries.

The entire range of the Soviet effort has proved amazing. The estimated $1,500,000,000 minimum that the U.S.S.R. and its satellites apparently spend on propaganda represent about two percent of its national income of $79,800,000,000. If America spent a comparable percentage, it would total roughly sixty-seven times the current cost of the Voice of America and all related U. S. information activities.

The case of France illustrates the scale of the Soviet-Communist program. Rough estimates place the total expenditure on Communist propaganda there at $150,000,000 a year. These include French-language broadcasts from Moscow, maintenance of cultural attachés, distribution of publications, locally financed publication of 200 Communist and pro-Communist newspapers (total circulation: 7,000,000), and activities of roughly 100 front organizations. The dominant purpose of all the pamphlets, posters, broadcasts, and lectures in France is to create a rift between the French and the Americans. The unending theme, sometimes open, more often subtle, is that the United States is maintaining a fascist-type occupation and is hell-bent on plunging Europe into a war that neither France nor the U.S.S.R. wants.

SUCH is the propaganda mechanism of America's self-styled enemy. Its output is cold, calculated, and virulent. It steals such terms as "peace" and "democracy" and distorts them. It is seemingly bound by no budgetary considerations. In some cases it has been too blatant and has hurt its own cause. In many others, it has infected the minds of vast masses with desired points of view—on outlawing the A-bomb, on resisting rearmament, on suspecting venal motives behind the Marshall Plan, or on the wisdom of neutralism.

On one point there can be no doubt: Malenkov, like Stalin, endorses fully the words of Lenin that "propaganda is of crucial importance for the eventual triumph of the Party."

13

The Defeatists' Myth

RECENT YEARS have produced much defeatist chatter to the effect that America is "losing the cold war." Those who have spouted such despairing generalities have simply helped the Kremlin to spread its favorite myth: the picture of an infernally clever, virtually infallible, and irresistible Soviet regime.

It is one thing to appraise the Soviet's great strength and vile intentions accurately in order to plan bold and resolute counter-measures. It is quite another to indulge quiveringly in loose defeatist talk that simply is not supported by the record. The blunt truth is that, even before Stalin's death, the Kremlin crowd had blundered repeatedly since 1945 and had fallen far short of their own aims, hopes, and expectations. We of the free nations have not lost the cold war; we are not losing it; we *can* win it. Despite our errors and our wavering, any careful examination of the free world's record gives cause for more hope and confidence than pessimism.

Of course, the cause of freedom lost ground in China. There can be interminable debate as to whether U. S. policies aided or slowed China's fall to Communism; there are respected students of fundamental trends who years ago predicted that if China were liberated from Japan she would automatically turn Communist. Today, some students see in China more

185

long-term problems than progress for the Soviet regime. They see potential Peiping-Moscow friction and the sheer difficulties of digesting the Chinese conquest as causing stomach-aches and headaches for the Stalinists in the long run. Nonetheless, Communism scored a vast gain in China, at least for the short run.

At the same time, while China was moving into the Moscow orbit, Tito's Yugoslavia was moving out. The forces of freedom snatched Italy, Greece, and Turkey from Stalin's grasp. Communist campaigns were repulsed in France, Scandinavia, and elsewhere.

Barbara Ward, brilliant foreign analyst for *The Economist* of London, wrote recently that "nothing is going according to the Kremlin's plan." In 1945, Soviet rulers gloated over a highly encouraging international outlook. They saw a world deeply admiring Russian wartime courage and endurance. They saw Western armies demobilizing at full speed. They saw the Far East seething with a new nationalism, Communists entering the governments of Europe, and the United States swinging into a boom of the sort that had preceded earlier crashes. They foresaw non-Communist forces losing their nerve in the face of Soviet might.

By 1946, the Soviet regime's own writings show, everything looked simple to Moscow. It had only to wait for the "inevitable depression" in America, employ its Communist minorities smartly in a depressed Europe, feed the anti-colonial flames of Asia, and ease one area after another into Communist control.

What has happened? China followed the pattern. Nothing else did. The U. S. economy continued to surge. The Marshall Plan helped to produce unprecedented recovery in Europe. Communist Party membership declined in every country of Western Europe. Western imperialism began to disappear in Asia, and the beginnings of technical assistance brought new hope to at least some parts of the area.

By 1953 fundamental changes had occurred—none of them in keeping with any Moscow master plan. Free nations, traditionally incapable of rapid arming in the absence of war, were far along in the building of powerful defenses. Nations that had met aggression with appeasement in the '30's banded together in costly but determined resistance in Korea. The basic concept of joint defense, as in the North Atlantic community, won support from political figures as diverse as Paul Douglas and Robert Taft, as Anthony Eden and even Aneurin Bevan; they quarreled only over the size of the effort. The idea of attacking poverty with technical assistance became a firmly established program of the U. S. Government and of the United Nations.

Credit for free-world advances had to be divided among a long list of Marshalls, Vandenbergs, Achesons, Trumans, and Eisenhowers, plus an array of Churchills, Attlees, Schumans, Adenauers, and Romulos. More credit still went to unnamed millions who had supported at least some far-sighted policies.

The Moscow rulers themselves helped by systematically undermining their own thesis that a Communist society is one in which conflicts between men disappear. Youths around the world, long tempted by the Communist short cut to Utopia, were rudely shocked by the shots of Communist firing squads, executing as traitors any citizens suspected of friendship toward the West. Would-be Stalinist puppets in democratic countries hesitated as they learned how the Paukers, Slanskys, and Eislers became scapegoats for the economic consequences of Soviet exploitation in satellite states. The religious forces already marshaled against Communist imperialism grew in strength as Communist persecutions continued and as Soviet anti-Semitism aroused new hostility among Jews everywhere.

The United States had not waged the cold war as well as it should have or could have, but it certainly was not losing. Indeed, by 1953, the Soviet Communists were trying to persuade the peoples of Western Europe that their governments had

sold out to the United States! In France, where the Communist Party could call a political strike at will in 1947, it had
failed to touch off a single strike of any importance for four
years. Despite constant agitation, France's Communist-dominated labor federation had lost two thirds of its members.
Circulation of the leading Communist newspaper had dropped
by sixty percent, and the second-largest Communist paper
stopped publishing altogether.

The same pattern emerged in other nations. The Communists lost ground in nearly every European election. West
Berlin, a democratic island in a Communist sea, showed unparalleled determination to resist Communism. Austria, one
third still under the Soviet Army's heel, voted to turn Communist officials out of office. Some of the Communist leaders
in Italy defected from the party.

Plain bungling by the Kremlin Communists had helped.
Moscow had gained complete domination over the populations of satellite countries and subjected them to six years of
intensive propagandizing, but it had dismally failed to win
them over. Almost every impartial analysis indicated that between sixty and ninety percent of the satellite populations
were strongly anti-Soviet. The Kremlin's blunt refusal to permit the satellites to share in the Marshall Plan had produced
more rancor behind the Iron Curtain. As word of Communist
brutalities seeped out of China, anti-Communism gradually
grew perceptibly in South Asia.

Kremlin propaganda, on the whole, had not only been un-
scrupulous; it had often been crude, stiff, and unimaginative.
While spending some billion and a half dollars a year on propaganda, Stalin had gradually alienated, rather than persuaded, the nations outside his immediate control. On one key
issue after another in the U.N., the United States and fifty-two
other nations voted together. The Soviet Union had eight nations voting with it. Andrei Gromyko, representing the
U.S.S.R. at the San Francisco Conference on the Japanese

Peace Treaty, started out with bluster, played the same old propaganda records, and ended up being laughed at by delegates and press alike.

Many of the Kremlin's blunders arose from its mammoth misconception of the mind of the outside world. Diplomats of many lands, who had dealt first-hand with the Soviet machine, seemed to believe that this misconception was becoming one of the machine's greatest weaknesses.

The terrific penalty for making a mistake in the Soviet system has caused even the ablest Russian functionaries to tell their superiors only what they think the boss wants to know. Hence, the Soviet masters in Russia get only limited knowledge of the nature of outside society, and even that knowledge is screened through Marx-Lenin-Stalin theory. The procedure has invited persistent mistakes in judgment.

Soviet postwar policy toward the United States was based, in large measure, on three fundamental assumptions, all arrived at around 1944. They were:

1. That the withdrawal of U. S. troops from Europe would mean America's return to isolationism;

2. That the U. S. could not shift from a war to a peace economy without an economic collapse;

3. That there would be increasingly bitter rivalry, instead of alliance, between Britain and the United States.

As a result of persistently holding to these beliefs (and even punishing citizens, like the economist Eugene Varga, who questioned them), the Soviets have blundered and continued to blunder.

As of this writing, the free world still has abundant troubles. In place of the fear of immediate war, there is a sense of uncertainty and stalemate. The momentum of the Atlantic alliance has slowed down. Conflicts between European powers and Arab nations are severe. Germany's role in European rearmament is still unresolved, and Britain faces renewed financial woes. Nations abroad are showing more vocal resentment at "being pushed around" by America. And there is still some danger that Americans, by turning suddenly defeatist and then frantic and irresponsible, could conceivably plunge the nation into full-scale war with inadequate arms and too few allies.

Yet, amid all these difficulties, the signs of steady, continuing progress show through. The short-term ups and downs do not obscure the fact that free nations are reluctantly but steadily accepting the concept of community action.

The world has not moved according to any Moscow Plan. It has moved appreciably in the other direction. There is ground for modest confidence that the forces of freedom, if they behave intelligently and resolutely, can steadily move it further along that route.

14

Suspicious Friends

"*Y E S,*" said our friend from Asia, "to be blunt, your proposal is sound and right—and we won't support it."

Sitting with another United States official and me in a Washington living room, a visiting diplomat from an Asian country was explaining why his government would probably decline a tentative American proposal. He could speak frankly, for the three of us were friends. "I like your government's suggestion," he continued. "Our Foreign Office likes it. It is bold, and it should help turn back Communism. But we can't go along with it—not now, anyway."

"Look. We are relatively new as a democracy. But we have to pay attention to popular opinion just as you do. Let's face it: Our informed people don't completely trust Americans. They don't want their government to seem to be just a junior partner doing whatever you suggest.

"Now, I'm not saying our people's prejudices are right. Often they aren't. But what are they? First, Americans seem to them to be still associated with the old colonial powers. Unfairly in most cases, they associate you with the arrogance and commercial exploitation practiced by other white men in the area in the past. Hence, even when you generously provide economic aid and technical help—you know, Point IV—they first suspect selfish motives; they fear we're going to have to pay for it many times over in some way. Second, they know vaguely of your immigration laws making Asians seem second-class human beings. They've heard much, most of it exaggerated by Communists, about your so-called mistreatment of your own Negroes.

"Then, too, it's not just the masses that cause trouble. Our educated people, intellectuals if you will, have their own prejudices. They look to Europe for cultural leadership. They think you are still a brash, young, uncultured people. Your Hollywood hasn't helped. Your films make it seem that all Americans are either pampered brats with swimming pools or cowboys, or gangsters and molls. Many of these élite just don't feel like trusting leadership to America—and don't forget they have an extraordinary amount of political power. So you see we who are in government can't always do what we think best, or we won't—well, we won't be in government any longer."

"All right," broke in the other American. "What are we going to do about it?"

Our Asian friend shrugged his shoulders. Then he added: "Of course, even now it's all not as bad as it once was. Telling and retelling the story of the Philippines and what you did there has helped. You didn't seem like any dreadful colonial imperialists there. Actions, of course, are most important, actions indicating not that you tolerate Asians but that you co-operate with them as coequals. Your little overseas libraries in our cities, with their books and art and fine recordings, have begun to impress educated citizens. I'm glad to see you are beginning to get some first-class American books translated and distributed. Those films—documentaries, you call them—about everyday American life and labor unions and even the Korean war are doing some good. I'm told that your visiting Negro speakers [including Edith Sampson and Walter White] who made some speeches impressed many of our people with how much progress, sensible progress, you are making on racial matters. They made more of an impression than a dozen eminent white Americans could. And—oh, say—some of your Point IV men are beginning to be fine missionaries, gradually making clear that they stand for helpfulness, self-help, and such, not just exploitation."

In blunter language than usual, it was an old story. In Europe, in Asia, in Africa, and in Latin America, cooperative-minded governments often had not dared work as closely with the United States as they wanted to. The masses of the people here, the so-called intellectuals there, or a few powerful politicians elsewhere were too suspicious of Americans. When the American Government and the other governments have failed to work systematically to combat such suspicions, they have passively sabotaged their own policies.

IN SOME WAYS, the recent doubts and suspicions have been less severe than they once were. Between World War I and World War II the United States Government had contributed to its own difficulties by sitting still and doing nothing while misconceptions about America were spread throughout the world by the propaganda machines of foreign governments—and sometimes inadvertently by its own private agencies of information.

For those twenty years people in other nations "learned" about the United States either from the systematic misrepresentations of others or from press wire services, American magazines, and, particularly, American movies. The news channels carried major news in true perspective. But they also naturally featured the sensational items for which there was greatest demand: news of strikes, gangster murders, lynchings, floods, and Hollywood divorces. Movies tended to portray gangster stories and penthouse escapades. They put little emphasis on the normal life of millions of Americans in between these two extremes. Much of the world came to think of America as the land of unlimited material wealth (at least for the upper crust) and little cultural wealth. It learned nothing about the typical

Americans who manned the factories, tilled the soil, and attended the churches. It heard almost nothing of American universities, libraries, museums, and symphony orchestras. It heard much about movie queens, gangsters, flagpole sitters, and dance marathons.

Some of the delegates at the London Economic Conference in 1933 referred to Americans as "La Delegation Cowboy." In an Oxford Union debate in Britain in the same year, a speaker brought down the house with the pronouncement, "The United States of America is the first country in history that has gone from a period of barbarism to a period of decadence with no intervening period."

Since that era there has been improvement. America is not now referred to as "Uncle Shylock." Assiduous information efforts by the U. S. Government have erased many misconceptions. More responsible conduct by private information channels have brought improvement. The enormous circulation of the *Reader's Digest* may sometimes have created the impression that Americans are oddly conservative by others' standards, but it has given a much wider impression of the vigor, decency, cooperative spirit, and inventive genius of Americans. On balance, other American magazines have helped. Even American films, still leaving much to be desired, have shown appreciable improvement.

But the burgeoning influence of the United States since World War II has given rise to new suspicions. Frenchmen, fearful in 1946 that the United States would soon revert to isolationism, later came to grumble about too much American solicitude. In contrast to official U. S. insistence on peaceful aims, a few blustering speeches by American political figures have created an exaggerated idea of American trigger-happiness. An incredible utterance by an American Secretary of the Navy, suggesting the possible wisdom of preventive war, provoked consternation abroad. In Italy and Belgium, in Pakistan and Burma, there have remained deep fears of "American

war-mindedness"—along with the usual envy so often felt toward a powerful young upstart. Englishmen, with 40,000 U. S.
Air Force men on their soil in 1953, revived the old wisecrack
objecting to Americans as "overpaid, oversexed, overdressed,
and over here."

The McCarran-Walter Immigration Act was mainly a cod-
ification of existing laws, but it repeated enough of the old
"national origins" features to indicate that Americans would
tolerate large immigration from some nationalities but not
from others. It was widely resented. Other new immigration
features involving unprecedented red tape or barring escapees
who had risked their lives to get from behind the Iron Curtain
stirred resentments. New visa restrictions conflicted sharply
with all the American protestations about fundamental freedoms. While America preached freedom of travel, it seemed to
many to barricade its borders with a "red-tape curtain." Americans could hardly continue to point an accusing finger at Soviet travel bans. Troubles also have arisen from other forms of
protectionism, notably, signs that Congress might be retro-
gressing on tariff matters.

As a sagacious Frenchman expressed it in 1953: "Thanks in
part to your Marshall Plan, we are getting back on our feet.
Now we want increasing trade, not continuing aid. But your
tariffs make that difficult. And I must tell you it's irritating to
find that your hordes of official representatives are forced by
law to ride your ships and planes, not ours, even if they have
to go miles out of the way. It's a small matter, but if you per-
sist in that sort of thing, how will we ever pay our own way as
you rightly say we should?"

Systematic surveys have shown a slight majority of Europeans having a high opinion of American generosity and
American motives. They have reflected undoubted improvement in attitudes toward the United States. They have also
shown, however, approximately a quarter of the people of
Europe believing the Marshall Plan "a scheme to promote

American domination of European industry." They have indicated that half the peoples of Europe consider Americans
"too materialistic," with most of these still believing U. S.
policy to be dominated by "Wall Street."

In sample countries of Europe and Asia, a majority of free
citizens said they did not believe that the Americans were
using germ warfare in Korea, as charged by the Communists.
However, minorities ranging from ten percent to thirty percent of these populations believed the charges *might* be true.
One underdeveloped nation of Asia was the delightful exception. There the charges were not taken seriously because
ninety-five percent of the population did not believe in germs!

WE AMERICANS have always been friendly people. From pio-
neer days when neighbors were rare and hence valued, we
have wanted to like and be liked. We find it a rude shock to be
feared, or envied, or disliked. Thrust into a position of world
power, we are deeply disturbed to find others regarding us as
"irresponsible" or "crassly materialistic" or "economic imperialists." We can understand being criticized by extreme right
and extreme left, Franco and Peron as well as Malenkov or
Tito or Mao Tse-Tung. But we are stunned to find ourselves
most persistently criticized by the intellectual élite of other
nations. We are baffled when we find affluent, well-educated
non-Communists in France or Sweden or India groping publicly for a middle course, a "third way" that is neither the
Soviet course nor the American course. Careful study of opinion trends abroad indicates that few except fanatics show hate
for Americans. Many, however, show doubts, distrust, and
even occasional dislike.

It is nonsense to pretend, as some do, that all of the existing
doubts and dislikes could be completely cured by a "bold information program." Some of the difficulties are little short of
inevitable. No nation which achieves enormous power can expect to be universally loved at the peak of that power. It can

win respect and perhaps even some trust, but not love. That was true of ancient Rome and Greece, of Napoleon's France, and of every other dominant power in world history.

As a buoyant, vigorous young nation, moreover, America can expect to have its energy, its confidence, and its friendliness and optimism highly regarded. Indeed, those are the traits most often commended by visitors from the outside. But as a dynamic and youthful nation, America will have to earn, with painstaking slowness, the privilege of having its judgment fully trusted.

My wife has a parallel she likes to draw. She says the attitude of other peoples toward America isn't hard to understand; it is exactly like the attitude of many American Easterners toward Texans.

The Easterner admires and likes the Texan's frankness, vigor, and unquenchable optimism. He finds the wealthy Texan unbelievably generous and willing to spend money, but doubts that this entitles him to tell Bostonians or New Yorkers how to run their cities. He is struck by the bigness of Texas projects, but laughs at Texas boasting. He regards Texans as valiant, courageous fighters and wants them on his side in event of trouble. He would hardly be eager, however, to entrust them with leadership in delicate international matters; he fears they may be a little headstrong and trigger-happy.

The Texan, in turn, sometimes looks on the East as a little effete and doddering, as not appreciative of the most modern techniques and of the value of bold, large-scale ventures. Texans particularly resent the American Easterner's suspicion that the largest state in the Union hasn't developed much of a culture.

Texas is "hated" by few, and its virtues are warmly admired. No amount of information, however, can suddenly erase the suspicion that it is exuberant, headstrong, and not "fully mature." In the eyes of the older nations, America faces the same problem.

OTHER misgivings about America will be inevitable unless and until the United States and its citizens undergo fundamental changes. The United States can impress others with the extraordinary progress being made in the relations between Whites and Negroes. But so long as it has segregation, so long as even a few political figures talk about "white supremacy," it can hardly expect to have its policies and objectives accepted unquestionably by even the friendliest of colored populations abroad. Endless talk about the theory that "all men are created equal" cannot alter that. It was Alistair Cooke, staunch admirer of this country, who once told his B.B.C. audience, "In America all men are created equal but some seem to be more equal than others."

Doubts as to American maturity and stability are bound to exist so long as Americans periodically take off on emotional binges like that surrounding the firing and homecoming of General Douglas MacArthur. Older nations are sure to question the depth of American belief in freedom when an internal Communist scare can throw the nation into a frenzy of character assassination, purges, name-calling, and blacklists. Why, ask others, can't Americans quietly and efficiently eliminate suspect characters from sensitive positions and forego such eruptions of national hysteria?

STILL other misgivings about America abroad will require more than effective information work. If Americans are to demonstrate a belief in freedom of movement in contrast to Iron Curtain philosophy, they cannot systematically withhold visitors' visas from every foreign scientist or sociologist who ever lent his name to a dubious letterhead. As a distinguished commentator pointed out, foolproof security can be and should be enforced around sensitive establishments within the country but hardly around an entire nation of 150,000,000 people. The latter may prove foolhardy security.

If others are not to suspect Americans of "taking over" their countries, there will have to be a conscious effort to reduce the number of American functionaries massed in the capitals of foreign lands. The Congress will need to recognize that there are many overseas jobs in economic aid offices, Point IV projects, and information centers which foreigners can fill at least as well as Americans without endangering security.

If American troops abroad are not to be an undue irritant, measures already undertaken will have to be carried through. During my tenure in Washington, the Pentagon and the State Department jointly initiated a program for better indoctrination of American troops, for the replacing of field commanders who were oblivious to local sensibilities, and for conscious good-will gestures between troops and the local populations abroad. A few cases of American units adopting local orphanages and of impoverished youngsters being entertained aboard U. S. warships have won vast good will.

If foreign friends are not to be frightened out of their wits, the U. S. Government cannot tolerate blustering threats by its officials. If other populations are not to be needlessly offended, American Congressmen will have to make more of an effort to understand others' sensitivities before rising to lecture allied nations. The wholesale traveling abroad by members of Congress has already produced vast improvement. The cost of such Congressional touring—even "junketing"—has proved one of the best investments taxpayers can make.

IT IS a mistake to expect information work alone to accomplish miracles. There remain, nonetheless, vast jobs that can be done only with efficient, discreet, and wide-spread information efforts.

Most of the world still thinks of American business in terms of the Wall Street of forty years ago. It does not yet recognize the new dispersion of ownership, under which great companies now belong not to a single family but to 500,000 and even to 1,000,000 stockholders. It does not recognize the emergence of professional hired managers to replace the fortunate heirs of the wealthy. It does not recognize what *Fortune* magazine called the "permanent American revolution" and what Frederick Lewis Allen recognized when he wrote in *The Big Change:*

> When the American system broke down badly in the Great Depression, the repair work and reconstruction was pretty drastic, and some was foolish. But the basic principle of unrevolutionary and experimental change prevailed. . . . When World War II came along, we discovered that if Washington jammed the accelerator right down to the floor boards the engine began to run smoothly and fast. And when the war was over, and Washington released the accelerator, it still hummed. . . .
>
> Through a combination of patchwork revisions of the system—tax laws, minimum wage laws, subsidies and guarantees and regulations of various sorts, plus labor union pressures and new management attitudes—we had repealed the Iron Law of Wages. We had brought about a virtually automatic redistribution of income from the well-to-do to the less well-to-do. . . . We had discovered a new frontier to open up: The purchasing power of the poor. . . .
>
> We recognized that our businesses are better run if they remain in private hands. The past dozen years or so offered a triumphant demonstration of the validity of this belief. For they have seen privately managed American business not only do a brilliant job of huge-scale war production but also foster a startling variety of advances in technology.

American business, private information channels, and government programs have only begun to put across that story. A few foreign editors and leaders brought to this country have sensed it and told their compatriots about it.

The outside world, even while deploring American "racial prejudice," has only begun to appreciate the gigantic strides in improving racial relations in America. It still is largely ignorant of the extraordinary upsurge of cultural developments in an America which frankly admits it cannot lay claim to ancient cultures like those of older nations. Again, the citizens of other lands, wincing at the sound-offs of a few irresponsible Americans, overlook the encouraging and rapid growth of responsible, broad-gaged, and internationally-minded American opinion.

In belief, severe misgivings about America's character and aims still impede efforts to achieve stability and peace. Some of the misgivings are inevitable; others can be erased only by action. Still others, however, are being or can be reduced or eliminated by effective information work—by persistently seeing that others learn the truth about new actions and about existing facts.

Home-Front Foes

"*D O N ' T* make the mistake, Ed, of believing that your Voice of America has to deal only with foreign enemies." One of the wisest, finest old gentlemen in Congress gave that advice as I sat in his office in the Capitol soon after taking office in 1950. "There are plenty of trouble-makers at home," he explained. "Most of them are just that way out of ignorance; a few are that way out of cussedness. Together, they make the job much harder."

Any official dealing with the American truth offensive in the years ahead will quickly learn the wisdom of the advice. Any one seeking to understand the use of words as a weapon will need to appreciate it.

The home-front foes who impede effective international persuasion fall into at least eight broad categories, not counting possible subversives. Individuals need not be named. Most are well-meaning, and experience indicates that many will improve if not forced everlastingly to defend their past positions. It will suffice here to identify the motley array of forces that can and do impede every intelligent effort at international persuasion.

1. *The Jingoists*

Few individuals in recent history have so neatly undermined America's standing abroad as the one Cabinet officer

who in 1950 blurted out that the United States should declare
its intention to "institute a war to compel cooperation for
peace." In that one suggestion of "preventive war," he gave
Kremlin propagandists the ammunition they had been seeking
for use on their own home front. He provided "proof" that
"the American imperialists planned to attack Russia and that
all hardships within the U.S.S.R. were necessary in the name
of urgent defense." At the same time, he strengthened those
cynics in friendly countries who argue that American leadership is bent upon dragging the world into war and cannot be
trusted. With American rearmament hardly begun, he re-
versed Theodore Roosevelt. He had America talking big and
carrying a soft stick!

He has not been alone. Occasional editorials and political
speeches about "dropping the atom bomb and getting it over
with" have enlarged the damage. They've been quoted shud-
deringly by America's friends and gleefully by Kremlin propagandists. One Congressional amendment, providing darkly, if
vaguely, for unorthodox U. S. activities toward Iron Curtain
populations, was both unnecessary and inflammatory. It reminded me of Tom Howard's old skit in which he crept
stealthily on stage with a six-inch sign on his hat reading:
SPY.

One American magazine, in 1951, reawakened European
fears by portraying garishly the horrors of "the war we don't
want" and distributing thousands of copies abroad. Its commendable editorial, telling of the United States' determination
to prevent a war, was lost amid pages of four-color nightmares
picturing American bombings, eventual American triumph in
a devastated Europe, and American occupation of other lands.

(Personal note: After that magazine issue had gone to press,
I saw proofs and shuddered to hear I had been quoted somewhere as having "unofficially approved" the project. I thereupon recalled a brief chat with a sub-editor of the magazine
many months earlier. I had then offhandedly observed that

there might be merit in a responsibly done magazine effort to describe the horror of another war and to emphasize American determination to prevent such a war. After the issue appeared, I swore off making offhand observations.)

Over recent years, irresponsible Congressional speeches have happily declined. They have not disappeared. Nor have other damaging outbursts. Too many Americans still forget that the real Voice of America is far more than a radio network. It is the sum total of the impressions given abroad by the American press, the Congress, government officials, and prominent citizens. Jingoistic sound-offs by Americans in positions of responsibility can still offset months of constructive persuasion.

2. *The Lecturers*

For the systematic alienation of friends abroad, almost no one excels the American leader who rises before some distinguished American audience to lecture some friendly foreign nation on its behavior. Press services naturally wire the news to the nation concerned. Sometimes the speakers demand that all aid to Britain be terminated unless the British denationalize all industries forthwith; sometimes they insist that Franco's Spain adopt America's rules of religious freedom; nearly always they demand that another nation model itself after the pattern of America. They generally propound the thesis that others are poor because they haven't aped America; they rarely speculate that others might have tried different systems because they were poor. Often the lecturers have justification (as when insisting on fundamental freedoms). Nearly always their tactics are ineffective—or worse.

It is too often forgotten that no democratic government can afford to seem to take orders from a foreign government. Even a dictatorship would be weakened by doing so. The demagogue abroad who wants to win added popular support has only to put on a show of refusing to take dictation from outsiders.

Every veteran information specialist sometimes yearns for the unlikely assignment of making some foreign nation *dislike* America. It would be so easy, and there are so many recruits who could bring peculiar ability to the work. At the head of the list on the domestic front, most veterans would place the pontifical American who specializes in lecturing other nations in public.

3. *The Do-Nothings*

To a sizable minority of respectable Americans, "propaganda" is still a word like "spit." It's just not nice. Even when totalitarians are busy undermining confidence in the United States, these Americans somehow feel this country should refrain from propaganda, counter-propaganda, or even "the propaganda of truth."

There is one elderly gentleman in Congress who sees nothing very wrong with a political party spending forty or fifty million dollars in a few months to win a national election. Yet he cannot bring himself to believe a government has any business spending twice that amount over the entire world in a full year to win cooperation and support for America and the cause of freedom. As most of his Congressional colleagues have come to recognize the need for international persuasion, the old gentleman has publicly changed his tune a trifle. He now says he opposes an American information effort only because it is "poorly done." To a few intimates he has been franker. He once spent a day, with an aid, studying the Voice of America operation and reading scripts. Later he reported to a friend: "It was very disappointing. We found nothing particularly wrong." He just doesn't believe in the idea.

As an individual, the old gentleman is not too important. It is more important that a substantial minority of citizens and legislators, though less extreme, still share his doubt that there is real need for a systematic program to persuade the peoples of other lands. Still more important, however, is the encouraging fact that the affirmative group is growing. More and more citizens and Congressmen are slowly coming around to the belief that it is a proper and necessary function of government to use the instruments of information systematically and honestly to assist the cause of freedom and peace.

4. *The Skywriters*

Almost as troublesome as the "do-nothings" are the rare but voluble enthusiasts who think that propaganda can work miracles alone and unaided. "We have developed the greatest advertising skills on earth," their argument runs, "so let's recruit all the best advertising and public-relations brains in America, allocate a billion dollars a year to the program, and go to town." They say, in effect, that it doesn't matter too much what American policies are, since they are pretty good anyway. All that's needed is to enlist the abilities that have made America a nation of great salesmanship and embark on a gigantic effort to sell the world on America, democracy, and freedom. Fundamentally, their theory is that what sells Chlorodent in Des Moines can sell liberty everywhere.

It is the same theory that led to the original blunders in the first days of every organized American propaganda effort. It early led to mildly offensive ads abroad, to misguided gift packets, and to inept broadcasts translated directly from English. It led to the effort of one high official of the current Administration to appoint the estimable Arthur Godfrey to a topmost international propaganda post because "he knows people." It even led one able but internationally naïve official two years ago to try to promote a plan for distributing in France a million colorful yo-yos bearing American propaganda slogans.

The skywriting school of flamboyant propaganda often overlooks the fact that the best propaganda is action intelligently executed and then fully publicized through information channels. As American-Arab relations worsened in 1952, continued talk of United States friendship for the Arab peoples would have done little good. But State and Defense Department officials accomplished near-miracles by slashing red tape and arranging emergency Air Force transport for 3,318 aging Arabs stranded tragically on their pilgrimage to Mecca. With that event, U. S. Information Service outlets throughout the Arab world had a magnificent story to tell. Better yet, by distributing the simple facts and pictures, the U.S.I.S. enabled Arab newspapers to tell the story in their own way. They did so glowingly—and with extraordinary editorial praise.

There are still some who would like literally to plaster the countrysides of Europe with American billboards and send sound trucks blaring through continental villages. Any one who knows Europe today recognizes these as dangerous techniques. They would encourage resentment at "American blatancy." They would strengthen the tendency of too many Europeans to think of the world conflict as essentially one between the U. S. and the U.S.S.R. And they would permit the enemies of freedom to shout that the United States is "just trying to buy the minds of men with American dollars."

There are great, enterprising things to be done in the field of persuasion. But blindly transplanting the techniques of super-sales and war-bond campaigns is not one of those things.

5. *The Boosters*

Among those seeking officially or unofficially to persuade others, the American "booster" type can do more harm than good. The proud American tourist who can't resist bragging of American wealth and material progress has long offended others. Many newcomers in international information work at first show the same tendency. They reason that if they can just tell the world enough about how the average American has thrived under democracy, then, presto, the world becomes fanatical about following the American example.

Fortunately, the booster boys in professional ranks soon

learn. They find that showing photos of $10,000 reapers, plus deep freezes and automatic washers, to a Pakistani farmer causes frustration or resentment—while a demonstration of simple contour plowing can win good will. They learn that some Europeans may actually prefer arguing in a cafe beside a bottle of wine to wheeling a new push-button convertible out to a drive-in movie. They learn that, with few exceptions, boasting of American material wealth can arouse more rancor than respect.

One exception is the discreet portrayal of American military might and defense production. If properly done, with due regard for timing and for audience sensibilities, this can convert the waverers and bandwagon-jumpers to support the side of freedom. Another exception lies in satellite countries, where Soviet propagandists have painted a picture of starving, down-trodden American labor. There honest photos of American workmen's homes can intrigue the populations. Five thousand copies of a Montgomery Ward catalogue quietly distributed in one satellite country were passed from hand to hand by fascinated citizens with jesting remarks about Soviet propaganda. In some captive areas, citizens chortled over a simple handbill. It showed a Soviet factory with one car outside, then an American factory with thousands of cars. Its caption: "In the Soviet, the factory belongs to the workers and the cars to the management. In America, the factory belongs to the management and the cars to the workers."

With such special exceptions, however, American information specialists learned years ago that boasting of material wealth is harmful. Contrary to rumors, it is not done in any significant way by the U. S. Information Service. Indeed, one prominent Republican leader in 1951 returned from a Far Eastern tour with a resounding pronouncement that American propaganda should stop "boasting of American wealth." Asked by me whether he had actually seen or heard any such official propaganda, he had memory trouble. Well, come to think of it, he couldn't recall any specific cases, but he somehow had that impression. He was sorry. He did not correct the speech.

Nonetheless, genuine American pride naturally fosters a tendency to boast. American officials, information officers, and plain American travelers need persistently to guard against it— and against the subtler tendency that William Allen White once called "the unconscious arrogance of conscious wealth."

6. *The Name-Callers*

On any list of propaganda bunglers, a high place goes to the devotees of You're-Another tactics, the eager characters who want to outdo the foe in the art of name-calling.

Moscow propaganda directed at the outside world has often defeated itself by waxing far too vitriolic in denouncing Eisenhower, Churchill, or "Wall Street." Unlike the less blatant output of many home-grown Communists in the West, the Soviet Union's own outpourings have frequently seemed ridiculous to Western eyes and ears. Recognizing that extremism can defeat the best persuasive efforts, those of us directing the Campaign of Truth in 1950 undertook a detailed study of all evidence on Soviet attitudes toward Joseph Stalin. Only after that did we finally permit the Voice's Russian broadcasts to aim mild gibes and ridicule at the Kremlin dictator personally. The time had come, we found, to start destroying his cloak of infallibility, partly by contrasting various incidents in his own record. Even that had to be only gradual. Tirades against the Great White Father in the Kremlin could arouse strong resentments. Indeed, strident broadcasts to Russia at the time of Stalin's death seem to have pleased one persistent Congressional critic of the Voice of America, but they probably did not help the Voice's cause in Russia.

Many an American propaganda novice is tempted to indulge in shrill denunciations. Even veterans are sometimes tempted, particularly after hearing or reading the diatribes from Moscow. All old hands have learned better; all know they should not alienate those they seek to persuade. If the Voice has sometimes erred on the side of stridency, as it unfortunately has, the tendency has stemmed largely from the pressures of novices on the outside.

In the United States, there are still influential figures who want the Voice to "talk back" vigorously, to denounce all Communists at every opportunity, and to tell off theoretical Marxism just as frequently and vehemently as they denounce Communist imperialism. They rarely sense that an effective technique in Communist areas is first to convince the dupes of Marx that Stalin and Malenkov have perverted Marxism and can't even lay claim to being pure Communists. The name-callers don't understand the wisdom of putting the weakening of the Soviet conspiracy ahead of the unmasking of all theoretical Marxism. They tend toward denouncing, and alienating, all who have been misled by Marx's teachings in any way.

Unfortunately, a few extremist name-callers still occupy influential spots in press and politics. They inevitably have some influence on Voice personnel. In the Spring of 1953, they went on a rampage and frightened some U. S. propagandists into putting out self-defeating vitriol. Even in normal times Voice broadcasters, continually being investigated and having their scripts combed by clumsy Red-hunters, know there is one easy defense. An occasional shrieking philippic against all types of Communism and Communists will remove any doubt. Naturally, they sometimes give in to the impulse. It may be poor persuasion but it helps keep one off of amateurs' "suspect lists." With benefit of hindsight, I fear I personally erred in sometimes yielding a trifle and permitting others to yield to the temptation of stridency.

In wartime, the Churchill government early recognized that indiscriminate name-calling, designed to appease misguided sentiment on the home front, could be self-defeating abroad. Accordingly, Churchill managed the incredible feat of classifying as "secret documents" the leaflets that were being distributed by the millions above enemy territory! America can hardly follow that course. It can learn lessons from it.

The firm conviction of most veterans in international persuasion is that, in talking to an "enemy," news should always take precedence over views. Straight, credible reporting of facts otherwise unavailable to the audience can be handled in a way to have enormous impact. The news should naturally include denial and disproof (often by indirection) of opponents' lies, but the tone should be calm. On the Voice of America, political satires have often proved appealing to satellite listeners, but they need to be deft, not violent. Vitriol, vilification, and name-calling often can be enjoyable. They rarely can win converts.

7. The "Causists"

For every nation or ex-nation now under Communist control there are two to twenty organized groups of emigrés in the United States. Most are made up of patriotic new Americans, but all naturally have fervent feelings about their old countries. Nearly all have a "cause" beyond that of America and freedom.

Latvians naturally tend to put the freeing of their homeland above everything else. One dedicated faction of Slovaks often seems more intent on dividing Czechoslovakia than on having it escape Soviet rule. Ukrainian separatists are among the most determined "causists." A few avid sons of Czarist Russians perennially beg the Voice to stress that the rule of the Czars was benevolent despotism beside the horrors of Soviet tyranny. Groups of Czechs and Sudetan Germans each want the Voice to "report fully" on the sins of the others.

Many of the "causist" groups have given helpful advice suggestions and aid to the Voice. They continue to do so. Others have been perpetual headaches, always demanding that the Voice support this or that factional cause. Often they insist that one of the brethren be given a regular period on the

Voice to spread one particular doctrine in the homeland. For many years now, Voice of America officials have stood firm, insisting that the Voice must be the voice of all America and not the voice of any particular factions. They say "causist" speakers might possibly be used on the Free Europe and Free Asia stations but cannot properly promote their causes on the official transmitters of the U. S. Government.

The very strictness of the system breeds trouble among the "causists." The fervent brethren who have been denied use of the Voice sometimes embark on systematic campaigns to inform Congress of the "inept" or even "seditious" output of the Voice toward the homeland. Congressman Doe, whose Slavic languages are less than perfect, has to take the complainers at their word. Next week he hears similar complaints from a Chinese whose job-seeking has been rebuffed. He soon says, "All the foreigners I talk to tell me the Voice is doing a frightful job." He may finally be set straight only when he reads special reports from behind the Curtain or the findings of one of the Voice's many panels of recent escapees.

One separatist sub-faction became singularly zealous in 1951. My colleagues and I patiently explained to its representatives that the United States was interested only in opposing tyranny in the homeland and could not take sides on whether the country should eventually be one, two, or three nations. Rebuffed, a few zealots in the group thereupon decided that, since the group was solidly Catholic, the Voice of America was "anti-Catholic." They somehow persuaded an influential priest of their theory, then two Catholic members of Congress who had unusual power. Before I realized it, they had jeopardized the entire information appropriation for the coming year. Only after extraordinary efforts and some constructive help from a high Church official did my colleagues and I convince the key Congressmen that they had been misled.

The "causists" in general have decent, understandable motives. These usually, however, are not the motives of the whole United States. In judging future complaints about the U. S. propaganda, any official should make it routine procedure to look into the background and the "cause" of the complainers.

8. *The Revolutionists*

About once a month one well-known columnist used to inform his readers that the U. S. Government, and particularly the Voice of America, was "soft" because it was not promoting revolt in Soviet-dominated areas. Almost as frequently, one or another of the small minority of Congressional extremists would likewise demand that the Voice start inciting rebellion. Without exception these "revolutionists" knew little about conditions in the Communist areas.

Not a single member of the Senate Foreign Relations Committee or the House Foreign Affairs Committee subscribed to the demands. Nor did a single member of the Pentagon's upper echelons. When I cornered the columnist and asked him to explain his views, he talked vaguely about it being "time to take the offensive," and revealed incredible naïveté about the power and character of totalitarian states.

In the last two years I have laboriously sought out the opinions of most recognized experts on Russia and the satellites, plus two veterans of underground movements in the last war. Without exception they held this general view: The plain fact is that the inciting of rebellion in Sovietized zones at this time would be an open invitation to the friends of freedom to commit suicide. To an extent unparalleled in modern history, the Soviet state and its sub-states have an overwhelming monopoly of physical force and no inhibitions about using it. Openly urging revolt behind the Iron Curtain would amount to inviting the Kremlin and its satellite governments to still more extreme forms of repression. To do so with no intention of coming to the help of the rebels would be a criminal act that would long be remembered. It would earn for America the same kind of hatred the Soviet got when it urged the "Polish Home Army" to rise up against the Germans in 1944 and then stood by and watched it get slaughtered.

Someday, conditions may well be changed, particularly as the backstage power struggle continues in Moscow. Today, however, the West's job of persuasion is clear: to encourage an *attitude* of resistance behind the Iron Curtain; to help foster, quiet, every-day resistance to Sovietizing, to collectivization, and to production drives in industries; to encourage slow-down tactics among the populations; and to help build the kind of satellite nationalism that can ultimately lead to Titoism in other captive states. That is what the Voice of America, Radio Free Europe, and the B.B.C. have been trying to do.

The efforts to date have not been flamboyant or spectacular. Neither have they been unsuccessful. We have seen a Voice warning of a forthcoming match shortage in Hungary lead to mass purchase and exhaustion of that nation's match supply. We have seen more than one case where Voice and Radio Free Europe warnings of forthcoming currency juggling in satellite states produced runs on banks—and later were proved accurate. There are indications that the free radios have helped produce slow-downs in critical satellite industries. Far more important, many students of Russia believe today that a major deterrent to all-out war has been the attitude of resistance among Sovietized peoples. These students mention the Kremlin's knowledge that U.S.S.R. and satellite troops could not be counted on if aggression took them beyond their own borders, plus the Kremlin's fear that its own lines of communication would be insecure.

In the meantime, irresponsible "revolutionists" on the American scene are performing a disservice. They are demanding a course that would get the friends of freedom killed off. They are ignoring the simple fact that, even if Western nations should help to build an organized core of resisters behind the Iron Curtain, the last thing on earth to do would be to advertise it. They are encouraging at least some Americans in false hopes of an "easy solution." And they are providing "proof" of the most extreme Soviet propaganda about American intentions.

THESE eight groups, of course, are not all-inclusive. There are others who make the difficult task of international persuasion even more difficult. These include the "inflexibles" in bureaucracy and in Congress who obstinately block any quick shifts in operations to cope with sudden changes in conditions abroad. They include a few Congressional dilettantes who make major decisions regarding international information work without finding the time to study it carefully. And they include the few ultra-nationalist newspapers which daily inveigh against Communism yet consistently oppose every governmental effort to fight Communism in the minds of men abroad.

No one can dissipate this array of home-front foes overnight. Some of them can be induced to mend their ways when they see the damage they are doing. All need to be recognized for what they are by any government or group which seeks to prosecute an effective truth offensive.

Part III

TIME TO WAGE PEACE

16

Resetting the Sights

MANY OF US who have labored in the so-called
cold war have learned lessons. Those of us who have taken
time out to sit down and rethink the worst problems have
found some answers that weren't so clear when we were grind-
ing away at high-pressure work. We hope that the lessons we
have learned may strengthen the vision of others.

It is the purpose of Part III of this book to set down in some
order the lessons learned from hard experience—and from
some concentrated rethinking by a number of cold-war veterans. Particular stress is put on the use of truth as a weapon,
but only as one of the weapons in a general offensive to insure
the survival of freedom.

IF EXPERIENCE has emphasized one clear lesson above all
others, it is a lesson for the nation as a whole. It is that Americans cannot expect some easy, quick solution of the world
crises; they must, rather, determine to wage a firm, persistent,
relentless campaign. To borrow Bernard Baruch's phrase
again, it is a matter of "waging the peace" for a long period,
intelligently and resolutely.

Top political figures have only rarely painted the picture so
darkly in their public utterances. That is because political
parties habitually portray themselves as the purveyors of hope,

219

confidence, and quick solutions, their opponents as the apostles of despair. Yet in many conversations and communications, I haven't found one truly informed government leader who privately foresees any easy short cut. Dean Acheson used to say privately, "We will accomplish a near-miracle if we turn back the Soviet forces without a war." John Foster Dulles, before he donned the restraints of high office, summed up the task bluntly: "An armament race is in full swing. If history is any guide, war will come out of this situation. . . . Future generations will look back with amazement if war is averted. It will be an achievement without precedent. Yet that is our task."

We voters and our Congress rarely see how difficult the task is. More actively interested in foreign policy than ever before, we still have a typical American yearning for some prompt, pat solution for every problem. We habitually call our problems, large and small, "headaches"—implying that all we have to do is find the right aspirin tablet and all will be well. In science and industry, this national trait of impatience has been an enormous boon. In international affairs, it can easily lead to frustration, vacillation, and tragic recklessness.

As a people, we usually forget one elementary point about foreign policy: *By its very nature, foreign policy deals with those things which are beyond the direct control and exclusive jurisdiction of this country.* This means that give and take, compromise and prolonged negotiation are necessarily involved. In foreign policy, one rarely has the chance to choose between black and white; he usually must deal in rather dirty grays.

We Americans can work with a country like Turkey, whose government is determined, and succeed in turning back Communism. In another country, whose government and people are not determined, we may try the same measures and fail. We can persuade a French, an Italian, or a Peruvian government to do certain things, and we can help them. We cannot just order them to do those things, even when we are shoveling millions in assistance to them. Any democratic government that openly takes orders from a foreign government would be tossed out of office, money or no money.

In dealing with a tyrant of the unpredictable type of a Stalin or a Malenkov, we cannot wisely employ empty bluster, threats, and ultimatums. That could too easily lead us into a war inadequately prepared and with our former allies frightened into either neutrality or impotence. We can, however, wisely employ inexorable firmness, continuing counter-pressures, and the steady building of economic strength, protected by necessary military might.

If we show a cool, set-jawed determination to carry through, some of the greatest problems may be solved sooner than we now dare hope. That is precisely what happened on a small scale with the Berlin airlift of 1949. When the Kremlin saw no sign of any wavering by Britain and America, it suddenly gave up and abandoned the blockade of Berlin. That is precisely what did *not* happen in the first thirty-odd months of the Korean war. Soviet Government and Tass cables from Washington doubtless told Moscow fully of American bickering about "the Truman war in Korea," of a few newspapers' scare headlines about casualties, and of stump speeches about the "useless war." No responsible American leader actually proposed abandoning the effort, but the impression given much of the world was that the United States was wavering. The distortions of Soviet intelligence unquestionably emphasized America's indecision. The Kremlin doubtless concluded it would be asinine to relent at such a time. The mere impression of American vacillation can frustrate the sturdiest of American efforts.

BUT, many ask, where do we end up? If we follow through boldly and resolutely, what will we find at the end of the tunnel? As of this writing, it is known that no responsible leader in either party can honestly give a precise answer. Eisenhower, Dulles, and Taft; Truman, Acheson, and Stevenson don't profess to have any complete blueprint for the ultimate triumph of freedom. Neither do Churchill, nor Eden, nor Attlee. Those few who do so profess have proved, upon examination, to be either soft-headed or slippery, sometimes both. Many, however, see hope in the lessons of history, in the knowledge that when a rapidly expanded, aggressive power overextends itself and then meets firm opposition, it can reverse itself or even crumble with amazing rapidity. This can happen particularly when troubles arise behind the aggressors' line. Something of the sort happened with the imperialist France of Napoleon; it happened to Genghis Khan's empire after his death; it can happen again—and perhaps without all-out war.

Soviet Russia may already have overextended itself. It has not won the loyalty of the satellite states—and probably cannot do so if the captive populations continue to be convinced they are not forgotten by the outside world. It has not proved a "good colonizer." The scanty intelligence that seeps from China indicates that the Chinese as a people are far from "converted." Even within the U.S.S.R., Latvians, Estonians, Ukrainians, and other nationalities, including those of original Russian stock, are more frustrated and resentful than willingly cooperative.

Any early armed uprising of the Russian masses against their Communist dictators is virtually out of the question. Those who expect such simply do not know the frightful effectiveness of the Communist police methods. Other developments are possible, however. Even before Stalin's death, a new wave of purges reflected unsteady nerves and violent rivalries within the Presidium. With Stalin gone, the Soviet has entered a new period of internal tensions, rivalries, and strains. A military dictatorship might conceivably emerge to replace the Malenkov regime. Mao in China, the East Germans, and puppets in other satellites could finally defect as did Tito—when they finally see the Soviet rulers blocked and bumbling. Internal economic pressures in an overextended Soviet empire could cause vast changes, going well beyond tactical "peace" talk.

Friends of freedom can help by keeping alive behind the Curtain a spirit of resistance, covert opposition, and plain "foot-dragging." And if peoples this side of the Curtain can be progressively convinced, through actions and words, of the fraud of Communism and the worth of freedom, Soviet hopes of easy conquest will disintegrate. The Kremlin rulers have already helped amazingly by their own actions—by their increasing ruthlessness, by their pogroms, by their own nervous conduct, and finally by a sudden flare-up of unconvincing "peace" gestures. Free governments can speed the process by continuing to build political unity and military strength, by persuasion, and by a variety of economic and political measures short of war.

The lack of a final, detailed blueprint at this stage is no cause for defeatism. The American Revolutionaries of 1776 did not see clearly the light at the end of their tunnel. Some asked whether life from then on was to be, at best, nothing but an unceasing business of withstanding British onslaughts, of being permanently on the defensive against a power with enormous reserves. When, however, the Revolutionaries resisted firmly and unwaveringly over a long period, completely unexpected events far away caused Britain to change course completely.

That parallel is far from perfect. It, nonetheless, illustrates a moral that has been pointed up by the determined resistance in Turkey, by the successful opposition to Communism in Greece, and by the Berlin airlift. In those and other cases, we found that when we followed the course we knew to be right and courageous, we may not have foreseen the ultimate outcome but finally we succeeded in turning the tide.

The first task of Americans and other free men, then, is to

reset the sights: to determine on a long, difficult campaign involving all the dedication, sacrifice, and zeal that are normally shown only in wartime. It will not be easy, but it will be necessary. By displaying such unwavering determination, ironically, free nations may well shorten the route to peace. The Kremlin rulers have been able in the past to sense resistance that is solid. They can do so in the future.

SOME SENSE and a great deal of nonsense have been written and spoken about "containment" versus "liberation." Of course, some campaign orators of 1952 blundered when they spoke of liberation in a way that implied U. S. armed aggression. Many more erred in overlooking the simple fact that it is necessary to halt an advancing foe before you can start rolling him back even by peaceful means.

By now it is safe to report a personal talk with Secretary of State Dean Acheson in early 1950. At the end of a wearing day, he observed: "Ed, we Americans will be insane if we ever again permit ourselves to get in our present relative state of military weakness. This job of trying to hold back those gangsters by diplomacy without having any real strength to back up our talk is about the most difficult thing imaginable." As he saw it, the big task then was to try to hold the line, to buck up our friends, and to get along with rearmament in a hurry. That's why he was a leader in the rearmament drive. As that drive moved along, American diplomacy did help hold the line, and Acheson was able to negotiate with increasing firmness.

Now, as America and its friends grow progressively stronger, they can move further and further beyond simple "containment"—and without in any way implying armed aggression. But to consider the so-called containment of 1950 as "soft" is like condemning an unarmed storekeeper who ingeniously stalls off bandits while his partner goes for a gun.

Dean Acheson's understanding of such realities was one of

the things that won him the admiration of informed men as diverse as Henry L. Stimson and Adlai Stevenson, Arthur Vandenberg and Learned Hand. He had flaws, including the political liability of feeling it was unmanly to yield in any way to Congressional and public opinion which he believed to be misguided. Yet he won the respect of other nations' foreign ministers to a degree true of few Secretaries of State. And my personal guess is that he will ultimately have a notable place in history books that will not even mention his noisiest critics.

A SECOND CLEAR LESSON, overlooked by too many, is hardly more pleasant. It is that the millennium will not have arrived when the present masters of the U.S.S.R. give up, are replaced, or otherwise are no longer a threat to the world. Conceivably, a decade from now Mao's China could be the main threat to world peace. We can imagine a world in which a Russian military dictatorship is allied with present Western powers in resisting Mao and other Communists of the Orient. Even if all present Communist aggressors should fade away, however, the free nations would still face huge problems. True, the massive expense of armament could be greatly reduced. But the enormously intricate job of building a peaceful, stable world would remain. If there are not to be new vacuums inviting the rise of other Stalins and Hitlers and Maos, the work of combatting poverty and easing tensions must continue. It has been wisely said but too rarely heeded that the only way to "stop Communism" permanently is to stop viewing it as the root of all the world's ills and to start aggressively assaulting the real root, human misery.

Even after Communist aggression is no longer a threat, the world will badly need large-scale technical assistance, political accords, economic agreements, and ever-improved machinery for settling disputes. Happily, the dollar cost of all this will be a fraction of cold-war costs. The difficulty of achieving it will not be appreciably less. When no longer stimulated by common fear of a ruthless foe, nations will more readily yield to apathy, misunderstandings, and petty frictions. Extreme nationalism might crescendo in some nations. Long-smoldering resentments in Asia could flare up seriously. The business of striving to understand others and to make ourselves understood will be correspondingly vital.

For both the short term and the long term, then, first-rate strategy and mechanism for informing and persuading others become essential parts of government. These can be developed and continually improved at a cost that is minute beside other international expenditures. They can be fully effective, however, only if they operate as an integral part of a much larger concerted strategy.

17

A Four-Part Offensive

T O   A N Y   O F F I C I A L , Republican or Democrat, who has dug deeply into foreign-policy problems in the last few years, one surprising point stands out: the near-unanimity among foreign-affairs specialists in both parties about the broad courses to be followed.

Campaign orators in 1952 tried their best to make it seem there were wide differences. With the help of hindsight, they did differ (or profess to differ) about the past—about Yalta and China, for example. As to the future, however, the differences were largely oratorical and illusory. No better proof can be found than in President Eisenhower's inaugural address of 1953, probably the most internationalist speech ever delivered by an American President. Democrats love it as reaffirmation of what they considered their policies. Its broad principles of cooperative Western rearming, international accords, and joint economic enterprises would have provoked fiery debate a decade or two ago. In 1953, they won plaudits from virtually every political and journalistic voice this side of the Chicago *Tribune*. Obviously, there would be initial differences about specifics, but the agreement on basic principles reflected a spectacular evolution.

Old-style isolationism no longer exists as a political force. Robert A. Taft, when he boned up to write a book on foreign

227

policy, emerged much more a proponent of collective security and the interdependence of nations than he ever seemed before. Except for a few older Americans who froze their views twenty years ago, almost the only prominent leaders who are still ultra-nationalists are those who simply have not devoted themselves to the study of world affairs. I confirmed that in dealing with the foreign relations committees of both houses of Congress, as well as with the State Department's top command (which few realized was about one-third Republican under the Acheson regime) and with outside groups of foreign-affairs specialists.

In their private conversations today, virtually all officials who are careful students of foreign problems see no alternative to a long, hard, international offensive for waging peace. Most of the informed see that campaign as having four important and interrelated parts: the diplomatic, the military, the economic, and the psychological.

It is not my mission to deliver a personal Olympian pronouncement on how to wage the peace on all fronts. I lack both the disposition and the flawless vision to do so. However, I can sum up, frankly and without official furbelows, the predominant findings of top-rank foreign-affairs experts, recent and present. And, against that essential backdrop, I can present some specific findings concerning the psychological campaign, without which the broad four-part offensive cannot succeed.

THE wise *diplomatic* course is at least clear in general outline to the majority of informed leaders. America must work incessantly to strengthen its sometimes wobbly alliances with like-minded free nations. It must seek to be friendly, helpful, reassuring, but not overbearing with less fortunate and near-neutral nations like India. It must continually make clear that Americans aren't trying to browbeat others into becoming U. S. satellites or even trying to dragoon them into following the American pattern. The United States, rather, is striving to work with them in order to help them become strong and independent enough to choose their own course—satisfied that they will, under those conditions, choose the course of freedom, not tyranny.

America should continue, without appeasing, to keep open some diplomatic channels to the Iron Curtain countries. We Americans have learned through bitter experience that it is a sad mistake to appease the Kremlin rulers or to hope to work in close harmony with them. Rightly or wrongly, we learned the futility of that course through the fiasco of once trying to encourage a workable coalition between Communists and Nationalists in China. At the same time, we learned, through such experiences as the Berlin airlift, that the Kremlin masters will use open diplomatic channels to work out a retreat when they have found their opponents determined to stand firm. They have done this so far on relatively small issues. They may do it later on bigger issues.

The United Nations has often been called a forum for Soviet propaganda. Actually, it can be and has been a useful forum for anti-Soviet persuasion. Continual haranguing by Vishinsky, Gromyko, Malik and Company has awakened the leaders of many smaller countries to the fraud of Soviet pretensions in a way that would not have occurred if they had not listened to such diatribes for long hours in U.N. meetings. In addition, factual, truthful presentation of the free world's case, by American and other spokesmen in the U.N., has paid dividends. Without that forum, it is unlikely that the nations of the world would have persistently lined up, 45 to 8 or 54 to 6, on the great issues of today.

Too few remember that the United Nations was not designed to *make* the peace but to maintain and organize the peace after it was made by the Big Powers. Because of Soviet obstruction, the peace has never been fully achieved. Meanwhile, the U.N. has at least helped to forestall some explosions

—as when it so focused world moral pressure that it forced the Soviet to withdraw its troops from Iran. The U.N. also localized and dampened explosive developments in Indonesia, Palestine and Kashmir which had threatened to tear the free world apart. It can continue to perform such functions.

It is well to recall that the U.N., stronger than the League of Nations, can always serve, at the least, the great purpose of marshaling world opinion on the side of decency. It was Stalin himself who once said even of the League of Nations, after criticizing its impotence, "The League might nevertheless serve as a place where aggressors can be exposed, and as a certain instrument of peace, however feeble, that might hinder the outbreak of war."

ON the broad *military* course to be followed there is now general agreement. It grows from a belated but thorough recognition of proven facts about Soviet Communist leaders: they recognize and respect power in others; they have only contempt for pleading that stems from weakness or fear. This means that if the United States is to survive, it has no choice but to continue the sort of military build-up on which it is now embarked and to press on with such cooperative military arrangements as have been made through NATO. It is the simple course of blocking war by making it obviously unprofitable and dangerous for the aggressors.

On that much there is general agreement by all hands. On other points there is cleavage between civilian officials and some of the veteran military leaders. In general, a sizable majority of the civilian foreign-policy specialists feel America must avoid setting its course too exclusively by military landmarks. In times like these it is important to meet military needs and provide a strong military mechanism. But it is essential not to yield so completely to the understandably narrow demands of military figures as to give the impression of subordinating all else to armed might.

The insistence of U. S. military men on complete strategic control of the once Japanese-mandated islands handicapped our whole diplomatic, and psychological, program to bring about peaceful colonial evolution instead of violent revolution in Asia. American military demands for a base in Panama, militarily sound, were pushed with such vigor that they brought setbacks on broader fronts—and failed to get the base. An air base costing vast good will can prove a bad bargain.

The U. S. Government needs the best military advice—and is getting it. But, as both Acheson and Dulles recognized, such advice must continually be weighed against other factors by leaders who don't believe war is inevitable. In times like these, we must carry a large and well-oiled gun. But we don't need to carry it aloft as our only standard

On the *economic* front, the nation has gradually groped through to courses of action that make sense to most enlightened leaders of both parties. There will always be argument among them on the amounts of money involved but relatively little argument about the principles. Those basic principles call simply for getting the world's old workshops going again, getting new workshops going where none existed before, and helping to invigorate both by improving the flow of materials and goods between the workshops.

Through the elaborate, rushed, and sometimes admittedly thriftless campaign of ECA, free nations turned back Communism in many a country by easing the economic conditions that invite Communism. Under the successor Mutual Security Program, the stimulus to economic revival has continued. Indeed, some decry the almost exclusive emphasis that has been placed on MSA's military purposes because they were the "easiest" to sell to Congress. They reason that the true justification of the program is at least as much economic revival as military defense.

I have heard Paul Hoffman argue persuasively that the eleven billion-odd dollars spent by the ECA under the original Marshall Plan did not cost the American taxpayers one cent. He reasoned that it sparked the economic and political revival of free Europe, without which the United States would have had to spend many billions more on armament.

There is no question that, particularly as military rearmament proceeds further, the economic aid of the ECA-MSA type must and should taper off. Other economic measures, substantially less costly, will have to continue.

Any who have studied the pilot Point IV projects in India, Liberia, and many parts of Latin America can have no doubt that the so-called technical assistance program can pay enormous dividends on small expenditures. Technical advice on improved soil practices, more irrigation, better use of simple tools, plus improved seeds, have brought visible production increases on farms. Simple health guidance went far toward stamping out preventable disease. Young foreign trainees studied here and then took their lessons home to help develop their own countries. Perhaps most immediately important, the downcast, discouraged natives of blighted areas began to see, in Point IV projects, spectacular illustrations of the advances that could be made by free men working together. They began to see hope in a course other than Communism. In underdeveloped areas there is no better public relations for freedom than the showcase of a Point IV pilot project.

Meanwhile, the whole array of efforts to free the flow of goods and materials has to continue: agreements on ending currency restrictions, international monetary stabilization, regional economic commissions, and reasonable, selective removal of tariff barriers (even in face of some revived opposition at home).

The broad economic course is now clear to most, but progress along that course will be difficult.

THE PSYCHOLOGICAL program, of course, has only recently gained recognition, even among enlightened foreign-policy leaders, as necessarily a full-fledged part of any campaign to wage peace. Many leaders still underestimate its importance and vastly overestimate its simplicity. A few, even in Washington, have unfortunately misrepresented psychological operations as a cut-rate nostrum that can obviate more difficult measures. At least, however, there is finally some general cognizance—even in both parties' platforms—that all the array of other programs will fail unless men are somehow persuaded of their justice and their promise. All now see, at least vaguely, the need for systematically combatting unjust suspicions about America; for enlisting popular support for the broad, constructive programs of the free nations; for the building among free nations of mutual confidence in their ability and determination to defend themselves; for helping to maintain stability and cohesion in areas where the ferment of change would invite exploitation by Communist conspirators; and for strengthening the attitude of resistance and the hope of eventual freedom among peoples who are captives of Soviet Communism.

All parts of the four-part offensive are difficult. No part is more difficult, more intricate, or less understood by the nation than the psychological task of persuading men.

18

Charting the Offensive

THERE ARE two wide-spread misconceptions which have often hampered America's spasmodic efforts to wield truth as a weapon. One has been the widely held—and recently fanfared—belief that propaganda is an isolated force that somehow can be employed without particular regard to other programs, or policies. Another has been the belief that the tactical planning can best be done in Washington—that some super-bureaucrats in the Capital can best determine not only the broad psychological objectives but also the best way to achieve those objectives in each country abroad.

Similar misconceptions have also impeded American economic and military programs. They could well gum up any future strategy.

One of the ablest U. S. ambassadors, a former businessman turned diplomat, once said to me: "I've decided one of our government's greatest faults is trying to do too much detailed masterminding in Washington. Those in Washington should leave the details much more to the representatives on the scene, remembering that the best expert on a foreign nation can be badly out of touch with conditions there when he has been home a few months. At the same time, Washington should do much more broad, long-range planning—setting up the chief objectives it wants to achieve in each area abroad.

"Thank heavens, we have made one great advance," he added. "We at least have started embryonic efforts at broad-gaged long-distance international planning. Now if we can chart the broad strategy at headquarters and shift the planning of detailed tactics more and more to our representatives on the scene abroad, we should be well on our way." In those words may lie the key to some of the nation's toughest international problems.

The years ahead will bring a continuation of the reorganizations and shifts that are a part of governmental development. Those changes affecting international relations should be most productive if sight is never lost of three simple points: (1) Washington should continue striving to lay out long-term objectives and policies, substituting more consistent planning for hectic improvising. (2) The government should seek to have specific programs abroad developed and directed by first-rate teams on the scene, operating always within the limits of basic policy. (3) Whether in Washington or the field, the planning of strategy and tactics should regularly encompass all four arms of the international effort: the diplomatic, the economic, the psychological, and (where appropriate) the military.

The government has made appreciable progress along these lines in the last five years. Much more progress is possible.

MANY OF US who served in government may have shuddered at some of President Truman's smaller actions, be they occasional inferior appointments, unseemly campaign utterances, or letters to music critics. We hasten, however, to credit him with certain great contributions to the science of running an immense government. Development of the Bureau of the Budget as a strong management arm of the President was an example. One of the most important and least publicized was the establishment of the National Security Council as an extraordinary body for long-range planning. Its basic study of the

Soviet Union's intentions and capabilities and its recommended plan of action, as mentioned earlier, was one of the most outstanding jobs ever done in government. Its less ambitious programs for dealing with various contingencies also brought a new sense of order into policy-making.

The National Security Council under Harry S. Truman had its faults. Made up of the President, the Secretary of State, the Secretary of Defense, and a few other agency heads, it consisted of overworked men already harassed with running large departments. Its "senior staff," charged with first-drafting many papers, was made up of subordinates of the members, but they also were busy men with many other duties. Hence, the N.S.C. was most successful at preventing contradictions and chaos between departments, less successful at hammering out basic new policies. At this writing the Eisenhower Administration is reputedly considering again various old proposals like that of recruiting "distinguished private citizens" to provide a permanent N.S.C. staff. That could help, if the outsiders are supplemented by others recently enough in government to make sure the staff doesn't go off into the clouds with no regard for current realities.

More important, the N.S.C. has proved an effective forward step, but it can be made more effective as ways are found to blend its personnel of busy officials with capable, realistic men who have time enough to plan. And it can function best if it charts the broad international course—including the objectives the United States wants to achieve in, say, countries A, B, and C of Europe and X, Y, and Z in Asia—and seeks to leave to specialists on the scene the drafting of precise programs for achieving those objectives.

THERE WAS a case in 1951 of a Middle Eastern country which had become grossly uncooperative. Since the country was hard up financially, old Washington hands assumed the proffer of a little more economic assistance would produce a more cooperative attitude. Even economic representatives recently returned from the country shared the assumption. What none knew was that the little nation was just undergoing a new flare-up of resentment at "subservience to America" and of suspicion toward U. S. help. The group in Washington decided to try dangling an economic offer; the newly arrived U. S. Ambassador accepted the scheme. There followed the spectacle of the Ambassador figuratively chasing the country's premier about the countryside with offers of help which the latter didn't want.

The incident recalled the story of the three boy scouts, each of whom cited as his good turn for the day the act of helping an old lady across a particular street. The scoutmaster complimented them but then asked why it took three scouts to help one old lady cross a street. At that, one of the scouts piped up, "Well, you see, sir, this particular old lady didn't want to cross the street."

There are some nations which don't want help and have, indeed, become suspicious of American aid—even aid that is badly needed. "Trade not aid" has become the new watchword. Other attitudes have changed quickly. A nation that a year ago welcomed large numbers of American functionaries as a sign of great friendship became disgruntled almost overnight at "having so many Americans around." Illogical perhaps, but real.

Only alert representatives on the scene can sense that sort of sudden development. Only a well-directed, coordinated team of American representatives on the spot can act wisely when they do sense it. Flocks of loosely related American representatives, reporting variously to an ambassador, a general, and an economic chief of equal rank, can rarely do so.

It is for that reason that the United States, in handling large peacetime programs in a critical country abroad, can well borrow a page from the painstakingly developed books of the military. In Country X, this would mean appointing a top-grade ambassador and establishing him as a rough equivalent of a wartime theater commander, with undisputed authority over all American workers in the area. It would mean giving him a first-rank administrator as a deputy or "chief of staff." And it would mean having, under both, four key staff members: the chief of diplomatic activities, of economic aid, of military activities (if any), and of psychological activities.

Under this system, the National Security Council in Washington would lay down the broad objectives desired in Country X: perhaps two added divisions for the NATO forces, a further fifteen percent increase in the nation's industrial production to assure stability, currency stabilization for the same purpose, firmer popular support for the NATO concept, and the removal of unwarranted doubts about "American unreliability."

The ambassador and his staff would set the objectives, study current conditions in the country, and evolve a detailed program for achieving those objectives. In that program they would include economic proposals, steps to be taken by the military, diplomatic moves, and a campaign of persuasion closely attuned to existing moods. They would clear the whole program with Washington, then go to work. On many projects, the staff would work hand-in-glove with appropriate officials of the country concerned; on all, the staff chiefs would cooperate closely with one another.

The problems America faces in its whole international program, when spread over a dozen critical countries and several dozen other countries, are just too enormous for any mind or group of minds in Washington to master in detail. To cope with them effectively will mean decentralization. It will mean adopting the course already followed by many great corporations: laying down broad policies at headquarters and leaving detailed planning and operations to the responsible chiefs of the widely scattered branches.

The idea has been tried, informally and almost unconsciously, in two key countries abroad. Those of us who studied the results considered them good. In both countries, the United States had splendid ambassadors of the type that would be indispensable to any such set-up. But the day is past, anyway, when this nation has any business entrusting top ambassadorships to mere political favorites, campaign contributors, or sinecure-seekers.

19

Set-up for Persuasion

WHEN asked what the United States should do about intensifying its Campaign of Truth, many a novice has given a glib answer: just set up a new super-duper agency, give it Cabinet rank, and start operating on a big-time scale. The glib answer is not necessarily the right answer—and certainly not the whole answer.

There are, of course, some valid arguments for such a "Cabinet status" propaganda agency. They have been put forward by conscientious groups who have wearied of seeing effective international persuasion handicapped by the State Department's cumbersome administrative methods, internal jealousies, and budgetary systems. Indeed, as of this writing, the Administration in Washington is considering setting up an independent propaganda agency.

The danger is that such a shift in status may be considered a cure-all. Independent status can remedy some faults, but it will create others. The obstacles to fully effective international persuasion are more basic than the question of where the work heads up within the Washington hierarchy.

Creation of any super-centralized agency will soon lead to wails for decentralization and for closer tie-ins with those making foreign policy. Most Americans forget that the nation

240

long ago tried it both ways. In wartime, the Office of War Information was a central agency of "Cabinet rank." As an official of O.W.I., I found that agency repeatedly hampered because too many policies were made and frozen, often in lower echelons of the State Department, before O.W.I. even learned of them. The Joint Chiefs of Staff, after years of wrangling, fully and officially recognized O.W.I.'s authority over international propaganda only two weeks before the war ended. After the war, the State Department ran the government's main international information program. As an official of that department in the early 1950's, I found the program suffered because of interdepartmental jealousies and inadequate status in the government hierarchy. No foreign-information specialist, for example, sat with the National Security Council.

As of this writing, a capable committee of Eisenhower appointees is systematically weighing the whole international information set-up. It is drafting some recommended alterations. Moreover, in later years, there inevitably will be successive changes. After all, every new official in the future, from President down to section chief, will feel compelled to effect some reorganizations. Whatever their nature, they will usually be called "streamlining." Such inevitable shifts can be made fruitful rather than wasteful if future "streamliners" will absorb and observe these basic principles:

The most crying need of the program is and will be an adequate number of first-rate executives and operators. This can be achieved only with decent pay for several dozen key jobs, improved "status" or prestige within government for those key posts, and some effort to protect and defend such executives and operators from wanton slander, particularly in Congress.

It is vital that those conducting the complex work of international persuasion shall have the support—and active interest—of the President, the Secretary of State, and other officials dominating foreign policy.

International propaganda, particularly the propaganda of truth, is not something that can be set up in a watertight compartment—whether it be a division of the State Department or a super-agency.

By its very nature, international persuasion is *inter*dependent with the other foreign programs and policies of government. If it should ever become truly "independent," it will become either ineffectual or perilous. This means that it must be intimately tied in with the top policy-makers of government, including the President and the National Security Council, but that it also must be closely allied with the lower levels of government at which foreign policy is so often made.

To understand the problem, it is necessary to grasp the whole process of what is called policy-making in foreign relations.

More than 315,000 words of cables go in and out of the State Department every 24 hours. Foreign policy is being made every day, most of it far down the line in the Department of State. Decisions have to be made daily on relations with some 75 missions abroad, with approximately 70 multilateral international commissions, agencies, and organizations, in addition to the United Nations. The President and his Secretary of State couldn't possibly handle all such decisions. So there has grown up a system of assistant secretaries, desk chiefs, standing committees, and *ad hoc* working groups to handle decisions and help evolve policies on new problems. The more important decisions go to the Secretary for approval; a few even go to the President; most get approval as a matter of routine. This is as true under Eisenhower as under his predecessors.

Some foreign-policy decisions actually are made in other departments—for example, when the Air Force decides to close a base in Country B, or when the Agriculture Department lends seven experts to Country X. But there has gradually developed a system of cross-checking that insures these decisions being cleared with the proper divisions in the State Department before they are frozen.

If America is to wield the weapon of persuasion effectively, world public opinion naturally must be carefully weighed at the time each policy is being decided. It is for this reason that, over the last seven years, arrangements have been made for international information specialists to participate in policy-making at all levels in the State Department. That was the only way to assure that world opinion factors were considered by those making policy. And it was the only way to assure that new decisions and policies were fully understood by the individuals who had to clarify them to the world public. Even when international information operations were mercifully freed of some of the State Department administrative red tape in 1952, care was taken to keep them in the State Department family and to preserve intimate ties with the policy makers.

Once during the war the O.W.I., as an independent agency, broadcast a quotation from a columnist referring (with some truth) to the Italian monarch as the "moronic little king." It became a *cause célèbre,* because at just that moment government policy called for inducing the King to cooperate with the Allies. In that case, and many others, there was trouble simply because the O.W.I., with all its independent-agency status, had not been intimately involved in (or even fully informed on) foreign policy developments. O.W.I. not only lacked opportunities to influence policy; it often lacked arrangements to be informed about policy.

Such difficulties gradually lessened under the system laboriously evolved since the war. But the attainment was painful. It was only when I took office in 1950 that, partly at the insistence of the U. S. Advisory Commission on Information, the Assistant Secretary of State for Public Affairs became automatically a participant in the topmost policy councils of the State Department.

To a lesser degree, something of the sort has been achieved within the Defense establishment, where the Army's Psychological Warfare division has finally achieved status, is listened to, and guides the Sykewar operations which have helped produce the 100,000-odd surrenders in Korea. MSA—successor to ECA—likewise finally arranged to have information operatives closely associated with its own policy-making. And similar arrangements have evolved in one or two other Federal operations, the nature of which are classified.

Any future reorganizations will amount to retrogression unless they somehow preserve these intimate tie-ins with policy-making. In addition, of course, there are other arguments against any sweeping reorganizations that aren't demonstrably necessary. Experience has shown that any vast reshuffling of operations in government results in near-stagnation of effort while countless bureaucratic characters struggle for months with mundane problems of office space, organization charts, liaison arrangements, budgets, and controls.

The central problem is to give the work of international persuasion maximum status, prestige, and flexibility, without weakening its tie-ins with policy-making. There are, fortunately, three measures which can make the job easier:

1. "Persuader-in-Chief"

Many basic problems can be made less troublesome by the President's having as a permanent member of his top staff a special assistant with the functions of "persuader-in-chief." Though serving in a "staff" rather than a "command" role, this individual, located at the President's elbow, would function as coordinator-in-chief of government-wide psychological planning.

Since the above paragraph was first drafted, President Eisenhower has moved in this direction by appointing a psychological warfare veteran, C. D. Jackson, to his immediate staff. The existence of that post, if properly established and preserved, can achieve much that could never be attained by the most elaborate reorganizations and "streamlinings."

Such a "persuader-in-chief" might well head a new psychological planning committee. Membership would include the chief of the State Department's international information and educational organization, the ranking representative of the military psychological warfare operations, and representatives of one or two other agencies. It might well include also two or three outstanding Americans with propaganda experience, who could give full time to broad psychological planning. It could well function as a subcommittee of the National Security Council, developing for the Council basic psychological objectives in keeping with the Council's over-all objectives. It should, of course, leave to the staff in each accessible country abroad the detailed programming for that country.

Most essential of all, the "persuader-in-chief" should be a person having the full confidence of the President, as Jackson apparently has. If he can work as closely with the President, as did George Creel during the first World War, his potential impact on the minds of men can be great. His status in the White House and his relationship with the President, as any experienced bureaucrat can testify, would leave no room for questioning his leadership in all government international information work.

With only a small immediate staff, the "persuader-in-chief" could assure the necessary coordination between the government's main-line campaign of truth under the State Department and the other related operations: the military Sykewar operation, as in Korea; any overseas information operations of the Mutual Security Administration; and any hush-hush operations that might deal with information dissemination abroad.

Most important of all, as the President seems happily to

have recognized, the individual should be in regular attendance at meetings of the Cabinet and the National Security Council. Some Cabinet members and others may protest at such elevation. If they do, Dwight Eisenhower can remind them of his own constructive campaign appeal for a "psychological effort put forth on a national scale." An important function requires important status.

2.   On-the-Scene Direction

Since the inception of the Campaign of Truth in 1950, fortunately, there has been a progressive shift of detailed propaganda planning from Washington to the field. Hindsight leads to the conclusion that the shift should be accelerated.

Soon after taking office in the State Department, I directed that no further U. S. Information Service publications, posters, or handbills should be produced in this country in final form for distribution in free countries abroad without first being cleared and edited by the information staff of the U. S. Embassy in that country. Texts, photo plates, and proofs were to be air-mailed abroad for clearance. When possible, translation and final printing were to be done overseas. The ruling brought some complaints. It nonetheless proved to be one of the soundest decisions for which I had responsibility. It largely eliminated information items that were "just off key." More important, modifications and adaptations abroad, usually different in each country, converted many "fair" items into "excellent" items.

That experience illustrated the wisdom of putting Grade-A men in the field, setting the broad objectives for them, then giving them maximum freedom for working out precise ways to attain those objectives. A trained information officer abroad can sense far more surely than any mogul in Washington the current tastes and the new moods of the local population. He detects quickly, for example, a sudden flare-up of displeasure at being "pushed around by Americans." He can make prompt changes in information tactics and advise changes in broader tactics.

My associates and I learned from hard experience that the most effective Voice of America broadcasts were invariably those which, even though originating in New York, were directed in detail by competent staff men at or near the points of reception. By cable and phone, such field representatives can send daily advice to emphasize news of this type, to eliminate humor of that type, or to try another announcer. It is like directing artillery fire from a point near the target—as opposed to trying to direct it from division headquarters behind the lines.

Similarly, many of the most productive U. S. radio programs have been shows locally produced by U.S.I.S. men abroad for local broadcast, even though they utilized heavily material recorded or written by the Voice of America in the United States.

The same point has obtained behind the Iron Curtain. Without question, the Voice of America's most effective broadcasting to an Iron Curtain country in recent years has been that directed at Country B, left unnamed. Arrangements existed there under which alert advisers sent daily suggestions to the Voice, including brief scripts on a treason trial or on local purges.

Even where no such arrangement existed in a Communist country, experience has shown radio can best do the job if its artillery is directed from a point just this side of the country's boundary. There the director-of-fire can keep himself fully informed by interviewing escapees, quizzing travelers, monitoring the nation's home-front broadcasts, and reading up-to-date daily papers from the country concerned.

Oversimplifying a trifle, it can almost be said that the effectiveness of international broadcasts is inversely proportional to the distance from the audience of those directing the broadcasts. That was why, when asked for advice regarding the new

Radio Free Europe in 1950, I urged that its broadcasts should originate largely in Munich or other points near the Iron Curtain. It was also why I arranged to have some of the Voice's satellite-language broadcasts originate at a U.S.I.S. branch in Germany rather than in the U. S.

Under the "theater command" concept discussed in Chapter 18, the information (or "psychological") chief in each key country becomes a member of the ambassador's four-man team. His program must be worked out as a part of the broader tactics for that country. With that kind of coordination and with maximum latitude given him by Washington, a good man should achieve effective results in short order. In fact, in two countries where the arrangement was tried, that is exactly what happened.

3. Advisory Commissions

One innovation in Public Law 402 (The U. S. Information and Educational Exchange Act of 1948) has proved of extraordinary value. This was the establishment of the two high-level advisory commissions: the U. S. Advisory Commission on International Information, and the U. S. Advisory Commission on Educational Exchange. Composed of eminent private citizens, these commissions have studied the international operations with great care, have detected weaknesses, have recommended changes, and have insisted that those changes be carried out.

They have been particularly important in demanding that the State Department and other agencies should give added status to international information work and should have information specialists sitting in on top planning councils.

They have made periodic reports, under the law, to the Congress. The principal reports have been intelligent, penetrating, and constructive. The one difficulty has been that many members of Congress, swamped with reading matter, never found the time to read the reports.

In my opinion, the advisory commission device deserves to be strengthened and increasingly relied upon. The detached view of capable, conscientious outsiders can always improve such an operation. It would seem wise to provide the commissions with able staffs to serve as their eyes and ears. It might also be well to elevate the commissions so that their field of jurisdiction covers not only the work of the State Department's information program but any international information and educational exchange work of other agencies. By such elevation, incidentally, the White House might at least increase the possibility that commission reports will be read by a substantial number in Congress.

To SUM UP THEN: Repeated demolition and reconstruction processes seem unnecessary. Many of the needs can be met by continuing to have a "persuader-in-chief" close to the President and high in government, by giving U. S. missions in key countries abroad the task of tactical planning within the limits of approved policies, and by utilizing fully the help of able advisory commissions.

It would be folly to contend that these three steps would solve all problems. They can achieve much. But their success will depend in large measure on the government's ability to get and keep capable, qualified men in the key positions. That in turn will depend, in the long run, on the treatment accorded both to new recruits and hundreds of experienced, skilled men and women already in the service.

Even ideal attainments in these respects will not assure success, however, until Congressional problems are at least partially solved. Those are the problems of keeping the Congress properly informed and giving it an opportunity to participate in planning without, at the same time, having the intricate and delicate program of international persuasion serve as a football in free-for-all political hassles.

The Role of Congress

THERE USED TO BE a story about a teacher saying to a student, "Since we know the prefixes 'pro' and 'con' have opposite meanings, will you give me a word containing each." The student paused, then replied, "Progress and Congress."

Many a government official has had moments of seeing truth in the story. One executive, a Republican who served with distinction in a temporary economic agency, told friends upon resigning in 1952, "I leave with one clear ambition: to shoot every damn member of Congress—and in the belly."

Actually, there are few men in or out of government who work longer hours or more conscientiously than does the average member of Congress. Both houses contain scores of first-rate men who are there only out of a sense of public duty and who sacrificed high income and risked the slanders of the opposition in order to serve. And the Congress, crude as its methods sometimes are, serves as a generally effective watchdog for the people.

Many of the injustices that make government executives bitter spring from the fact that the Congress, which does not choose its own members, has found no effective way to curb the small minority who are incompetent, arrogant, or even venal. Every bureaucrat has seen able men give up good jobs to become Washington executives, only to find themselves insulted and badgered by one of the small minority of irritable or arrogant members of Congress. Many Washington insiders fumed when the able and devoted William Foster, as ECA chief, was publicly denounced as a conscienceless wastrel by a Senator who needed publicity as an "economizer" in his home-state election campaign. They were troubled but not surprised to see a Civil Defense appropriation reduced by ninety-five percent after the Administrator had been unwise enough to return in kind some insults from Congressional inquisitors.

Newcomers to Washington have sometimes been stunned to see Congressional hearings turned into farces by some hopelessly senile committee chairman. Once an aging chairman, after I had uttered my first two sentences of testimony, said, "Young man, I've been listening to you all morning, and you haven't made any sense yet." I was never able quite to convince him that I hadn't even been present that morning when he heard another witness on a completely different subject. Again, a State Department official explained to the same chairman that the expenses of the Embassy in Warsaw had gone up because the Polish Government had revalued the *zloty*. It was at this point that the old gentleman banged the table and demanded, "Young man, what part of the Constitution or the laws of these great United States gives you the right to go around revaluing other people's currencies?"

In addition, all of official Washington knows of two or more mountebanks who have attained great power in Congress just by staying there long enough to earn seniority. One is famed for abusing his power over two departments in order to wangle jobs for supporters and to divert government business to "friends." I have heard irate Senators of both parties say that the mink-coat and five-percenter episodes of downtown Washington would look like playful pranks beside the practices of a few members of Congress. Yet the clubhouse spirit in both houses keeps colleagues from going after the few malefactors in their midst. The Department of Justice, needing every vote it can get for its appropriations and legislation, shies away from "persecuting" Congressmen.

That is the seamy side. In soberer moments, even the most embittered official comes to recognize that the Congress, however helter-skelter its methods, performs an essential function as a watchdog. He knows that without Congressional committees some bureaucrats would become lax and wasteful, if not corrupt. And he knows there are numerous decent men in Congress for every one that has grown petty or arrogant. I myself received what I considered grossly unfair hazings from two key members of Congress but extraordinarily responsible and objective treatment from a dozen other key members.

Of course, it's all a surprising experience for most newcomers to government. In business, as Eric Johnston once pointed out, a company executive normally has a board of directors pulling for him. In government almost half of the 531 members of Congress, who control his authority and finances, have the natural political goal of trying to discredit the present management and oust it at the next election. Yet in accepting a government post, a man accepts accountability to the public and its representatives. He must be prepared for detailed and suspicious supervision, sometimes even arrogant treatment, by members of Congress. It is all part of a system that, on balance, generally serves the nation's interests.

Moreover, those concerned with international affairs have noted an extraordinary broadening of Congressional horizons in two decades. The irresponsible insult to allied nations is only rarely heard in Congress today; it was a frequent occurrence a few years back. In the same halls where the League of Nations was once rejected, Congressmen have voted for the United Nations, for the Marshall Plan, and for a score of other world-minded measures. A dozen Senators and a few House members have mastered intricate foreign-policy issues and have sometimes led all of government in helping to evolve enlightened policies.

ON BALANCE, Congressional actions provide at least a rough approximation of justice and of wise legislation. They cannot provide much more unless and until the Congress itself can manage the difficult feat of updating its own mechanism, of policing the ethics of its own members, of finding some way to give key posts to the ablest hands instead of to the oldest hands, and of providing salaries that its members can live on decently without wangling outside income.

As most members recognize, many of the difficulties stem from outmoded Congressional mechanisms. Committees which nominally oversee gigantic operations have no appreciable staffs to serve as their eyes and ears. One committee in each house deals with a department's policies; completely different committees oversee appropriations for those policies. Most members admit privately that the typical appropriations committee, understaffed and overworked, metes out at best a crude sort of justice based more on impressions than on systematic findings. Custom still gives the chairmen of committees such power that a committee report often reflects just the beliefs—or the prejudices—of one man. That explains why it was not unusual in 1952 for one committee to issue a detailed report denouncing the Army Engineers for one project, while another committee, in almost equal detail, praised them for the same project.

The understaffing of key committees should be subject to easy cure. Other evils, like the seniority system, are not. Most members recognize that seniority sometimes tosses up into a key chairmanship a befogged old gentleman or an occasional small-timer who, badgered by critics at home, seizes upon his day of glory as a chairman to "take it out" on a hapless bureaucrat. Most members, however, have found no simple remedy. A measure to abandon the seniority system could get through Congress only with the unlikely approval of chairmen who hold their own positions through seniority. Moreover, every alternative plan for selecting chairmen proves upon examination to have serious drawbacks.

There are equal difficulties on other problems. In a government that is a thousand times more complex than it once was, the volume of work is such that present Congressional machinery would bog down if committee chairmen didn't have extraordinary power to act. That is why there is increasing truth in Woodrow Wilson's statement, "If I were forced to give a brief description of the United States Government, I would describe it as a government by the chairmen of standing committees of Congress."

THE WEAKNESSES of present Congressional mechanisms affect to some degree all operations of government. Because of special considerations, however, they hamper the operations of international persuasion with particular severity. The reasons are simple:

1. The sensitive nature of international information and propaganda is such that its effectiveness suffers whenever it is dissected and worked over in the halls of Congress while Tass correspondents and others busily scribble notes in the gallery. Obviously, it is harmful to telegraph the punches by staging full Congressional debates on plans, strategy, and tactics toward the totalitarian states. Less obviously, it is often undiplomatic, at best, to spell out on the floor of Congress the details of some Campaign of Truth plan for a friendly country—or to proclaim publicly the details of cooperative information arrangements with governments or private organizations in allied lands.

2. Anyone who has dug into the full strategy and mechanism of international persuasion will testify that the problems cannot be even reasonably comprehended in less than sev-

eral weeks of intensive study. Today in the whole of
Congress I know of less than twenty members who have
found the time to study the subject carefully, abroad and
at home. It is impossible, therefore, for the full membership of Congress to acquire even a reasonable understanding
of the field and its intricacies. Hence, full-scale Congressional debate is usually uninformed debate and often dangerous debate.

3. The work of international persuasion is naturally intangible business that is suspect among "hard-headed" and "practical" men. Appropriations committees, whose members
generally do an enormous amount of tedious work with
little public credit for it, specialize in granting funds for
post offices, highways, buildings, munitions, and routine
office workers. They are the "practical" men of Congress,
always under pressure to cut costs. They are the men who
demand hard evidence of the use of last year's funds before
granting next year's.

It is inevitable that propaganda work will always have
trouble with "practical" appropriations specialists. It is impossible, as noted earlier, to show them a cage filled with
ex-Communists converted by the Voice of America or to
display millions of Indians and Italians who are a little less
suspicious of America than they were a year ago. A campaign of persuasion that makes sense to a foreign relations
subcommittee as part of world strategy is just as apt to
strike a hard-pressed appropriations committee as "fuzzy"
and "impractical." Traditional rivalries between the two
committees does not make the obtaining of appropriations
any easier.

4. "The controversial Voice of America" is currently a cliché.
Actually, the Voice and all related propaganda and information matters will *always* be controversial. The accuracy of a
gun or the speed of an airplane is subject to clear proof.
The effectiveness of persuasion rarely is. That is why the

campaigning tactics of Dewey and then Eisenhower, of Truman and then Stevenson were roundly criticized by some elements of press and public, even while winning fulsome praise from others. National elections helped "settle" those differences. There are no international elections to prove the effectiveness or ineffectiveness of international persuasion.

Such operations can hardly be made less "controversial" by being publicly debated by all of Congress or by some uninformed committee holding televised hearings. It is as though the full Republican National Convention tried to debate publicly the precise campaign tactics of its candidates.

A BRITISH Member of Parliament who long specialized in psychological warfare has said, "Any propaganda program which is run primarily to please the uninitiated on the home front will be severely handicapped." That is equally true in America.

Yet, under the American system of government, the Congress has a right and an obligation to satisfy itself that any world-wide information activities are being intelligently administered and that, with due allowance for occasional errors, the funds are being wisely spent. It has a right to keep tabs on the activities and even to participate in the planning. For the full membership to attempt to do so, however, leads to severe confusion at best.

If a great American corporation faced unprecedented public-relations problems, it would hardly expect the stockholders to have meetings, debate every phrase in past company announcements, and decide what to do. It would not even expect the full board of directors to debate perennially the complex problems of the company's public relations. Rather, it would name a small select committee of directors to work closely with company executives on the problem. That pattern may well provide the answer for the Congress. It is not an easy answer within the present Congressional framework, but it is the only sound answer that I and other veterans in this field have been able to find. It amounts to establishing a special "Joint Committee on International Information" to act on behalf of the entire Congress in the whole field of international information, educational exchange, and psychological strategy.

This nation made remarkable headway in the inordinately difficult field of atomic power by devising a new Congressional mechanism to meet a new need. It did not subject the atomic program to policy supervision by one group, budgetary supervision by an entirely independent group, and frequent free-for-all debate by the entire Congress. Instead, a new Joint Committee on Atomic Energy, under the able leadership of the late Brien McMahon, assured the kind of progress that would never have been possible had the complex issue been subjected to usual procedures.

Chairman Gordon Dean of the Atomic Energy Commission once called his commission's work "the second most important task in the world." He added, "The first, I think, is somehow or other to pierce the Iron Curtain and let the ordinary Russian know our real and peaceful intentions." President Eisenhower has gone even further than his predecessor in underscoring the need for a "psychological offensive." It seems logical, therefore, for Congress to do what it did with atomic energy—to adopt an extraordinary measure to meet an extraordinary problem.

The Joint Committee on International Information should have membership informally agreed upon by the Congressional leaders of the two parties and by the President. The members should be selected with enough care to assure the safety of the kind of classified information which is necessarily involved. They should be members who are not too harassed and who signify in advance a willingness to devote a minimum of several weeks each year to the problems of psychological strategy. The membership should include at least two members each from the committee on appropriations of each house of Congress and from the foreign relations committee of each house. These could well act on behalf of those committees. The appropriations committees' representatives, for example, should be in a position to guide those committees in the allocation or non-allocation of funds.

It would appear necessary and logical to supply the Joint Committee on International Information with a modest permanent staff for continuously studying operations at home and abroad. If the members themselves would devote at least one full day a month to the subject they could hold all-day sessions with the executives of the nation's psychological programs, going over with them fully and frankly the problems they face. The committee, incidentally, would provide a place for healthy interplay between foreign-affairs specialists, thinking in terms of global strategy, and budgetary specialists, who necessarily think in terms of guarding the taxpayers' dollars.

As frequently as can be arranged—perhaps once a year—the committee could be divided into teams of three, with each team sent on inspection tours of U. S. information operations in various parts of the world. Since publicity is essential to elected officials, each team should be expected to make a public report on its return. The full committee should have a conference at least once a year with the President to keep him informed on its thinking—and, incidentally, to give the members a chance to have their pictures taken on the White House steps.

As THE COLD WAR grows more complex, the nature of psychological strategy and information activities grows more intricate. Only by some such device as a special committee can the Congress play its legitimate role in the effort without jeopardizing what is being done and much that might be done.

On occasions in the past, groups of Congressmen or special committees of private citizens have studied with great care the problems and the mechanisms of international persuasion here and abroad. On every such occasion (not counting, of course, the one-sided McCarthy hearings), the findings, I believe, have been sound. After much experience extending over a decade, I would not hesitate to entrust broad decisions on this field to any group of intelligent and balanced Americans —or any cross-section of responsible Congressmen—*if* they have devoted long weeks to studying its intricacies. I would not willingly entrust such decisions, however, to the wisest men in America if they had not similarly studied it. That, in a nutshell, is the basic argument for a special joint committee of Congress.

A few members of Congress have told me such a joint committee arrangement is "impossible." A number of others have told me it would be difficult to establish but would be eminently justified and quite possible. Some suggest the sensible alternative of a special committee in each house. At any rate, if the whole field of psychological strategy is truly worth what Dwight Eisenhower calls a "great national effort," it is also worth an extraordinary set-up within the Congress of the United States.

The Quest for a Formula

L A B O R E R S in the ideological struggle have long recognized that the free world suffered from one handicap: the lack of a dynamic appeal that would fire men's imaginations with a zeal and fervor approaching that of the Communists. Some have even yearned for Communist-like fanaticism, though others view fanaticism as a dangerous element incompatible with true freedom.

Volunteer advisers grope for the same sort of thing. They often talk confidently, if vaguely, of the need for "a new psychological crusade," of "starting an offensive that captures the imaginations of mankind," and of "mobilizing the vast spiritual forces of freedom." In their speeches and articles, these gentlemen unfortunately neglect the matter of just how to do all this. Indeed, after reading a few of these clarion calls, one distinguished and wise friend recently put tongue in cheek and wrote me:

> Of course, we can always fall back on the recently proclaimed formula of acquiring a sense of mission and purpose which will unloose such moral and spiritual forces that the edifice of despotism will crumble into dust, without anybody having to work at it. Lovely work if you can get it, though some of our fellow citizens might find that building up their spiritual natures was about as painful as paying war taxes.

Of course, the free world's ideology needs—and deserves—more wide-spread, fervent, and enthusiastic support. Some slight and very gradual progress has been made in that direction. Certainly, however, in some years of work in the field I never found any simple formula. Nor did I come upon any one else who had done so. At most we began vaguely to detect a few clues. Studies of the great fanatical mass movements of history have helped to clarify some of those clues—and have cast light on the whole problem, including the grave question of whether a truly fanatical counter-movement is really wanted. Analyses of the world's mass movements, particularly the extraordinary study of *The True Believer* by Eric Hoffer, have led to fascinating conclusions. Among them are these:

Frustrated souls have always provided the backbone for the truly fanatical mass movements. Most of these individuals come from among the intensely discontented poor, the misfits, the outcasts, the inordinately power-hungry, the bored, the temporarily frustrated youths, the resentful minorities, and the sinners seeking escape from a guilty conscience. All are trying to "get away" from themselves; all seek sweeping change.

By the time such frustrated characters are ripe for a fanatical movement, they are usually ready for any such movement without regard to particular doctrines or programs. The fanatic seems generally to embrace a cause not chiefly because of its righteousness or holiness but because of his violent need for something to hold onto. He wants to lose himself; in what cause he does so is relatively unimportant. In the 1930's it was a toss-up as to whether many discontented German youths would go Communist or Nazi. Moreover, the adult fanatic who deserts his holy cause can rarely return to normal existence. As Eric Hoffer put it, he is "an eternal hitch-hiker on the highways of the world, thumbing a ride on any eternal cause that rolls by." He is even ready to enlist in a fanatical crusade against his old cause, provided it is a full-scale crusade—strident, uncompromising, intolerant, and devoted to the one and only truth. Hitler recognized this when he ordered that ex-Communists should be admitted to the Nazi Party without delay. Communists are recognizing it today in proselytizing ex-Nazis in East Germany.

(The nature of the Communist fanatic, incidentally, makes one wonder about current tendencies to lionize American ex-Communists and put them on pedestals from which to lecture all citizens who had sense enough never to become Communists in the first place. Some of us suspect the typical ex-Communist—particularly the recent Communist—has great value as an informer and tipster but hardly any as a propounder of eternal verities.)

In their susceptibility to mass movements, both the extreme reactionary and the extreme radical have more in common with each other than with sober liberals or moderate conservatives. Both extremists loathe the present and both seek change. Though one seeks innovation and the other seeks what he considers glorious restitution, they often can wind up in the same cause.

Freedom is not a first-rank goal for fanatics in such movements. Those seeking to escape themselves usually want equality and fraternity far more than liberty. Equality provides the anonymity of being an equal part of a great whole; individual liberty and freedom of choice leave the blame for any failure on the shoulders of the individual.

Ingredients of the fanatical mass movement include extravagant hope for the future, symbols and make-believe, and a sense of great power growing either from an "infallible leader" or some powerful doctrine. The effectiveness of the doctrine generally depends less on its logic than on its certitude. The most effective doctrine usually is vague or unintelligible. At the least, it is unverifiable in that its truth can be proved only in heaven or in the remote future. In any case, it must be advanced as the one and only truth.

Religious faith and nationalism are often the sources of mass enthusiasm. But fanatical mass movements can rise and spread without belief in a god. They never do so without belief in a devil. Hatred of a devil, preferably a tangible one, indeed, appears the most universal and powerful force in such movements. Hitler said Jews would have to be invented if they did not exist, because "it is essential to have a tangible enemy."

One way to stop a mass movement is to substitute another movement for it, preferably a good one for a bad one. But the method is sometimes dangerous. The counter-movements can get out of hand. As Hoffer pointed out, practical businessmen in Germany and Italy behaved logically when they encouraged Nazism and Fascism in order to stop Communism. But by so doing these practical people promoted their own liquidation. Again, Premier Mossadegh of Iran, as of this writing, has become the captive of the runaway nationalism he helped to arouse.

Viewed thus, the fanatical mass movement may well be an instrumentality the free nations don't want and should not attempt to use. In political fields, what attracts fanatical men often repels reasoning men. Most such movements can get out of hand. Moreover, the things in which Americans believe and for which they will fight are the antithesis of simple dogma and unreasoning conformity. Basically, the free nations are struggling for an *absence* of rigid doctrine, restraints, and regimentation.

Nonetheless, there are degrees of zeal and fervor short of the type of dangerously fanatical "movements" dealt with above. Analysis of these movements, plus practical experience in combating them, at least provides clues to possible methods of generating enthusiasm of the sort too often missing from the free world effort. If there is no pat formula, at least four clues seem worth particular mention.

1. *The Force of Religion*

As one surveys the battle against Communism in various areas, he cannot fail to note that religious forces have been in the vanguard of effective opponents. The Catholic Church has proved a powerful deterrent in many nations. Father Keller's Christophers have aroused great zeal for the anti-Communist cause. The Moral Rearmament movement, whatever its critics may say on other scores, has shown notable anti-Communist efficacy in parts of Europe and in Japan. Buddhist priests have often been among the most effective exposers of Communism's flaws.

In my recent term in Washington, my colleagues and I came to recognize that too little attention and too little support had been accorded to the great appeal of godliness versus godlessness, the spiritual appeal against the solely materialistic. We formed a Catholic-Protestant-Jewish advisory panel. With great help from that panel, the information program then began to emphasize appropriate religious matters far more than formerly. Materials stressing Communism's incompatibility with any of the world's great religions began to flow from the U.S.I.S. The government encouraged the production of Arthur Goodfriend's moving book, *What Can A Man Believe,* and facilitated its translation into eleven languages in Asia and the Far East. In words and pictures, it dramatically contrasted the faith and ideals of the world's religions with the cynical ruthlessness of the Kremlin gangsters.

Many other steps were taken. They were only a beginning. With Soviet Communism more clearly ranging itself against all religions each day, the potential of religious faith as a counter-force to Communism becomes enormous.

I will venture no simple "formula"; I doubt that any exists. It is now evident, however, that the spiritual content of America's Campaign of Truth deserves not only part-time help from a wise religious panel but full-time creative work over an extended period by a group of the ablest churchmen in America. And, as the great religions of the world chart their parallel counter-offensives against the common foe, they will deserve all the support and assistance that free governments can properly give.

2. *The "Devil's" Role*

"We should stop being negative," say internal and external critics of government information efforts. "We should emphasize what we are *for* rather than what we are *against*." The advice has become a truism in propaganda. Each time it has been heard, I and others have nodded our heads in thoughtful agreement.

With benefit of perspective, I am not so sure. The negative task of exposing the gigantic hoax of Soviet Communism is important and, in many areas, more persuasive than any honest picture that can be painted of democracy and freedom.

Americans and other champions of freedom cannot honestly promise that Arabs and Burmese and Pakistani will automatically partake of the Abundant Life two years, or even ten years from now, if they only will spurn Communism and follow the course of freedom. The only honest promise is that free men working together, with mutual assistance, can slowly but steadily improve the economy, health, and well-being in their areas—and without enslaving themselves.

At the same time, it is possible, practicable, and persuasive to reveal the fraud of Communist promises and to expose the conditions actually existing in Soviet-dominated areas. Among the peoples of Asia, I know of no single item of persuasion that was more powerful than the authentic and credible story called "When the Communists Came." It told simply and authoritatively the story of Communist promises to a Chinese village, of the village's capitulation to the Communists, and then of the privation and brutality that followed. It was "negative propaganda." Yet, without it, the mild affirmative propaganda about the promises of freedom would have lacked appeal. "When the Communists Came" proved so persuasive that the United States Information Service reproduced it in twenty-odd languages, first as a booklet, then as a comic book, and finally as a film. When the U.S.I.S. assisted native groups abroad in obtaining and disseminating similar authentic material, the "negative" propaganda became even more persuasive.

As has been seen, the great mass movements have always had a devil. Hatred of that devil has usually proved more potent than any affirmative element. In the free nations' campaign of persuasion, no devil has to be invented. The Soviet tyrants already constitute one—more ruthless and more brutal than most men can believe. Perhaps the most important single step in enlisting zeal and enthusiasm for the free nations' cause is full revelation of the nature of Kremlin Communism. Particularly important is it to demonstrate that a people can't just choose the Soviet path today and reverse the decision tomorrow; once in the clutches of Soviet tyranny, there is no easy turning back. When that realization has sunk fully into men's minds, the mild and hardly flamboyant promises that can be made on behalf of democracy begin to look pretty tempting. Berliners have been the most zealous foes of the Soviet in all of free Europe not because they have a more optimistic view of freedom but because they have had the closest view of Kremlin-style tyranny.

Precise methods of exposing the devil are another subject. Often exposés can be most effective when they are done by fellow citizens of the audience group. The blunt fact remains that portraying fully and accurately the bogey of what we are *against* is often more effective than any "affirmative" material in arousing determined resistance to Communist imperialism.

3. *The Presidential Symbol*

It is extremely difficult to create enthusiasm for a complex and intangible cause. It is much easier to do so when there is a dynamic personality to serve as a symbol. That has always been true. Woodrow Wilson acquired great symbolic importance in World War I; public squares and streets were named for him in much of Europe. Churchill and Roosevelt likewise became important symbols in World War II and made great psychological contributions to the eventual triumph.

In the past, political critics have been quick to pounce on the efforts of any administration to dramatize its own chieftain around the world. In the last war, many complained vociferously at O.W.I.'s "using the taxpayer's money" to publicize F.D.R. in other lands. One might have thought the citizens of Germany, Iran, and Thailand had decisive votes in U. S elections.

There is no room for such nonsense today. Had the last election gone to the Democrats, Adlai Stevenson's personality and his deft, inspiring prose should have been dramatized around the world. As matters stand, Dwight Eisenhower's talent for leadership, his infectious smile, and his air of confidence should be publicized to the hilt. Despite captious critics, the President and his subordinates should have no qualms about it. As a symbol of free-world confidence, determination, and friendliness, he can be a priceless asset. Overseas promotion of that asset will not swing a single precinct to Republicanism; it can help swing entire nations to democracy.

4. *A "Creed of Freedom"*

For some years, officials engaged in the propaganda of truth have looked for what might be called an "American Creed" or even a "Free World Creed." Paul Hoffman, in winding up his ECA stewardship, called for such a creed which would "walk up and down in the hearts of men." John Foster Dulles groped for it in his book *War or Peace*. Lesser lights, including myself, have attempted drafts—with discouraging results. One of the efforts in which I participated was designed to become a ringing declaration by the North Atlantic Council of Foreign Ministers. By the time that draft was modified to meet the criticisms of all the governments concerned, it deserved just the treatment it got: being buried in an official communique.

There can be interminable discussion of whether any ringing and reasonably brief creed is possible without resort to gross oversimplification. Some will argue that freedom-loving peoples who produced a Magna Carta and a Declaration of Independence, both drawing upon principles of Confucius, Plato, and Christ Himself, *should* be able to produce a rousing twentieth-century document. Others, including men of intellectual stature, argue that no simple, reasonably brief credo is practicable, that free men stand basically for diversity and resistance to rigid doctrine. They add that the best way to "sell" the cause of free nations is by continuous statement and restatement of the whole array of beliefs that differentiate the way of free men from the way of tyrants.

At any rate, many continue the quest, convinced that the effort to clarify basic beliefs will be a healthy force even if it does not produce a ringing document. The Ford Foundation has underwritten an effort by a panel of leading citizens to restate American principles and purposes. *Fortune* magazine has made efforts in the same direction. So have others. The U.N.'s Universal Declaration of Human Rights is a significant document, if not one that stirred men's hearts. It deserves renewed attention. Eisenhower's generally admirable Inaugural Address contained some elements of great international appeal. But the modern creed that is both fully honest and emotionally thrilling has not yet been produced.

The main principles are not too obscure or too controversial. They were embodied, clearly if not briefly, in a draft statement of foreign policy by members of the U. S. Advisory Commission on International Information in early 1953. Many individuals contributed to that draft, and a few fragments from it found their way into the President's Inaugural Address of 1953. It was hardly a ringing document. But, as an indication of content rather than as any stirring appeal, the opening paragraphs are worth printing here:

The foreign policy of the United States must be based on three universal cornerstones:

The first is the Principle of Self-determination. The second is the Fact of Interdependence of all peoples. The third is a deep and abiding faith in mankind under God.

Our nation, like many others, stands committed to the principle of self-determination. Our nation stands committed to it for *all* nations, and above all for *small* nations.

It is a principle upon which our own government is founded. But it is not something new and unique with the United States. It is an idea borrowed from the ages. It is a legacy from many lands. It is the common heritage of all freedom-loving people.

The Principle of Self-determination affirms, in moral terms, the privilege of all men to choose their own way of life, subject only to the condition that the rights of one individual shall not violate the rights of others. It affirms, in political terms, the territorial integrity of all nations. It means, in social terms, a concept that leads ultimately to government based upon the dignity and supremacy of individual man.

The second cornerstone is the fact that all free peoples are interdependent. This is a great and important realization of the twentieth century—that the political, economic, and moral well-being of all men relates directly to our own.

It involves the need for the full, free, and continuous flow of ideas across boundaries. Only through the interchange of ideas can the free nations progress together toward a common understanding, and a mutual plan of operation to achieve a common cause. There must be no iron curtain on ideas between the free nations of the world.

The third cornerstone is faith in our fellow men throughout the world —faith in the innate decency, honesty, and integrity of men in all nations and of all creeds who are guided by the God of their fathers, and not by any mortal man who seeks to destroy every God under which reverent men worship.

No universal brotherhood of man would ever be possible if the freedom to worship in the churches, the temples, the mosques, and the tabernacles of our ancestors were denied us.

These are the cornerstones. We gladly accept the duty to recognize and implement the Principle of Self-determination, the Fact of Interdependence, and to let faith in God and faith in our fellow men guide us in all of our policy making.

The formula for a rousing, yet meaningful, new "creed of freedom" may or may not be found. Any one-and-only document is unlikely. But constant, clear, and forthright restatement of principles like these can help produce, if not fervent enthusiasm, at least solid understanding, faith, and resoluteness.

Behind the Curtains

IN JUNE, 1941, the Nazis launched their "Operation Barbarossa," the invasion of Soviet Russia. Immediately there occurred an extraordinary development that is still little recognized by most Americans, yet a development that points to great vulnerabilities in Soviet areas.

As the Germans advanced, Russians surrendered by the thousands. The outside world learned little about the mass defections. After the war, secret German documents showed that 320,000 U.S.S.R. troops had surrendered in one eight-day period in the Bialystok-Minsk pocket. In the battle of Smolensk on July 16, some 300,000 gave up. Between July and October more than 2,000,000 Soviet men went over to the Germans. In addition, in one town after another, peasants hailed the German troops as liberators. They enthusiastically welcomed the invasion as meaning the end of the collectivist system. They seemed little affected by the stream of anti-German propaganda which the Kremlin regime had poured forth all during the 1930's.

Hitler soon muffed his opportunity. Against the advice of his own former ambassador to Moscow and others, he insisted on winning by arms alone. He said he wanted to make the conquered territory "a German India." He made no concessions. He retained the collectivist system as being easy to

271

manage. His troops mistreated their prisoners, abused the welcoming civilians, and devastated property. Word of this soon leaked through the lines. The Soviet regime, when it recaptured a few prisoners, sent them on speaking tours to tell of "German brutality." The tide of surrenders and welcomes quickly abated.

In 1943, the Nazis belatedly tried to recover lost ground. When the Soviet General Andrei Vlassov surrendered and proved to be rabidly anti-Stalin, the Germans vacillated for a while but then tried to use him as the center of a new anti-Soviet army of Russians. They achieved moderate success, but they were too late. They had thrown away their big chance at the start of the invasion.

THE HISTORY of that period gives a clue to the many vulnerabilities of the Soviet monolith. Naturally, there are means short of war for taking advantage of those vulnerabilities. Such measures can lessen the Soviet rulers' threat to the free world and can help to weaken their tyrannical grip on the areas they dominate. A few measures have long been in process; others cannot even be precisely planned until developments are further along.

This is not the place to spell out the various peaceful measures that free nations might take. To advertise techniques sometimes is to defeat them in advance.

Nonetheless, by taking a closer look at the Soviet's vulnerabilities, it is possible to chart a few basic guidelines. Here is a condensed list of such vulnerabilities:

1. *Popular antagonism to the regime.* Among European satellites, there is little doubt that seventy to ninety percent of the peoples are anti-Soviet. Within Communist China statistical estimates are sheer guesswork, but there is grave doubt that anything like a majority of normally articulate citizens are pro-Mao, let alone pro-Soviet. Within the U.S.S.R., the

mass defections at the start of the German invasion gave some clue to potential opposition. At this date most individuals within the U.S.S.R. appear to outsiders to be frustrated and cowed. Yet there are signs that millions harbor deep resentments. If hope is kept alive, those resentments could burst into flame when (but only when) any of the captive peoples see some alternative to continued enslavement.

2. *The regime's internal anxiety.* Surrounded by hostile or suspicious populations, the Communist élite have become addicted to intense suspicion of one another. Hence, they indulge in eternal vigilance, repressions, purges, and liquidations. Involved in this has been what James Burnham has called a "fearful chasm"—the fact that there was no theory to justify the choice of this man rather than that man to succeed Stalin. The absence of either an hereditary or a democratic formula for succession could lead to violent delayed explosions long after Malenkov's succession of Stalin. The jockeying for power that may continue for years springs in part from the fact that Malenkov had no "legitimate" claim to his job.

3. *The power of religion.* As noted earlier, the most severe repressive measures have badly failed to eliminate religious faith within the U.S.S.R. itself. Within the European satellites, faith has survived even more vigorously. The inherent conflict between Communism and all religions is well known to the captive populations of Europe, probably less known at this moment to those of China. In neither Europe nor Asia, however, can the millions of religious faithful ever be happy under Soviet rule. As long as religious faith lives, it threatens the regime.

4. *The menace of Titoism.* In June, 1948, when Tito and his Yugoslav Communist colleagues successfully defied Moscow, they delivered a memorable blow at the myth of Stalin's infallibility. It was the greatest humiliation ever experienced by the Kremlin tyrants. If Titoism appears hardly imminent

today in the other satellites or even in Eastern Germany, it exists as a real potential in all.

Behind the Bamboo Curtain of China, meanwhile, Mao Tse-Tung already has more the status of a junior partner than that of a puppet. As a master of political maneuver, as an abler Marxist theoretician than Stalin, Mao reputedly has had to be persuaded, not ordered. With Malenkov succeeding Stalin, Mao became relatively more powerful.

Within all the satellites, Communists worry increasingly over the gap between theoretical Communism and Soviet imperialist domination.

5. *Economic weakness.* The deterrent effect of Soviet economic weaknesses is often exaggerated by those who forgot that a dictatorship can allocate its resources far more arbitrarily than can a democracy. Yet the Soviet's economic shortcomings are real. Even under forced-draft production, oil output in Soviet areas is no more than a sixth of U. S. production. Soviet and satellite steel output totals less than one third of the U. S. total. Despite prodigious efforts to increase farm production, there are few signs of Kremlin success in stockpiling food for future emergencies.

Even after great progress in training personnel, the U.S.S.R. still has an acute lack of skilled workers, engineers, and technicians. And native mechanical sense is scant. The simplest problems of gasoline engines, almost second nature to the American GI, baffled the majority of Soviet G-Ivans in World War II.

And, in the satellites, Soviet looting and the sheer inefficiency of much of the Communist-controlled production mechanism causes perennial grumbling.

6. *The regime's rigidity.* Every operator in international affairs knows of at least one case of a Soviet official representative who dared not make a decision on the smallest issue without getting instructions from on high. Many problems have to go from the lowest functionaries to the highest councils, then

back down again. The complete centralization, the monolithic structure of Soviet society, makes possible rigid control and abrupt changes of policy when expediency dictates. At the same time, however, it sharply limits spontaneity, initiative, and inventiveness. It gives the whole machine a cast-iron character—making it capable of enormous, crushing strength but also capable of cracking under well-directed blows. Less flexible than other systems, it is probably more likely to disintegrate rapidly once it meets powerful counterforces.

AGAINST such vulnerabilities, the Soviet system also has its strong points, particularly in terms of efficiency. These include iron discipline, avoidance of the "waste" of democratic procedures, and ability to allocate limited resources ruthlessly. The assets should not be underestimated. The weaknesses, however, are most important to those seeking ways to curb the Soviet menace by measures, including propaganda measures, that are well short of war.

Without specifying detailed measures, I think these broad points deserve mention:

1. For the immediate future, the non-Communist nations have no intelligent course but to continue the drive to make themselves unassailably strong. This means pressing forward with the build-up collective security forces. And it naturally means continued measures to protect their sensitive agencies against infiltration. The latter, of course, is a job for professional subversive-hunters, not for loquacious headline-hunters.

2. As the strength of anti-Communist nations grows, those nations can afford to accelerate measures for putting the Soviet rulers on the defensive. They cannot afford to be lulled by Soviet "peace gestures." Military threats and bluster are not called for. Other measures will be increasingly in order. One small example will suffice: In 1950, when I helped hammer together a program for erecting a network of new transmitters

around the fringes of the Soviet empire, some allied governments urged caution. They feared such steps would amount
to dangerous "provocation," and a few U. S. officials inclined
to agree. If such extreme caution was then justified, it isn't
now. If the free world is unwilling today to risk even the fullest open use of truth as a weapon, it can have little hope.

3. Great efforts to keep alive and encourage religious faith
within the Soviet empire will be in order. Some progress has
been made; much more should be possible if the best minds
in the world's great religious movements will concentrate on
the problem. One possible measure: setting aside periodically
one day when everywhere in the world all faiths believing in
a God will offer prayers for the enslaved peoples. The services
could be reported in broadcasts over all free-world transmitters and summarized in balloon-dropped leaflets sent over
Communist areas by private groups. The impact could be
great on both sides of the curtains.

4. Intensified efforts to weaken the economic underpinning
of the Soviet tyrants seem in order. Embargoes and similar
measures have already partly succeeded. As in other fields,
propaganda can help. It can increasingly encourage the defec-
tion of engineers and technicians (even while not encouraging
mass defections); it can cause runs on short commodities, as
Radio Free Europe and the Voice have already done; it can
intensify the already useful efforts to encourage slowdowns in
critical industries. Again, by increasing Voice of America
strength in particular ways, the United States can force the
Soviet rulers to spend five to the U. S.'s one, in terms of money
and of scarce technical manpower.

5. In action and in propaganda, the free nations should
hammer home the distinction between the Soviet rulers and
the peoples they rule. Recently, a newspaper pundit urged
forgetting this distinction and thinking of all Russians as the
enemy. In the eyes of nearly every careful student of Russia,
this would be a tragic blunder. The vast majority of members

of the U. S. Congress recognized this when, in July of 1951, they passed the McMahon-Ribicoff Resolution, expressing friendship for the Russian people. President Truman recognized it when, in response to urging from myself and others, he transmitted the Resolution to the Russian people through a message to President Nicholas Shvernik, then nominal head of the Soviet state. The Kremlin rulers recognized the power of the message's content, and of the V.O.A.'s repeated question: "Why has your government not reported this to you?" On the thirty-first day, the Kremlin finally publicized the message, along with a labored reply over President Shvernik's name.

Today the masses in the U.S.S.R. are the victims, not the accomplices, of the Soviet rulers. They are potentially our allies, not irrevocably our enemies. To treat them otherwise is to buttress the Kremlin's own propaganda.

6. As escapees come out from behind the curtains, the wise course is to treat them as well as possible, to employ their services as greatly as possible, and never again even to consider forcible repatriation of any kind.

Many escapees have proved superb sources of intelligence (even when allowance is made for possible "plants"). Some retain incredible "pipelines" to their homelands. A few can do highly useful broadcasting. Though government loyalty regulations make such broadcasting difficult, the defectors can be used safely when they are screened and their broadcasts prerecorded. Radio Free Europe has successfully used many of them. In addition, able-bodied defectors can well be placed in units of the NATO armies. On all scores, happily, at least some progress is being made.

The tragic forcible return of thousands of Russians who fell into American hands at the end of the last war was then considered necessary in order to insure the freeing of American prisoners in Soviet hands. It, nevertheless, set the cause of freedom back immensely. By contrast, the determined stand of

U.N. negotiators against forcible return of Korean war prisoners has gone far toward regaining the faith of dissidents within the Soviet empire.

There are good grounds for discouraging indiscriminate, mass defections now, since draining off all dissenters would simply ease the Kremlin's internal job. There are few grounds for shoddy treatment of defectors after they have come over. And there are good reasons to encourage selective defections— of technicians and troops, for example. Word of friendly treatment of defectors is bad news for the Soviet. It travels fast— even through the Iron Curtain. It says in effect:

YOU HAVE FRIENDS ON THE OUTSIDE.

7. In propaganda and related operations, the Communist élite themselves should not be overlooked. Within any disciplined organization, successful opposition is impossible unless there is a division in the ruling group. As many have pointed out (notably James Burnham in *The Coming Defeat of Communism*), the unorganized masses cannot easily become a serious opposition. And behind the curtains, particularly in the U.S.S.R., effective leadership is most likely to come from within the Communist élite.

It is the élite who have easy access to powerful radios and even to official reports on Western broadcasts. (I recall countless interrogations of defecting soldiers who reported that it was the Red officers who listened to the Voice of America regularly. The G-Ivans got their news by eavesdropping.) The possibilities of divisions within the élite clearly exist and have multiplied since Malenkov's ascension. And a World War II experience may be illuminating. Of all the broadcasts that we in O.W.I. beamed to Japan, undoubtedly the most effective were those in which Captain Ellis Zacharias, speaking calmly and clearly to Japanese ruling groups, spelled out the reasons why they should change their course. They listened; they read;

and increasing numbers of them believed. They ultimately forced their government's hand.

To be effective, this means that the broadcasts should contain a minimum of shrillness, a core of cold hard news, and a fair quota of dispassionate, high-level discussion of such subjects as Western aims, Titoism, and ideals versus practices. During my tenure, we took important steps in this direction, but we progressed only part of the way. Much more can be done.

8. The Western nations should seek increasingly to play on the monolithic, inflexible structure of the Soviet empire. There are vulnerabilities in any vast organization which is so rigid, so unwilling to risk even small decisions without having them go all the way up through the hierarchy and down again. There are ways to capitalize on these weaknesses.

9. Lastly, in action and words, it is vital for the anti-Communist forces to show maximum resoluteness, maximum determination, and maximum confidence that a victory of freedom is inevitable. On balance, the events since 1946 chart a general trend against the Communists. So the free nations have reason for *feeling* confidence. They also have reason for *showing* confidence. We of the West have gained ground in the past when we stood up to the Communists. We have lost ground when we wavered before them. We dare not—and need not—waver now.

23

Unofficial Persuasion

A L M O S T as bad as having no government program of international information would be having one that tried to do the entire job alone. Much of the task can best be performed under private auspices.

Of course there is work—vast work—that can be done effectively only by government. This is true of much of the enormous assignment of getting the truth into Communist-ruled countries. In open areas, moreover, the *official* U. S. position can best be presented by government agencies. Concerted "campaigns" related closely to high strategy can be carried out only by government. Finally, the total world-wide information effort requires expenditures far beyond the reach of private organizations.

Nonetheless, the tasks that can be performed under non-government auspices are extensive. They far exceed the routine operations of American press services, publishing houses, and movie companies. This would be true even if those agencies were performing far more perfectly than even their warmest supporters say they are.

As of early 1953, many private agencies were already performing valiant service. The Institute of International Education sponsored large numbers of educational exchanges in addition to helping in the government's exchange programs.

Radio Free Europe, as noted in Chapter 6, provided an effective voice for escaped Czechs, Poles, Rumanians, and Hungarians to talk to their own peoples and to say things that the government can't say. The Committee for Free Asia showed promise of ultimately performing similar useful functions.

In the last three years, the government has had notable success in enlisting the help of private organizations, commercial concerns, and American communities. At the last count, 102 business firms, 19 non-profit organizations, 10 cities, 30-odd trade organizations, and hundreds of schools and colleges were playing large or small parts in the total campaign of truth. A few examples illustrate the range:

Twenty-two very well-known American newspapers * arranged to employ temporarily on their staffs foreign journalists whose transportation for three-to-six months visits is paid by the U. S. Information Service.

The city of San Francisco "affiliated" with Caen, France, exchanging unofficial "ambassadors" and cultural and industrial exhibits. Citizens of Chester, New Jersey and Kumrovek, Yugoslavia have exchanged more than 300 good-will letters; Chester sent seeds, school supplies, and sewing equipment. Kumrovek responded with children's books and Yugoslav handicrafts.

The American Heritage Foundation, with help from the Young and Rubicam advertising agency and the New York *Herald Tribune,* initiated distribution of 175,000 booklets for U. S. travelers suggesting ways in which they could serve as helpful "unofficial ambassadors." Airlines, travel agencies, and shipping companies cooperated in the distribution.

The Common Council for American Unity encouraged

* St. Louis *Post Dispatch,* San Francisco *Chronicle* and *Call Bulletin,* Hartford *Times,* Denver *Post,* Toledo *Blade,* Riverside *Enterprise* and *Daily Press,* San Jose *Mercury,* Milwaukee *Journal,* Louisville *Courier-Journal,* Boston *Globe,* Nashville *Banner,* Winston-Salem *Journal,* Newark *News,* Syracuse *Herald Journal,* Portland *Oregonian,* Albany *Knickerbocker News,* Chicago *Sun-Times,* Indianapolis *Star and News,* Trenton *Times,* Baltimore *Sun.*

and guided a large program under which first- and second-generation Americans correspond with friends and relatives abroad in such a way as to combat misunderstandings about American practices, policies, and aims.

Fifteen American symphony orchestras arranged to play "musical salutes" to cities in Western Europe, Latin America, the Near East, and Far East. Such salutes, consisting of two-hour radio programs, with exchanged greetings from the mayors of each city, have been heard via national radios in Luxembourg, Copenhagen, Strasbourg, Ankara, Teheran, Florence, and other cities.

More than a dozen large American corporations arranged to emphasize "free enterprise" themes in their overseas advertising.

The General Federation of Women's Clubs began donating community-type receiving sets to such overseas communities as would genuinely welcome them.

In the aggregate, such activities have already played an appreciable part in the effort to sway men's minds. Many more such projects would be useful.

There are, however, fields in which a much larger-scale coordinated effort under private auspices appears to be in order. Past experience points to three particular needs:

1. *Encouragement, direction, and coordination of a large-scale program in the cultural field.* In Chapter 12, the Soviet Union's extraordinary cultural offensive was outlined and its dangers noted. The United States has lost by default in many international cultural competitions. Congress, understandably, is not prepared to have the government underwrite any sizable procession of American musicians, art exhibits, and ballet performers to other lands.

Yet those who have most carefully studied the subject generally agree that extraordinary American performances abroad somehow enhance respect for America and the desire to co-

operate with America. They find this particularly true \
the performances or exhibits are clearly American rather \
slavish imitations of the arts of other lands. They have no
how the splendid performances of Ibsen's *Wild Duck* in Scandinavia by a group of young Negro actors from Howard University won acclaim—and served to offset false impressions
created by Paul Robeson in his earlier European tour. They
have noted the enthusiastic reception given the American-style
ballet presented in twenty-one cities under auspices of the
American National Theater Academy. They recall the enthusiastic European press comment, including that of the Rotter-
dam *Nieuve Courant:*

> Europe has been inclined to look down on the country across the ocean
> with pity and ridicule for appropriating old traditions and adapting them
> to their own tastes with foolish misunderstanding. But last night the
> Americans demonstrated our error. Instead of changing old ballet tradi-
> tions, the Americans have used them as a base on which to experiment and
> construct an individual style. . . . We wondered whether the Americans
> could sustain this special quality of teamwork. . . . Much to our admira-
> tion they did—with superior results!

Such undertakings, however, have been notoriously few. The
American talent for a much wider effort exists; so does the
desire—and even the potential underwriting. What is lacking
is a well-organized, well-financed organization to serve as stim-
ulator, clearing-house, and co-sponsor of a wide range of such
exchanges in the arts. By stimulating such enterprises, by helping to schedule overseas engagements, and by enlisting the
help of American airlines, shipping companies, and others, a
central private organization could achieve much.

2. *Mobilizing of American business representatives abroad.*
The British have long had a tradition under which thousands
of British business representatives scattered around the world
felt they had the auxiliary mission of representing their nation, combatting misinformation about it, and helping win
support for its aims. They have taken part in activities of the

British Council and other unofficial or semi-official groups dedicated to combatting misunderstandings. There has been no such universal tradition among overseas representatives of U. S. business, who now total many thousands and are rapidly increasing. In fact, many an American business representative abroad has not even made himself an effective explainer of modern-day American capitalism—American industrial democracy as contrasted with the "Wall Street" mirage.

A non-governmental organization could achieve substantial results if it would undertake the large job of inducing American corporations and other organizations to mobilize their overseas representatives in the national effort. The program could well begin with simple instructional courses for employees about to be sent abroad. A small handful of companies have already experimented with this, with some success. The program could also embrace a regular flow of useful background reading to overseas representatives—material, for example, spotlighting the great and continuing changes that have taken place in the American economy since the days when Andrew Carnegie's annual income was $23,000,000 (with no income taxes!) and the average worker's was $500. It could include formation of an increasing number of binational groups (Egyptian-American clubs or Indian-American associations) abroad, dedicated to improved mutual understanding. It could include exchanges of selected researchers and technicians. It could embrace increased speech-making by the more articulate representatives of U. S. businesses before leadership groups overseas.

The total possibilities are great. The inducements are substantial, particularly in this day when enlightened business leadership is well aware of its stakes in the world struggle. All that is needed is broad-gaged leadership, guidance, and assistance from a respected private organization which is willing to take the initiative.

3. *Sponsorship of an institute for research and training in*

the whole field of international information and persuasion.
There is now no real training center for young workers in the
complex work of international persuasion. Government agencies generally must recruit young men having only a few of
the skills and attributes needed; they learn by osmosis while
they work. A war, in which America would have no time to
improvise as it has in the past, would find the nation with
inadequate reserves of young men knowing anything about
combat psychological warfare.

At the same time, the nation lacks any comprehensive, yet
realistic, research program in the increasingly complex field of
international persuasion. In recent years, social scientists, particularly psychologists and anthropologists, have made excit-
ing progress in the study of the factors that influence men's
actions. They have compiled fascinating data, for example,
showing how direct personal persuasion, man-to-man persuasion, is the most effective means of changing attitudes, and
appraising various means of approximating this on a broader
scale. A few of America's international propagandists have
exposed themselves to these new developments, but the exposure has been brief. The administrators of government programs, up to their ears in day-to-day problems, have generally
gone their way, while the academicians, up in the clouds without concrete problems, have continued exchanging papers and
holding stimulating, if somewhat incestuous, discussions. Only
in one or two limited experiments has the gap been bridged.
M.I.T.'s Project Troy, discussed in Chapter 8, was one case, as
is a current project in its Center for International Studies. The
promise shown by those developments underscores the wisdom
of a much broader undertaking.

A new and adequately financed Institute of World Opinion,
perhaps attached to one of the great universities, could go far
toward meeting these needs. It could have a teaching and research staff comprising both able social-science scholars and
veterans of the government information agencies. To insure

against its becoming too detached, the Institute could borrow "practical propagandists" from government operations for one-year terms and, in turn, lend its own staff members to the government as replacements. It could provide a one-year course in international information and psychological warfare for college graduates. In all likelihood, government, civilian, and military agencies could lend assistance in the teaching and could underwrite the training of selected groups of recruits.

If one assumes that the United States will face a difficult world contest for years, he must also assume that international persuasion will be a problem for a long time. Under those conditions, few can doubt the need for an institution devoted to large-scale research and training in the field.

ONE broad, all-embracing answer to all these needs suggests itself. It is the formation of a United States Council on World Opinion, with a board of directors made up of outstanding American leaders conversant with international problems. Through well-staffed divisions, it could undertake: (1) direction of the cultural effort abroad, (2) the mobilization of business representatives, and (3) sponsorship and direction of the Institute of World Opinion. Operating abroad simply as "The United States Council," it could parallel some of the more fruitful activities of the experienced British Council.

I suspect there are few projects more deserving of the time of distinguished citizens or more worthy of financing by the great American foundations.

THERE ARE at least two other missions that such a United States Council on World Opinion could appropriately undertake. Certainly it could do both far more effectively than could any government agency.

Film Improvement

If its directors saw fit, the U. S. Council could well use its influence to persuade American film distributors to make more of an effort to see that their exports contribute to understanding rather than misunderstanding.

A few American films have been so poorly gaged to foreign tastes that the Communists have actually acquired and distributed extra prints of them. The basic reason is simple. When an American sees a movie about penthouse playboys or about incredible intolerance, he has the background to know the cases are not typical. Many a foreign audience has no such perspective. Hence, American films have given millions overseas a badly distorted picture of American softness, gangsterism, inhumanity, and materialism. They have bemused as well as amused. Often such film stories can be put in perspective for foreign audiences by minor additions and slight editing.

Both Hollywood companies and American publishers who export their wares have made appreciable improvements in the last five years. They can do vastly more without dishonesty or distortion. When the government endeavors to influence private film makers in this direction, however, its efforts are understandably suspected as "Washington censorship." Similar persuasive efforts by a council of distinguished citizens would be more likely to yield results.

New Approach to Languages

No mention of major projects for private organizations could be complete without including the necessity for someone, somehow, to do something about the state of American training in foreign languages. No one who has had broad experience in administering international programs can fail to note the acute dearth of Americans with true knowledge of the tongues of other nations. And no one who has studied the wide-spread American misunderstandings about other peoples can fail to realize that it stems in large part from utter lack of interest in the tongues in which others speak and think and live.

The teaching of foreign languages in American schools and colleges today is an incredible joke. Anyone dealing with job applications for foreign service has noted scores of applicants who have studied some foreign tongue for one to four years and yet cannot speak it, write it, or even read it with facility. If some American foundation is looking for worthy projects as desperately as some of them occasionally appear to be looking, here is an answer. The time is overdue for a comprehensive survey of the reasons for failure of American training in languages, for some research into the most effective methods employed in other lands, and for pilot projects to test ways and means for making effective language instruction both possible and practicable in American schools.

Whether the job be undertaken by the proposed U. S. Council on World Opinion is not important. What is important is that it be undertaken vigorously by some private organization.

24

Lessons Learned

THERE ARE many problems still to be solved
and lessons still to be learned in the conduct of international
persuasion. All the accumulated experience, for example, has
not yet developed ways to draw adequately upon the great
power of religion in the current cold war.

There is as yet no accurate method of measuring the impact
of propaganda behind the Iron Curtain, though some guidance is provided by such techniques as the systematic use of
"listener panels" made up of escapees. Even in open areas,
there are not yet satisfactory ways of testing the persuasive
effects of poster, handbills, or films. The audience can be measured; the impact on that audience so far can only be crudely
estimated.

The elements of dynamic appeal and emotional impact are
still too largely missing from American output abroad. As
noted earlier, the free-world "message" appeals very much to
reason, very little to emotion.

Nonetheless, hard experience and analysis have yielded some
answers to some questions. These conclusions, set down by
categories, seem to be justified:

Concepts

In today's world, the government would be guilty of profli-
gate waste if, while spending billions abroad, it failed to use

organized international persuasion to explain its actions, aims, and policies, to help build unity among free peoples, and to weaken the power of its foes. To act without explaining why is folly.

At the same time, propaganda * operations alone can accomplish little. They are most effective when closely meshed with specific actions, clear policies, and grand strategy. A free-wheeling propaganda operation could be worse than none. (Educational exchange and cultural activities need not be closely meshed.)

Against any enemy area, the psychological weapon is an aggressive weapon. In a defensive or stalemate period, psychological operations against enemy areas should be directed principally to building up confidence in the source (through truthful reporting even of setbacks), to sustaining the hope of friends in the enemy areas, and to encouraging attitudes (not open acts) of resistance. Psychological weapons cannot be used as substitutes for military or diplomatic measures without destroying confidence and good will.

Propaganda to enemy areas should not be directed in a way to please the uninitiated on the home front. That too often leads to the kind of stridency that alienates those who are to be persuaded. To be effective within enemy areas, propaganda often requires a tone that appears "soft" or "appeasing" to the uninformed at home. (On the other hand, such effective propaganda generally wins the approval of any group of intelligent Americans who have thoroughly studied conditions, attitudes, and moods within the enemy area.)

* The word "propaganda" throughout this chapter is used in the sense of truthful propaganda—the dissemination of information in order to influence. Technically, such propaganda breaks down into four main categories: (1) combat propaganda, such as has been used to influence enemy troops in Korea; (2) information directed to populations behind enemy lines or behind such barriers as the Iron Curtain; (3) information to friendly areas to combat divisive forces and to strengthen existing ties; (4) information directed into neutral areas. This chapter deals chiefly with the last three categories, in all of which many of the same principles obtain.

Strategy

In any official U. S. Government output abroad, truth is the indispensable ingredient. Only factual honesty builds the confidence that is necessary for long-term effectiveness. The policy is not too confining, since truth is generally on America's side today—and truthful items can be so selected and emphasized as to support the basic objectives.

Contrary to wide-spread cant, effective persuasion need not be overwhelmingly, or even predominantly, "affirmative." The "negative"—the exposure of the foe's actions and policies—is frequently more effective than any other factor in building determined resistance to a common enemy. Both the positive and the negative are needed.

It should be standard government policy to have specialists in foreign opinion participate in decisions on international policy. Sound policy should not be changed in order to win popularity, but it can at least be so formulated, announced, executed, and explained as to win maximum good will. The United States will sometimes need to be firm, even "tough," in dealing with its allies. It never needs to do so in a way that uselessly irritates them. Continuing attention to foreign opinions can prevent this.

The simple matter of wording official announcements has great importance. A good rule in drafting announcements of new actions or new policies is to "think back from the headline." Conceive of the most desirable headline or radio bulletin possible under the circumstances; then draft the announcement to achieve that.

Organization

While no flat rule can be laid down for desirable U. S. expenditures on international information, the practical experience of many indicates that a good broad estimate today would call for annual expenditures running to about two-tenths of one percent of the government's total "international" expend-itures—that is, of the total spent on economic aid, interna-tional activities, military defense, and the like. Today this would mean an expenditure of about $120,000,000 for *all* such governmental operations. Experience indicates that a consis-tent program at this level can be effective without being un-duly wasteful—if it is well managed in each area. The figure is low compared with the percentage of budget allocated to pub-lic relations by the average American corporation. When wisely spread over eighty-odd countries, such expenditures would entail neither extravagance nor flamboyance. Some stu-dents of psychological strategy would consider it low.

In recent years the international information program, while having relatively few of the flaws alleged by noisy irre-sponsibles, has had deeper faults that require conscientious, adult treatment. Most of those faults stem from four causes:

1. The enormous difficulty of developing sound evaluation techniques—ways of testing the persuasiveness of various items of output.

2. The continuing inability to recruit enough first-rate execu-tives—because of the low pay and because of the fear of being slandered.

3. Too much red tape, budgetary rigidity, and bureaucratic rivalry—perennial problems in government, but not alto-gether incurable.

4. The fact that top executives in the program have always had to spend more time combatting irresponsible charges of nonexistent faults than they could devote to the correc-tion of real and basic faults.

Exactly where information operations are located in the gov-ernment hierarchy is less important than many suppose. Sim-ply relocating and reorganizing operations will never provide a cure-all.

More fundamental, the U. S. agency or agencies conducting

international persuasion cannot be set apart in some water-tight compartment, however high its status. It should be meshed in at every level with those making and carrying out international policies. This means, in peacetime, being keyed in particularly with the State Department. It means that combat propaganda in wartime must be *a part of* the military operations. It means that peacetime information operations abroad must be coordinated with other activities under U. S. embassies. And it means that the whole, in peace or war, should be pulled together by a staff coordinator at the President's elbow.

In addition, it is essential that the organization, wherever located, be given enough status and enough decent-salaried jobs to attract and hold an adequate number of first-rate executives. This has not been true in the past.

Precise tactics in international persuasion can best be mapped out and executed by capable men in the countries concerned—or (in the case of inaccessible areas) as near as possible to the countries concerned. Too much master-minding from Washington is an evil. Broad objectives for each country should be laid out in Washington. Detailed programming should be left to the field, where the information chief should be one of the three or four top-rank officials immediately under the ambassador.

Congressional responsibilities in the field can best be exercised by one permanent and well-staffed joint committee, replacing in-and-out inquiries and harassments by multiple Congressional groups. America cannot conduct an effective information operation if it is to be pulled up by its roots and dissected by various groups every few months to see how it is getting along. One responsible committee that would genuinely study the intricacies of international persuasion could forward the work, rather than impede it.

Any effective information operation should include improved mechanisms for testing the persuasiveness of its output. To date, the best devices have proved to be: (1) public opinion samplings and panels of typical citizens in friendly areas, (2) panels of escapees from inaccessible areas, and (3) skilled interrogation of war prisoners in combat areas.

Personnel

For a "firing line" propagandist the most necessary skill is intimate knowledge of the audience—its language, attitudes, myths, politics, and *current* beliefs and grievances.

Other desirable attributes are media skills (in radio, press, leaflet writing, etc.), a basic knowledge of U. S. policy and its background, a flair for effective expression, and, when possible, some knowledge of such social sciences as psychology and anthropology.

Skill in American advertising, public relations, and journalism do not automatically make a propagandist. Such ability helps, but persuading other peoples on primarily political subjects is vastly more intricate than persuading Americans to buy this or to believe that.

In general, there is no substitute for first-hand experience in active international persuasion. The individuals who most approximate ideal international propagandists combine such long experience with knowledge of the audience, plus media experience.

Since all the ideal attributes haven't yet been found in one man, the ideal propaganda operation for each area requires a team headed by one of those rare individuals skilled at getting the best out of others.

There is no pat answer to the perennial question of whether the effective international radio speaker should be a "native" who speaks the broadcast tongue flawlessly, or whether he should be clearly an American, speaking with an American accent. Often the American accent is best for giving official American views, the flawless accent best for intimate person-to-person persuasion. Only trial and error and audience sampling, however, can provide the specific answers for a specific country.

Media

No one medium of information is universally more effective than others.

Such unspectacular activities as the exchange of persons program and overseas libraries have far more importance than is generally recognized. Their importance can be short range as well as long range. Some United States Information Service libraries literally serve as arsenals of ideas for those abroad currently fighting Communism. The exchange of persons program has probably converted more influential persons into staunch allies of America than any other single activity.

Long-distance radio is most effective today in the Communist-dominated areas where men *want* to listen because they are being cut off from the truth. It is least effective in the completely open areas. There international radio speaks chiefly to a small group of stalwarts, whose friendship is potentially important. It generally reaches large audiences only when selected programs are relayed over domestic stations—as now happens in twenty-odd countries.

The effectiveness of other (non-radio) media varies widely. Films are extremely useful in most countries, because they combine visual and aural impact. Posters, pamphlets, exhibits, photos, magazines, and books have important places in any international program, but their effectiveness varies from country to country and even from district to district.

Personal contacts, as social scientists have found, generally change more attitudes than any other method. Hence, the exchange of persons between countries has vast potential effectiveness. Hence, also, there is great value in personal contacts of American public-affairs officers with editors, commentators, and intellectual leaders abroad.

Some of the most effective activities are those carried out

jointly with like-minded organizations abroad—and without American labels all over them.

Tactics

There are few universal principles to be applied on a world-wide basis. (One of the few is the simple moral and practical principle of sticking to the truth.) Even the concept of freedom, highly effective in many nations, is almost meaningless in others. A broadcast that is too militantly anti-Soviet for the Swiss will be surreptitiously applauded by the Czechs. Accordingly, American information output should be carefully tailored, edited, and translated (where possible) by experts in the countries concerned. Even broadcasts from America should be subjected to regular criticism and guidance by persons on the scene or near the scene.

It is meaningless to judge the persuasiveness of international information output by purely American standards. A booklet or poster carefully tailored to meet the needs in one area abroad may seem naïve to Americans. Another that seems too "high flying" and intellectual to Americans may be just right for influential editors and leaders in a half-dozen countries of Europe. The type of humor that is most effective in two satellite states is often a type at which Americans would scarcely smile.

To gain maximum effectiveness, an international information program should have maximum flexibility. It should not be tied to spending this much in France and that much in Burma, or this amount in radio and that amount in posters simply because an eighteen-months-old appropriation specifies those proportions. A changing world situation requires rapid changes in emphases. Ideally, the Congress should allow maximum flexibility, relying on a watchdog committee to be sure the latitude is not abused.

To achieve effectiveness, international information operations, particularly radio, must build and hold an audience.

This means that effective broadcasts, for example, must include moderate amounts of music to one area, of gossipy chit-chat to another, leisurely features to another, and considerable news containing no "message." Uninformed critics often single out such audience-bait for ridicule. Experience shows it to be of substantial value when appropriately employed.

Small items of intelligence on happenings in a Communist area help immensely to build audiences in that area. Though too few intelligence officers realize it, there is justification for declassifying much information in order to use it in this way.

International persuasion needs to be acutely tuned to the tastes of the immediate audience. Cosmic concepts mean nothing to natives who think only in neighborhood terms. In one underdeveloped area, a simple poster on farming improvements or on what Communism would do to local customs can achieve more than ten posters heralding the virtues of liberty.

A prime requirement of effective persuasion is to have the best possible information on the current attitudes and moods of the audience. Hence, for propaganda operations directed to enemy or inaccessible zones it is essential to have an apparatus providing the fullest and most accurate intelligence on the target audience. Without this, the propagandist is blindfolded.

LASTLY, it is a mistake to think of the "Voice of America" as being just a radio network. Even the formal government operations in international persuasion embrace far more. They include leaflets, posters, magazines, films, lectures, books, exhibits, libraries, information centers, exchange of students and editors and teachers and leaders, press releases, day-to-day contact with commentators and other opinion-formers, scientific newsletters—in brief, every medium that can sway men's minds. More broadly, the real voice of America is the total impact abroad of our attitudes, our conduct, our press, our political figures, our business representatives, and our prominent private citizens.

The Task Ahead

FRANKLIN D. ROOSEVELT was an accomplished propagandist in his own right. He set up the wartime agencies that ultimately carried out a vast propaganda offensive. Yet he never fully understood the organized use of persuasion in a total war. On two occasions within my personal experience, he showed signs of confusing the function with censorship. He knew its value but not its methods.

Harry S. Truman, far from a master-persuader himself, came to understand well the organized use of international persuasion. He strengthened the machinery for international information. He also made notable efforts to bring the multitude of government voices into some semblance of harmony. When my colleagues and I prepared guidances to inform all Cabinet officers of U. S. aims and strategy directed toward world opinion, he cooperated fully. He subjected the guidances to careful review, then distributed them at Cabinet meetings. He was quick to cooperate in issuing statements that we found to be needed around the world.

Dwight D. Eisenhower, fortunately, came into office with a broad-gaged appreciation of psychological strategy. In London, in 1942, while planning the North African landings, he had told O.W.I., "I don't know much about psychological warfare, but I want to give it every chance." In later years he came to

give great credit to the weapon. By the time of his inauguration as President, he had developed an appreciation of international persuasion in its broadest sense. Eisenhower had said
during his 1952 campaign:

> We must realize that as a nation everything we say, everything we do,
> and everything we fail to say or do, will have its impact in other lands. It
> will affect the minds and wills of men and women there. . . .
> We are not going to win the struggle for men's minds merely by tripling
> Congressional appropriations for a super-land Voice of America. Rather,
> it will be the message which we give the Voice to speak. Rather, it will be
> the spiritual strength, the understanding, and the compassion which we
> Americans can summon to put into that message. Rather, it will be the
> planned and effective use of every means to appeal to men and women
> everywhere.

A large order, to be sure. Nonetheless, Eisenhower's statements showed he recognized that an effective Campaign of
Truth needs to be as broad as government itself. While seeing
the need for a strong apparatus, he also saw the need for much
more, as he demonstrated in his early speeches.

Of course, neither Dwight Eisenhower nor any other official
in a democratic nation can achieve the sort of perfectly balanced psychological campaign he envisaged. But at least it is
possible to move steadily toward that goal. To do so will involve unprecedented meshing of the activities and utterances
of agencies throughout the government. It will involve delegation of Congress' responsibility to a small group of members
who will specialize in the complex business of persuasion.
Finally, it will involve increasing recognition throughout government that winning the hearts of men is at least as important
as winning the formal cooperation of their rulers or leaders.

This means continually striving to keep the nation's actions
in harmony with its high principles. When the actions *seem* to
conflict with the principles, America must spare no effort to
explain those actions fully. The United States has no intelligent choice but to keep its case continually before the world.

And, in doing so, there is no substitute for a strong mechanism staffed by trained specialists whose skills cannot be acquired overnight.

When we Americans consistently put our case before the people of the world in a way which shows we respect their intelligence, we will be well on our way. In the world of today there is an enormous stock of good will toward us. There are, even in Communist-enslaved nations, millions who want to believe in us if we will only help them by persistently making clear our aims, our policies, and the reasons for our actions. America can mobilize this force of good will effectively when it determines to pursue vigorously and *consistently* the aim reflected in the Declaration of Independence—to behave and to speak out of a decent respect to the opinions of mankind.

Author's Notes

CHAPTER 2

It was the original Psychological Strategy Board, an interdepartmental committee set up under the authority of the Secretary of State, that particularly urged sending Dwight D. Eisenhower to head the NATO forces in Europe. This board consisted of Brig. Gen. John Magruder, representing the Secretary of Defense; Vice Admiral Leslie C. Stevens, representing the Joint Chiefs of Staff; Mr. Frank Wisner, representing the Central Intelligence Agency; with myself representing the State Department as chairman. A few other agency representatives sat with the board as observers and advisers. In late 1951, President Truman, responding to the pressures of other departments, set up a new Psychological Strategy Board, presided over by a specially appointed chairman. The original board then became the Psychological Operations Coordinating Committee. Both did some good in coordinating strategy and operations. Both have thus far fallen far short of being cure-alls. In retrospect, it appears that both have attempted too much Washington masterminding of complex tactical problems that could best be solved by first-rate men in the field.

CHAPTER 3

26   Among the O.W.I. films, one of the most moving was *Hymn of the Nations,* featuring the N.B.C. Orchestra, and Arturo Toscanini, who donated his services. There were many official reports of crowds in European theaters standing and cheering at the end of this film.

26   With regard to American strength, O.W.I. continually pounded home to world audiences through all media one key theme. This was that America, in World War II, had demonstrated the greatest eruption of national strength in world history without sacrificing its basic principles of freedom and respect for human dignity. Films, pamphlets, and broadcasts told the story of the nation's astounding production of planes, tanks, ships, and guns. The same items emphasized that, through it all, America had kept a free press, free

Page elections, and freedom of worship. The mere story of what was
going on was living refutation of dictators' perennial claims that
"emergencies" make necessary the "temporary" abandonment of
democratic principles and practices.

27   As the war progressed, American-British propagandists learned
particular techniques. We found, for example, that it paid off to
commit the enemy to achieving something that he might or might
not actually achieve. Thus in broadcasts to the Germans, we "committed" them to holding the Atlantic wall at all costs. We told how
Hitler's forces were going to extraordinary lengths to strengthen the
Atlantic wall because of its enormous importance to them. We glori-
fied the strength of the wall, quoting the Nazis' own statements.
These tactics presumably would enhance our victory when we pene-
trated the wall and would minimize any temporary failure to do so.
After glorifying the wall, we began working in references to the German leaders' "Maginot mentality" and to the "Maginot complex,"
seeking to raise doubts in the minds of Germany's soldiers and citizens. We found we were hitting pay dirt when the Nazis started issuing home-front denials that they were "Maginot-minded." We got
further confirmation on June 10, four days after D-day, when the
Stockholm *Aftonbladet* reported news from Berlin: "The Allied
breach in what was called the impenetrable Atlantic wall was a cold
douche for German public opinion. . . . People remark more and
more openly: the high command gave us the Maginot psychosis and
this is the result."

Allied propagandists also learned how to pick out items in German home-front news to underline the theme that "Germany's leadership is confused." As the war progressed, they learned to cite
evidence of the "overwhelming force" of the Allies and of the "hopeless odds" against Germany—all to accustom enemy minds to the
idea of surrender and to make it seem reasonable.

The Allies also learned to develop the hope theme by describing
day after day, in broadcasts and leaflet newspapers, the good treatment accorded German soldiers who had "gone over," or German
civilians who had fallen into Allied hands.

Again, Allied propagandists developed a particularly effective
theme when, on July 20, 1944, a group of German officers made
their famous attempt on Hitler's life. This was treated as just an
outward sign of a "peace movement" in Germany—a growing movement among people of all classes to save the remnants of German
manhood and of Germany itself by getting rid of Hitler. Allied

Page propagandists pounced on every scrap of information that would buttress this theme and reported it back to Germany. Subtly implied in every report was the thought that it was now becoming respectable, in fact patriotic, for Germans to plot for peace.

27   One ABSIE (American Broadcasting Station in Europe) broadcast warrants particular mention. Immediately concurrent with the announcement of the surrender on V-E Day, ABSIE went on the air, in all languages except German, with this statement: "The order to 'cease fire' has been given. We, speaking to you now, are Americans. Our dead lie with yours. Our men fought, and those who died, died for their own freedom and for the freedom of the American people, who armed and sent them into battle. Their fight was just and worthy in their own interest. But in fighting for their own freedom, they died for yours, too. And so, may we all think today about those Americans who lie beside the Britons, the Belgians, the French, the Russians, and your own compatriots, beneath crosses on the hillsides of Europe. Whoever you are, think of these Americans as being your dead, too. The cause that brought them into battle was the simple proposition that your freedom is inseparable from their freedom, and that your enslavement held the threat of their ultimate enslavement. Now, you who were enslaved are free, and those men who belong to Kansas and Mississippi and New York must turn, not homeward, but eastward to the last battleground, in Asia. From the lands of Europe their fathers came to America, seeking freedom, and to Europe the sons returned, still seeking it. Now that they have helped secure it, now that the 'cease-fire' has sounded, let us post sentries and never again dismiss the guard that watches over our indivisible freedom."

27   One of the most fascinating enterprises concerned an O.W.I. magazine, *Photo Review*. A group of Danish patriots arranged to obtain copies, duplicate the plates, and print and distribute the magazine under the noses of German occupation authorities in Copenhagen.

28   The extent of radio penetration of wartime Germany, despite jamming of broadcasts and punishment of listeners, was indicated in findings of the U. S. Strategic Bombing Survey. In postwar polls, this group found that fifty-one percent of the adult population of Germany had listened to the B.B.C., the Voice of America, or other Allied broadcasts. Moreover, the danger of being caught listening caused the audiences gradually to develop a bond of sympathy and a sense of unity with the broadcasters.

Page   There were numerous reports by American forces of hearing newly
28   liberated Europeans in Brussels and Paris whistling "Yankee Doo-
dle," then the air signature of the Voice of America.

32   It was at the end of the 1945 House appropriations hearings that
Representative Clarence Cannon, the veteran chairman of the Appropriations Committee, volunteered these words: "When I look
back on the month's work, there is one thing that stands out to me,
like the headlight on a locomotive at night, and that is when a man
is appointed to take charge of one of these agencies, or to accept
one of the key positions under them that he is automatically di-
vested of that immunity which hedges about the character and
standing of any private citizen. He is fair prey from that time on, to
any casual passerby who cares to comment on or criticize with
rancor either him or any of his actions. . . . Of all the unsung
heroes of the war, the men who take these positions rank among
the highest. . . . Whether or not they receive it, they are deserving
of the thanks and the appreciation and gratitude of every American
citizen, and along with the few and very meager compensations
which go with this character of service—about the only consolation
we can offer them is the assurance that when history is written . . .
it will be realized that they have rendered a service second only to
that of the men who have led our forces on the battlefield of the
western and Asiatic fronts."

33   At war's end, Major Pedro Lopez, Philippine guerrilla leader, testified: "Without the daily (Voice of America) broadcasts of the
Office of War Information from San Francisco, my people would
have lost their last vestige of hope. And, because of O.W.I., the
spirit of my people still lives."

CHAPTER 5

60   It was to meet the need for increased world understanding that
the United Nations Educational, Scientific and Cultural Organization was born. UNESCO has not been as devoid of accomplishment
as many imagine. Its research projects into the tensions between nations have laid important groundwork. As a clearing house for educational, scientific, and cultural exchanges between nations, it has
proved valuable. It has charted possible new advances in fundamental education and in the teaching of science. Its Coupon Plan has
made possible substantial exchanges of books, educational films,
and scientific equipment between countries, despite the existence of
currency barriers. Yet UNESCO's achievements have seemed small

Page beside its potentialities. Set up to increase understanding between men in a world that promised to be peaceful, it found itself in a world sharply divided between hostile elements. If UNESCO is disappointing, at least this much can be said for it and for the U. S. investment in it:

1. By providing about one third of UNESCO's budget—about two cents for every U. S. resident—the United States participates actively with intellectual leaders from some sixty-five other countries in joint planning, discussion, and research. These intellectual leaders, to an extent far greater than in the United States, have real influence on the actions and attitudes of their governments and fellow countrymen. Some have real political power. (For example, Professor Radakrishnan, a member of every Indian delegation to UNESCO, is now Vice President of India.)

2. Americans reach these intellectual leaders in UNESCO by meeting on the common ground of education, science, and culture. Under the auspices of such a multilateral organization, many of the old prejudices and suspicions between the U. S. and other nations begin to disappear.

3. The Government of the United States itself benefits by the direct link between the United States National Commission for UNESCO and the sixty-odd great private organizations represented on the United States National Commission for UNESCO. Through this device unique in political science, there is a continuing interchange between the leaders of such groups and the United States Government. A close association has produced and is bound to produce important results on the home front.

In brief, UNESCO has fallen far short of the high-minded goals of its founders. It appears, however, at least to have proved worth the small American contributions to it.

CHAPTER 6

80 As we explained to appropriate Congressional committees, my colleagues and I, as individuals, would have greatly preferred to spend the coming year or two perfecting the organization—making changes in certain key positions, recruiting improved manpower for some positions, and changing the whole tone of output. But, we explained, we couldn't afford the luxury of waiting for expansion. That would be as if the air force wanted to take two years to perfect its thirty-five groups before beginning to build the fifty or seventy groups that almost everyone considered necessary.

Page
95 The U. S. propaganda operations in the little island of Berlin, deep within Sovietized territory, deserve special emphasis. There the great RIAS (Radio in American Sector) station carried on a continuing barrage into Soviet-ruled Germany. It was able to do so effectively because Germans from the Soviet zones continually visited the RIAS headquarters and briefed the staff. It was also able to do so because ninety-five percent of the staff was made up of thoroughly investigated German Nationals working under the broad direction of a few Americans. They spoke the language and knew the inner thoughts of their audience. RIAS won an audience by broadcasting the best music, the best entertainment, and the most complete news in all of Germany. It helped its audience in Soviet Germany by alerting listeners to Communist agents within their midst, by warning them of forthcoming Communist plans, and by advising how they could deter Communist plans without risking their necks.

From the Information Services Division of the U. S. establishment in Germany came a continual flow of material that found its way behind the Iron Curtain. Its publication *Ost-Probleme,* containing documented evidence on Communist aims and methods, became a standard tool of free-world propagandists in a score of countries.

The U. S. information specialists under the U. S. High Commissioner had opportunities to enjoy their work, too. They distributed miniature newspapers by the thousands through covert channels within the Soviet areas. They even effected an arrangement under which telephone subscribers throughout Berlin, including those within the Soviet sector, could dial a particular number and get a digest of RIAS news. Once German organizations who were working with them set up a gigantic electric sign facing the Soviet sector of Berlin. It bore the heading, "The newspapers of free Berlin provide the news." Beneath, a moving electric sign carried the latest news bulletins. This so nettled the Soviet authorities that they put up a gigantic sign nearby in such a way that it obstructed the view of the free Berliners' sign. To make the obstruction complete, they hung a huge sheet of canvas from the sign. Their free-German opponents were ready, however. They started immediately using a high-powered projector which flashed the latest news on the canvas in such a way that it showed through the other side.

CHAPTER 7

Page

105   The directive, which Senator McCarthy implied amounted to "sabotage," had actually been proposed by an advisory committee headed by Dr. Martin R. P. McGuire of Catholic University, and including Cass Canfield, chairman of the board of Harper and Brothers; Robert L. Crowell, president of Thomas Y. Crowell Company; Robert B. Downs, director of libraries at the University of Illinois; George P. Brett, Jr., president of the Macmillan Company; Lewis Hanke, director of the Institute of Latin American Studies at the University of Texas, and Keyes D. Metcalf, director of libraries at Harvard University.

106   The witness's letter on the mobile studio follows:

1790 Broadway

March 6, 1953

Mr. Roy Cohn
Legal Counsel, Permanent Sub-Committee
U. S. Senate
Washington, D.C.
Dear Mr. Cohn:

In my testimony on February 17, 1953 before the Committee, I find that I was in error, regarding figures on the mobile unit. I should like to correct my testimony and hope it will be corrected in the record.

The true figures on the original cost of the mobile unit was $40,414.22 plus $625.00 for paint and lettering. A total cost of $41,239.22.

When it was decided to modify the unit and add a tractor, this work was done by R.C.A. at no cost to the Government other than $590.00 for paint and lettering after it was modified. Therefore, the total cost was $41,829.22.

I trust you will accept my apology for being in error as I had been misinformed and regret any embarrassment I may have caused you or the Department.

Sincerely,

(Signed)
Assistant Chief,
Domestic Transmitter Division

CHAPTER 9

CHAPTER 12

Page "many general statements and few clear facts." Nonetheless, as of this date, it is an extensive and growing operation.

CHAPTER 14

192   Like Edith Sampson, Walter White, secretary of the National Association for the Advancement of Colored People, has helped combat anti-American feeling arising from racial developments. When asked how he, a Negro, could defend American democracy, White has repeatedly told overseas audiences, in effect: "We do not claim to have achieved perfect democracy yet. We still have lynching and discrimination. But more and more Americans are ashamed of these practices and are doing something about them. In America organizations like mine are permitted to function, often in disagreement with our own government. Contrast this state of affairs with what happens in totalitarian states, where critics of government are exiled or shot. We prefer to take our chances and fight our way in a democracy, whatever its shortcoming, for we are making steady progress."

193   There has been much exaggerated nonsense to the effect that international understanding is a cure-all and a preventive of wars. Experience shows that understanding each other doesn't necessarily mean two nations will never fight each other. We know that Canadian-American understanding has been great and that the Canadian-U. S. border is a model of peaceful relations between two nations. We also know, however, that the French and Germans understand each other pretty well and yet have been at each other's throats at frequent intervals. Again, the most determined fighters against Soviet Communism have been West Berliners, who know and understand Kremlin ways better than any other free Europeans. Professor Frederick Dunn of Princeton likes to tell the story of a minor European monarch who was engaged in a boundary dispute with a neighboring monarch. When this monarch was urged by his neighbors to try to settle the differences and misunderstandings, he replied that there were really no differences or misunderstandings between them, that they both wanted exactly the same thing. They understood each other perfectly! Social scientists studying this whole broad field have generally reached this conclusion: Knowledge of other peoples does not necessarily guarantee harmonious relations with them. However, understanding another nation's cultures, traditions, and reasoning does at least greatly increase the chance that intelligent decisions will be made on basic

Page questions of foreign policy. Such understanding is an important corrective of the too-common tendency to fit one's own cultural values onto other peoples. In the case of America, popular ignorance of others was not too serious a matter for a long time. Then, however, the United States found itself suddenly thrust into a position of world leadership. The parochialism of large segments of the American public suddenly became a serious handicap. It can almost be said that only through knowing something about other people can the U. S. lead them in a way that they will *willingly* follow.

CHAPTER 15

206   The Mecca airlift project has been criticized as meaningless by the astute and fluent James Burnham in his book *Containment or Liberation?*. He contended that the project won no good will for America, because all Moslems say, "All good things come from Allah," and that it was a half-baked stunt concocted by some bright psychological warrior. There is much evidence that, in this case, James Burnham is wrong. His logic could be no better if he said it is impossible to win good will from Christians because they say, "Praise God from Whom all blessings flow." Actually the project was enthusiastically endorsed by veteran diplomats thoroughly conversant with Moslem customs. One of the many favorable press comments in Arabic newspapers said: "The Jidda airlift is Beirut's chief topic. All Lebanese Arabs are talking of America's heroic gesture. Never before in Islam's history has such a humanitarian act taken place. America has really touched Arab hearts. Religion is our weak point. We are all sentimentalists. We want the U. S. to understand our mentality and continue its good work."

CHAPTER 19

244   Regarding the importance of a "persuader-in-chief" close to the President: It is noteworthy that much progress in psychological strategy under Harry S. Truman was attributable to the fact that he had a young assistant, George Elsey, who happened to be deeply interested in international persuasion. Elsey, as an intelligent and energetic assistant to the President, repeatedly performed noble services on the psychological front. He conveyed suggestions from my office to the President, helped incorporate special passages in Presidential speeches, persuaded the President to clamp down on irresponsible statements by officials, and himself originated a num-

Page ber of worthy projects. Indeed, many of the functions to be performed officially by C. D. Jackson under the Eisenhower Administration were performed informally under Truman by a White
House trio consisting of Elsey, Joseph Short—press secretary—and
Charles Murphy—counsel to the President.

244 The original proposal in this book for a Presidential staff assistant
concentrating on international information was drafted some weeks
before C. D. Jackson was appointed to the job. The draft was discussed with several members of the Eisenhower entourage. It is not
known whether they influenced the President's action in appointing
Jackson or not; in fact, there is evidence that the President was
thinking along these lines many months earlier.

248 It is, of course, essential that there be integration of the official
U. S. information activities in each country abroad. This will mean
having one chief information officer, ranking just below the ambassador, and supervising all U. S. information operations in that country. Such a set-up would preclude the ridiculous kind of overlapping
between the U.S.I.S. and ECA (later MSA) information operations
which long existed in Europe and which was ultimately overcome
only by painstaking and protracted negotiations.

CHAPTER 20

257 Incredible though it seems, there has never been any standing
provision for security clearance of Congressional staff members who
search through the classified papers of government agencies. Some
Congressional committees have sometimes employed as staffers individuals who could probably not pass the kind of clearances required
in the Executive Branch. It is elemental, of course, that any Congressional staff members dealing in the confidential business of an
international information program should be subjected to the same
security clearance as are all members of the agency.

CHAPTER 21

264 The special religious panel, which provided extraordinary assistance, consisted of Dr. Edward Pruden, pastor of the First Baptist
Church of Washington, D. C. (former president of the American
Baptist Convention); Msgr. Thomas McCarthy, director of the Bureau of Information, National Catholic Welfare Conference, Washington, D. C.; and Mr. Isaac Franck, executive director of the
Jewish Community Council of Greater Washington. Dr. Albert J.

Page McCartney, religious advisor to the information program, chaired the group.

CHAPTER 22

272   There is no doubt that German vacillation over the use of General Vlassov constituted a severe blunder. Alfred Rosenberg, the Nazi Party's "philosopher," distrusted him as a "Great Russian." Only after months of delay did Rosenberg become convinced that Vlassov, openly willing to concede self-determination to the minorities within the U.S.S.R., could be useful. By that time, however, the Soviets had scored a victory at Stalingrad, and the Nazis had lost the initiative.

276   On December 8, 1952, Radio Warsaw screamingly admitted Voice of America effectiveness on the economic front. It complained that the U. S. Government "learns that there is a temporary shortage of certain commodities." Then it added: "A few days later the Voice of America triumphantly blasts that in this country such a shortage exists. The result is overcrowding of the stores and great difficulties."

CHAPTER 24

290   Propaganda, to be effective in the long run, must be not only factually true but credible to the audience. This quality, sometimes called "empathy" by veterans in the field, involves not only knowing the audience, but feeling *with* the audience so as to avoid statements and forms of presentation which would create hostility and suspicion. By and large in World War II, Anglo-American propaganda outstripped its rivals in this respect. The totalitarian states seemed somehow to be unable to understand fully the sentiments in opposing nations.

295   As to the effectiveness of various media, the New York *Times* in 1953 conducted a survey in forty-four countries this side of the Sovietized areas. It summarized its findings in these words: "Almost everywhere educational and documentary films distributed by the U.S.I.S. and the Mutual Security Agency were regarded as the most effective propaganda device. Libraries where lectures and discussions are held, as well as books made available, were said to be growing in popularity everywhere. Exchange programs under which students, teachers, professional men, business and union leaders and others exchange visits between the United States and foreign countries were found to have had good results. Similarly, joint cultural

Page institutes sponsored by both the United States and a foreign government, and magazines, pamphlets and leaflets, and in some places anti-Communist, pro-democratic comic books, were found effective." The *Times* reported that, while the Voice of America was not particularly effective in some free areas, it was obviously more useful in Iron Curtain countries. It added: "Twenty different Hungarian refugees interrogated about the effectiveness of Western broadcasts as a whole agreed it was high. . . . As a morale builder in satellite countries, the Voice ranks high." At the same time, the *Times* added in its survey that in many areas the press material was "too elaborate and too extensive" to be highly useful.

295 Examples of unexpected good will won by the Voice of America turn up repeatedly. One such case: When Professor Leonard Doob of Yale, in 1952, visited the Sultan of Zanzibar, the tiny British protectorate near Tanganyika, he was welcomed with much pomp and ceremony. The Sultan started the interview with these words: "I am so glad to see an American. I have wanted to thank you for the Voice of America broadcasts. I have listened to them regularly for the news and find them extremely helpful."

CHAPTER 25

298 Regarding Truman's role: In the forum of world opinion the United States was beginning, in the early winter of 1950-51, to appear both confused and dangerously headstrong. The Secretary of the Navy, by virtually calling for a preventive war, had caused untold troubles. General MacArthur, by a series of public statements and communications to American publications, had seemed to call for broadening the Korean War by bombing Manchuria. An occasional American diplomat had sounded off with purely personal views. The net effect of all of these was, at best, to make America seem confused. At worst, it made America seem on the verge of willfully broadening the war, contrary to official policy.

At a White House meeting early in December, I jotted down on an envelope the kind of Executive Order that seemed to me to be essential if the U. S. Government was to avoid increasing this sort of confusion. It read in part: "In the light of the present critical international situation . . . officials overseas, including military commanders and diplomatic representatives, should be ordered to exercise extreme caution in public statements, to clear all but routine statements with their departments, and to refrain from direct communication on military or foreign policy with newspapers, magazines, or other publicity media in the United States."

Within a few days this had been incorporated in a Presidential order to the Joint Chiefs of Staff, the State Department, and other appropriate agencies of the government. The records indicated that all overseas representatives followed this, with the exception of General Douglas MacArthur. By a series of broad statements issued in Tokyo without clearance, he seemed to disregard the President's order. In a publicized communication with Joseph W. Martin, Jr., minority leader of the House of Representatives, on March 20, 1951, he appeared to violate it again. It was on the basis of these actions that he ultimately was relieved. The theory, of course, was that however right or wrong his views may have been, no government can function effectively if its representatives abroad express publicly views that conflict with the official policies of their government.

Appendices

A—TYPICAL COUNTRY PLAN

(Following is a hypothetical plan to illustrate the approach used by U. S. Information Services in tailoring the information program to a target country)

COUNTRY PLAN—X

Revised August 1952

Country X—Priority III, Y million population.

Situation Analysis

The primary political objective of the United States is to keep Country X an independent, sovereign nation, free from domination by an aggressive Communist power and to encourage social and economic betterment which will stem social unrest in the country.

To this end U.S.I.S. objectives are:

1. To convince the people of country X that the United States provides positive and stable leadership in the free world, that our policy is not imperialistic and respects the sovereignties of the nations with whom we deal.

2. To expose the nature of communism, its debasing effects on living conditions and its negation of freedom and human dignity, its threat to national sovereignties and particularly country X.

3. To stimulate optimum use of the assistance available under American and U.N. technical and economic assistance programs, to encourage the people of country X to raise their standard of living by developing their own resources.

4. To give full publicity to the work of American technicians in X and to inspire confidence of X in itself to solve problems arising by virtue of its "transitional" state and accompanying social unrest, in cooperation with the technical assistance available.

5. To support X's participation in the U.N. framework.

6. To build an enduring foundation of understanding between America and the people of X based on mutual respect and appreciation of the respective cultural heritages: to correct distortions of American scene, particularly with regard to color problems.

BASIC ATTITUDES

Aspirations.—Freedom from unwelcome pressure or interference from any foreign source; intense pride in their national heritage, former influ-

315

ence and culture; the improvement of political, economic and social conditions by the gradual adoption of modern methods; avoidance of provoking any foreign power to take action which would impair or destroy the sovereignty of country X; more constructive government leadership at all levels with increasing responsibilities and power in rural officials, combined with attempt to hold neutralist position, insuring X's independence through maneuvering big power interplay.

Toward U.S.S.R.: Traditional mistrust of Russian motives; concern about Communist menace though not sufficient to inspire government action to prevent growing strength of Communist-infiltrated popular-front movements.

Toward Britain: Previous ties have been prejudiced by resentment at Britain's "colonial attitude"; frequently depreciated in nationalistic press as waning power which tends to cling to outmoded empire; some doctors and professionals British-trained.

Toward Germany: Respect for come-back in industrial potential since the war; some of X's professionals are German-educated.

Toward France: Residue of cultural leadership though no longer looked upon as great political or military power.

Toward neighboring states: Traditional rivalry, friendly veneer.

FACTORS AFFECTING U.S.I.S. OPERATIONS

Favorable.—Traditionally friendly relations with United States based on United States philanthropic, educational, and medical activities; increasing evidences of benefit from American economic and technical assistance; growing realization in provincial areas of the benefits of aid projects; distrust of age-old Russian imperialism; basically energetic people when self-advantage can be demonstrated; national characteristics—quick mind, lively imagination, adaptability, facility to learn quickly.

Unfavorable.—Almost morbidly obsessed with importance of X as a peg of international security; unstable and inefficient government which takes credits for all successes, blames foreigners for all mistakes; paradoxic combination of characteristics of mercurial emotional range and widespread defeatism; concentration of wealth, backward attitude toward women; private capital unwilling to invest widely in national projects; lack of social consciousness among rich business interest; excessive illiteracy in rural areas; youth is unstable, cynical, socially insecure, energetic but untrained for citizenship responsibilities or work; heavy bombardment by Soviet radio propaganda (clandestine and openly operated) and subsidized press in the capital.

Soviet Communist activities.—Local Communist Party, though outlawed, actively agitates, has reportedly increased in strength during past year, concentrates among restive student and labor groups, particularly in factories in provincial areas and among large groups of unemployed who have flocked to the capital as a result of recent national economic difficulties. Publishes clandestine newspapers, organizes demonstrations, has several front organizations. Soviet broadcasts in X dialects total 24 hours a day blanket some portions of the country. Extent of covert activities not known but believed wide-spread.

Other foreign interests, activities.—British and French continue efforts to maintain influence through information and cultural services; B.B.C. has good signal; Reuters, BIS, and AFP news agencies operate.

Other United States programs.—United States Military mission has trained X army, reorganized military practices; substantial economic and technical assistance program.

Non-Government United States factors.—Rockefeller Foundation has operated some health and educational programs; now being coordinated with United States technical assistance programs. Minimum American business activity—local representatives of larger United States firms in international field, especially automobiles. United States News Services, AP and UP.

Mass communications channels.—Press: 109 dailies and weeklies, estimated 175,000 circulations; 19 magazines. Radio: estimated 90,000 sets, mostly in cities; four government stations operate locally, V.O.A. heard shortwave, signal medium to strong. Films: Hollywood mostly—occasional Soviet, some British and French; censorship required. United States publications; some in the capital but expensive. Other: rural coffee houses.

Attitude-forming groups.—*Religious:* 95 percent belong to state religion, especially effective rurally. Education: elementary system growing though still inadequate; shortage of trained teachers, school buildings, archaic curricula (all learning by rote); danger Communist penetration among teachers and secondary school groups. Labor: approximately 200,000 industrial workers; government-supported union formed to counter Communist-dominated union, but government program ineffectual. Military: conscription; attempts now being made to give positive educational value to military service period. Governmental: leaders, 4,000 and civil servants, 100,000.

Priority target groups—
1. Leaders in: (a) government; (b) education; (c) press.
2. Leaders of: (a) farm organizations; (b) labor unions.
3. Intellectuals and professionals.
4. Youth: university level.

Significant current documents—
Reports on mass media and public opinion study by Bureau of Applied Social Research, Columbia University.

OIR Report, CS 5.5, Part III, December 25, 1951 (Secret).
NIS Survey (Secret).
U.S.I.S. semiannual reports.

B—RESOLUTION OF FRIENDSHIP

(Following is text of the resolution introduced in 1951 by Senator Brien McMahon and Representative Abraham Ribicoff, both of Connecticut, and passed by the Eighty-second Congress.)

[S. Con. Res. 11, 82d Cong., 1st sess.]

CONCURRENT RESOLUTION

Whereas the goal of the American people is now, and ever has been, a just and lasting peace; and

Whereas the deepest wish of our Nation is to join with all other nations in preserving the dignity of man, and in observing those moral principles which alone lend meaning to his existence; and

Whereas in proof of this the United States has offered to share all that is good in atomic energy, asking in return only safeguards against the evil in the atom; and

Whereas this Nation has likewise given of its substance and resources to help those peoples ravaged by war and poverty; and

Whereas terrible danger to all free peoples compels the United States to undertake a vast program of armaments expenditures; and

Whereas we rearm only with reluctance and would prefer to devote our energies to peaceful pursuits: Now, therefore, be it

Resolved by the Senate (the House of Representatives concurring), That the Congress of the United States reaffirms the historic and abiding friendship of the American people for all other peoples, including the peoples of the Soviet Union, and declares—

That the American people deeply regret the artificial barriers which separate them from the peoples of the Union of Soviet Socialist Republics, and which keep the Soviet peoples from learning of the desire of the American people to live in friendship with all other peoples, and to work with them in advancing the ideal of human brotherhood; and

That the American people and their Government desire neither war with the Soviet Union nor the terrible consequences of such a war; and

That, although they are firmly determined to defend their freedom and security, the American people welcome all honorable efforts to compose the differences standing between the United States Government and the Soviet Government and invite the peoples of the Soviet Union to cooperate in a spirit of friendship in this endeavor; and

That the Congress request the President of the United States to call upon the Government of the Union of Soviet Socialist Republics to acquaint the people of the Soviet Union with the contents of this resolution.

318

C—SENATE QUESTIONS AND AN

In late 1951, Senator Pat McCarran, as chair
committee on State Department appropriatio
list of highly detailed questions on the interna
tion and educational exchange program. The
cers prepared extensive answers. Some of those .... not
classified throw such light on the aims and methods of the program that they are reprinted here from "Objectives of United States Information Program":

QUESTION 1

*What are the basic themes which serve as a guide to our
psychological warfare and to the Voice of America?*

Will you list these themes according to the following categories:
  a. Themes directed to the Russian people.
  b. Themes directed to the Chinese people.
  c. Themes directed to the people in the satellite countries.
  d. Themes intended to influence the Soviet bureaucracy.
  e. Themes intended to affect the Soviet Politbureau.
  f. Themes intended to disaffect the Soviet Secret Police.
  g. Themes intended to reach Communist Party members in Russia
       and the satellite countries.
  h. Themes intended to disaffect the armed forces in these countries.
  i. Themes intended to influence the members of the Communist
       Parties in Western Europe and countries outside the Iron
       Curtain.
  j. Themes intended to inspire confidence and morale among the
       people of Western Europe in nonsatellite countries generally.
Answers to this question will be found in the classified "Attachment
to Question 1," submitted with this report.

QUESTION 2

What media are used for this purpose?

Targets of the themes listed in question 1 fall into three major groups:
  The Communist areas—Russia and its European and Asian satellites.
  Communism in the free world.
  The people of Western Europe and in nonsatellite countries generally.
Radio broadcasting and, to some extent, publishing operations reach
the first target group.

SIE media—radio, press materials, pamphlets and leaflets, posters, n pictures, photographic displays and filmstrips, the information ters and their services, and the exchanging of persons—reach the two latter groups.

The remaining questions in this document, and their answers, provide detailed examples of how our basic themes are brought to life in products and activities, and how these weapons are then delivered to their targets. The over-all nature of the media used is reviewed below:

Radio broadcasting

As the medium best able to hurdle communism's iron curtain against information, the Voice of America devotes a high proportion of its total effort to delivering our basic themes to the Russian, Chinese and satellite peoples, the Soviet bureaucracy, Politbureau and secret police, and the Communist Party members and armed forces throughout the Red world.

To Soviet territory, languages and hours of programing per day are:

Russian	2½	Latvian	½
Ukranian	½	Estonian	½
Lithuanian	½	Azerbaijani	¼
Georgian	½	Tater	¼
Armenian	½	Turkestani	¼

or a total of 6¼ hours of original programs per day. To increase their effectiveness and counteract Russian jamming, these programs are re-broadcast again and again through the day and night so that a total of 55 hours of programs go out each 24 hours—most of them over several high-powered transmitters at once.

To Red China and other Soviet satellites, program hours are as follows:

Chinese:		Hungarian	1¼
Mandarin	3	Polish	1½
Cantonese	1½	Czech and Slovak	1¼
Swatow	½	Rumanian	1
Amoy	½	Bulgarian	¾
Korean	1¼	Albanian	¼

or a total of 12¾ hours daily.

Another 30 hours and 20 minutes of programs, divided among 24 language services, are devoted to targets in free world areas.

Potential audiences for these programs as a whole is estimated at 300 million, and the evidence of surveys, letters from listeners, and reports from press correspondents, travelers, and our own foreign missions indicates that many millions listen regularly. Letters from listeners total as many as 40,000 per month.

In addition to VOA-operated transmitters and relay facilities abroad, Voice of America transmissions are picked up and broadcast by the national networks or leading stations of some 25 foreign countries—thus becoming part of the domestic radio fare of listeners in these countries.

Local radio activity by USIE officers in the foreign missions is steadily on the rise. Our information services are granted time on local stations for news, discussion, and musical programs. They provide transcriptions, radio scripts, and information materials for the stations' own programs, and supply both anti-Communist and prodemocratic materials to local radio commentators and speakers. Some purchase air time, as well.

Publications

An increasing quantity of USIE-originated or inspired leaflets, pamphlets, and news material is finding its way behind the iron curtain, with the aid of various agencies here and abroad. Both organized channels and "loopholes" in the curtain give access to these materials. For the Soviet Union, the Russian language magazine "Amerika" constitutes the only open franchise into the U. S. S. R. by any free world country. As has been reported to the Congress, the Soviet Government has seriously crippled its distribution recently. However, more than 30 bitter press attacks by "Pravda" and other official Kremlin-controlled journals on articles in "Amerika" attest to Soviet concern over its potential effectiveness on the "élite" of the Russian people—the bureaucracy, Politbureau, secret police, and party members.

For other channels, USIE has created a small fold-over leaflet in Russian on the so-called "McMahon resolution" of friendship. A pamphlet now on the presses, printed in Russian, will be distributed to certain anti-Communist circles outside Russia. It is so designed that the entire pamphlet or individual pages may be easily carried about, and also may serve as models for leaflets or other anti-Communist materials produced by these circles themselves. . . .

Chinese people under Communist domination offer a somewhat more open target for publications, and indirectly some of the other media listed below, because of certain loopholes, and also through the presence of Chinese populations in the southeast Asia countries who maintain close ties with relatives, friends and business associates behind the bamboo curtain. . . . The nature and extent of propaganda fed into these channels is outlined, with examples, in answer to question 5.

Publications materials, produced or written by USIE, mainly brief, hard-hitting leaflets, also are reaching the European Communist satellites on a continuing basis through one special channel. . . . A total of 17 subjects in thousands of copies each have gone by this route. More such projects are in progress.

For the remaining target groups—Communists in the free world, and the free peoples whom we seek to inspire—the 36 pamphlets, 37 leaflets, and "Amerika" magazine in Arabic and Yugoslav languages initiated by the Department have been supplemented by several hundred pamphlets and other printed materials created by USIE officers overseas for special local appeal. Distribution of these materials from both sources together is running higher than 10 million items per month, and the great majority of them are being delivered to the final reader by his own local prodemocratic and anti-Communist organization.

Motion pictures

Motion pictures are used in Western Europe and other countries outside the iron curtain both to attack Communist influences on groups infected or threatened by communism, and to inspire free peoples everywhere. This is accomplished through both the techniques for distribution of films as well as by actual program content.

Films are directed to workers, a prime breeding ground of Communist influence, as a primary target. This audience is reached through showings sponsored by labor unions and factory management, through churches and other community organizations where labor can be reached, and through use of commercial theaters for special showings in neighborhoods where industrial workers live. Mobile units present programs in rural agricultural areas where the Communists attempt to win a following.

The films used are specifically aimed at destroying confidence in the U. S. S. R. and communism generally. For example, the Department's film stories of Communist action in Germany, Korea, and the U. N. show that that action is in marked contrast to the stated "peace aims" of the Soviet Union. Moreover, the visible truth about life in the United States, activities of the free nations in the U. N. and under the North Atlantic Treaty is seen to be so different from what the Communists would have other people believe that confidence in the veracity, infallibility and inevitability of communism is shaken.

To inspire confidence in the United States and in the ability of the free world to achieve a good and peaceful future, the Department's films portray the inherent moral, political, and economic strength of the United States. These films vividly demonstrate the character of the American people, their great energy and will to uphold the basic values which free peoples everywhere cherish. This is manifest in pictures of our free institutions—schools, civic clubs, government services, religious and cultural life —in the many practical ways in which we work with other free nations and in our willingness to share our economic and military resources and technical know-how for the common good.

Films being produced abroad aim specifically to strengthen the democratic forces within these countries and to develop confidence in their ability to improve their own living conditions without recourse to communism.

Through the showing of documentary short subjects and newsreels, through loans of films to private organizations and local government agencies abroad, and by its own mobile projector units, USIE is reaching its audiences with these messages at the rate of 400 million persons per year.

Other visual media

Posters—both inspirational art types and photographic news posters— are created for local anti-Communist campaigns, to tell the story of the free world's fight against aggression in Korea, and to carry other themes throughout the world. In special cases, picture-leaflets have been delivered into the heart of Communist-menaced areas. . . . Total audiences run into the hundreds of millions.

Filmstrips and photo displays are used by USIE information centers everywhere, and extended out through the population by use in labor organizations and schools. They carry such messages of warning as "They Always Say No"—the record of Russia's obstruction to U. N. action—and such messages of hope and confidence as "General Eisenhower" and "A

Better Life for Farmer Lin"—the story of the joint Chinese-American program to assist farmers in Formosa.

Press materials

Factual information on the lies and treacheries of international communism and on the strength, progress, and ideals of the United States and other free nations flows steadily into the press of all non-Communist areas from USIE press operations in each country, expressing the basic themes in news, feature articles, photographs, and cartoons. Such material reaches approximately 100 million people through some 10,000 foreign newspapers and magazines, which among them print an average of about 400,000 column inches—equivalent to 2,500 full-size newspaper pages—of USIE materials per month.

Examples of the many types of press material adapted to various purposes and audiences will be found in the answers to later questions. The chief categories are—

News.—A 9,000-word Wireless Bulletin, in five regionalized transmissions, is delivered instantaneously by Morse wireless each day to 67 USIE missions, which in turn distribute it, in local languages, to editors for publication and background information. USIE news reports accurately and with direct quotations the activities of the Congress and executive branch, the United States role in United Nations activities, the programs and acts of recognized private American organizations which combat communism or strengthen the free world cause, and United States editorial comment on world affairs. Supplementing it is an alert and rapid special news service to individual countries and regions, dealing with United States events of special interest to each such country, visitors to the United States, and information requested by USIE officers abroad to help them carry on local programs. Photographs of major events in Washington, the United Nations, in Korea and elsewhere are also provided for foreign publications everywhere.

Feature materials.—Outstanding articles from American magazines and newspapers attacking communism or demonstrating United States principles and accomplishments are copyright-cleared for reprinting by foreign publications. Air Bulletins (clipsheets of brief articles addressed to special audiences such as labor, farmers, etc.) and a variety of staff-written articles are provided, as well as sets of photographs demonstrating long-range themes. To reach remote areas, provincial newspapers and small publications abroad are given ready-made printing plates, made of plastic and carrying both photographs and stinging anti-Communist cartoons from the American press, at the rate of 60,000 per month.

Information centers

A less direct but no less effective method of influencing both target groups outside the iron curtain is provided by the network of USIE information centers and binational centers abroad, currently reaching a total of 180 in 78 countries.

With average libraries of more than 5,000 books, periodicals, Government publications and other printed materials, they are used by national leaders of all types in obtaining information with which to improve their local institutions and combat communism. Government officials engaged in drafting their constitutions and national laws consult corresponding American documents; labor leaders fighting Communist infiltration in their own unions get ammunition on the evils of communism and United States methods of combating it from American books and periodicals.

Through these centers also, local publishers have been encouraged and assisted in printing editions of significant books ("Constitution of the United States and Other Historical Documents," for example, and Kravchenko's "I Chose Freedom"). American books, many of them contributed by United States publishers, are given to key foreign government officials and organization heads; 800,000 or more in this year's program.

Last year, information centers throughout the world recorded a total of 24,000,000 visitors.

Exchange of persons

Most selective of all media, and therefore capable of enormous direct influence on key target groups, is the bringing of foreigners to the United States and sending Americans abroad to exchange knowledge and ideas.

To carry out our basic themes, special attention is being given to visits to the United States by foreign government officials, labor leaders, and important members of the communications professions such as journalists, radio broadcasters, and publishers. More than one-quarter of the some 8,000 exchanges being programed in fiscal year 1952 are in this "leader" category—each of whom can personally influence thousands or millions of his countrymen on his return home. USIE cooperates with the technical exchange program, the foreign economic program, and NATO in such activities. Exchanges serve not only to strengthen the democratic cause outside the iron curtain, but also to undermine Communist strength in free countries. By selection of carefully screened union leaders from labor groups which are Communist strongholds abroad, USIE arms their men with information and know-how, gained from conferences with American anti-Communist leaders in the labor movement, to go home and "clean out" their own unions—to drive out Communist organizers and win back workers who have been duped into following them.

In addition to the great influence which these visitors themselves have, the observations and reactions of leaders, students, and other exchangees are exploited in all media—through radio interviews, press and photographic stories, films, and in information center lectures and other programs—after they return home.

Accomplishments and specific applications of the programs briefly outlined above are illustrated in detail in the responses to questions 4 through 13, which follow.

QUESTION 3

Have you published a handbook of facts and themes against communism used by your employees as a guide in the field of psychological warfare? If so, please attach copy.

The most recent example of such a publication is Guides in Influencing Mass Opinion, produced for the Department of State through the Business Advisory Committee to the Information and Educational Exchange program, of which Mr. Philip Reed, of General Electric, is chairman. The actual work was done by the Young & Rubicam advertising agency through the following circumstances:

At the first meeting of the committee, Mr. Sigurd Larmon, president of Young & Rubicam, offered to assist in improving the Department's program. He was invited by Mr. Barrett to conduct any sort of investigation necessary to arrive at a sound opinion on the entire scope of operations. Mr. Larmon appointed a task force from his agency, who were cleared for security and set to studying our operations. With generous expenditure of time, effort, and expense they prepared this booklet which has now been distributed to USIE staffs in all overseas posts and in Washington and New York.

Another type of material distributed to our employees overseas serves both as a guide to propaganda campaigning and as a source of campaign materials. These are the monthly "kits" which are prepared by the press and publications operation. The first of these kits was wrapped around the title "Essentials of Peace," and exposed the spurious nature of Soviet peace proposals point by point.

The next kit, "Peace of Reconciliation," dealt with the Japanese Peace Treaty as an example of a genuine and just instrument and concept, underlining the contrasts with U. S. S. R. dealings with its conquered peoples.

This was followed by one on "Freedom or Slavery," which cited chapter and verse on Soviet practice, even to including an accurate map of U. S. S. R. slave-labor camps.

The October kit was entitled "Korea: Pattern for Aggression," and showed in detail how the Communist python swallows the colonial sheep.

The kit for November dealt with the history of minority problems in every quarter of the globe, showing (1) that this problem is not uniquely one involving Negroes nor one confined to the United States (whose treatment of Negroes has been viciously slandered by Communist propagandists); (2) that, on the contrary, the problem is universal, and that efforts to wipe it out must be universal; and (3) that, in concrete efforts to wipe it out, the United States is doing rather more than most, and certainly more than the U. S. S. R.

The December kit is a "We-and-they" year-end review of accomplishments versus talks with the obvious implications.

In these kits we use every scrap of telling material, whether from trade books and publications, or specially prepared for us by qualified outside authorities, or assembled by our staff from the wealth of anti-Communist materials used in our regular flow abroad. These kits are particularly useful since the essence of successful propaganda lies in hitting hard on specific issues such as those dealt with in the kits.

Other recent publications distributed include:

"100 Things You Should Know About Communism": Revised December 1, 1950. Prepared and released by the Committee on Un-American Activities, United States House of Representatives.

"The Strategy and Tactics of World Communism": Report of Subcommittee No. 5, Committee on Foreign Affairs, House Document No. 619, with supplements I and II, 1948.

"Confuse and Control—Soviet Techniques in Germany": Department of State Publication 4107, 1951.

All of the regular series of press materials contain factual articles on communism and, in addition, there are two special series devoted exclusively to this subject. . . . These provide USIE offices with material which not only can be infiltrated into publications and radio programs abroad, but also can be used in lectures and personal conversation.

Another series of documents which may be cited in answer to this question is the "USIE Country Program Plan" for each country—more than 80 in all—where USIE operates. These papers are prepared jointly by the field officers under the direction of the chief of mission and by State Department officers. . . .

These country papers contain:

I. Priority information aims and objectives (in each country).
II. Priority target groups.
III. Relation of priority target groups to media.
IV. Statements of evaluation of program.

These country plans are *confidential* and are not printed, but hectographed.

Our employees are provided with a varied arsenal of aids and guides in their work, including not only handbooks and formal policy direction but materials from many sources which will round out their indoctrination in information techniques and the Communist tactics, with which they must cope. One final and interesting example was an article by Jean Paul David, the famous director of the hard-hitting French anti-Communist movement "Paix et Liberté," on the theory and practice of Russian psychological warfare, which was reproduced from the publication United Nations World and distributed to USIE staffs here and abroad.

QUESTION 5

What effort is being made to inform the Chinese and North Korean peoples that they are being used as "cannon fodder" in the interest of Soviet imperialism?

The USIE program, in coordinated action with psychological warfare operations, has driven this theme home daily during Korean hostilities, by radio, leaflets, and airborne loudspeaker units in the fighting areas of Korea, and by radio and printed material channeled to the civilian populations of Red China and North Korea. The same theme is given widespread currency, through a variety of media, in Hong Kong, Formosa, and the Chinese communities of Southeast Asia. We know that without question . . . material so distributed filters back to the Chinese mainland.

Over and over, the Chinese and North Koreans are reminded of the ignoble role that the Kremlin has given them. Acting under specific guidance, USIE media have pointed out the prodigality with which the Communist command has expended Chinese and Korean lives in carrying out Moscow's power drive; the brutal indifference of the Commie rulers to human life, and specifically to the lives of their own forces; the criminal subservience of the Peiping puppets in the sacrifice of Chinese youth on a foreign battlefield in the sole interest of Soviet imperialism, and the senselessness of the Chinese Red's so-called "human sea assault" as a military tactic—a tactic which wins some battles but no decisive engagements, and which bleeds to death the nation employing it.

We have repeatedly pointed out the crudity of the way in which Peiping has aped its Moscow masters, and the tragic manner in which it has thrown away Chinese and Korean lives. We stress that the Chinese people are being used for purposes directly against their own interests, through the servitude of the Chinese Communist leadership to the Kremlin.

We have stressed the truth that Moscow, and Moscow alone, gains from Chinese losses in Korea—in that Chinese dependence on the U. S. S. R. increases as these losses mount, while China's ability to say "no" to her Kremlin bosses vanishes as her manpower is decimated.

Broadcasts driving home these themes have been a regular part of the Voice of America's message to the Far East. The following excerpts from Chinese language transmission are examples:

From News Footnote: "General Chu Teh on the Red Army Day," broadcast 11–11:30 a. m., August 1, 1951:

> All the Chinese people know, say the observers, that Stalin is singularly responsible for the death of untold thousands of young Chinese men and women in Korea.

From News Footnote: "Soviet Use of Chinese Troops," broadcast 8–9 a. m., August 17, 1951:

> The Soviet Union has absolutely no regard for the welfare and safety of the average Chinese Communist soldier in Korea. Most Chinese troops are considered merely "cannon fodder" by their trainers, and they are sent into "human sea" battle with almost no training and a minimum of supplies * * *

It is clear from General Michaelis' testimony—based on 10 months of personal observation—that Chinese Communist troops in Korea are being sacrificed by the Soviet leaders in order to weaken China at home and abroad and make Soviet colonization of China more easy.

From Feature: "Advice from American Longshoremen to Chinese Workers," broadcast 1–1:30 a. m., August 9, 1951:

> * * * the Chinese workers are asked not to serve as socalled "volunteers" in the Communist Army to kill the Koreans and to die in the cause of Soviet territorial expansion. They are asked not to transport military supplies for the Chinese Communists. They are also asked not to participate in any Soviet aggressive activities. Mao and his followers "have gone so far as to put all the Chinese lives at stake and join an aggressive war in Korea against the United Nations."

Instead of aiding Korea as alleged, the Chinese Communist troops are joining the defeated Korean Communists in trying to convert Korea into one of the Soviet colonies * * *

From Commentary: "Comrade Stalin and Mao", broadcast 7:30 p. m., August 13, 1951:

And, as this [Korean] war has dragged on, with a consequent decimation of the flower of China's young manhood, the suspicion has grown within the Chinese Communist Party that the Soviets are allowing the Chinese armies to be decimated in order to harm not only the United Nations but also their Chinese competitors themselves.

Direct tactical propaganda to break enemy morale in the fighting area is always the responsibility of the armed services, although all appropriate USIE resources in Korea are contributed to it.

That the Chinese in Korea are dying for Soviet Russian, not Chinese interests, has been an important propaganda line used by army psychological warfare operations in Korea since the beginning of the Chinese aggression. This message has been driven home by dropping leaflets in the Chinese language behind the Communist lines, by loudspeaker units mounted on low-flying planes, and by radio broadcasts. Chinese prisoners report that propaganda operations have played an important part in inducing Chinese soldiers to surrender in Korea.

The State Department has helped the psychological operations in Korea by lending some of its highly trained Chinese personnel for translation and writing; by supplying suitable printed materials in the Chinese language; and by VOA broadcasts in Chinese designed to stir up discontent and disaffection in the Chinese homeland. State also provides basic guidance on propaganda lines as well as guidance on how to handle special situations which arise.

One leaflet, for North Korean troops, shows North Koreans and Chinese being herded into the Korean battle area by a giant figure of Russia. It asks five "Questions that every North Korean soldier should answer for himself," ending with: "What will your family and your mother country gain if you lose your life fighting for Soviet Russia's imperialism?"

Another Korean-language leaflet showed the Soviet "old brother" pushing North Korean and Chinese troops into battle, then refusing them military aid, and finally handing them a cease-fire pact and saying, "Talk about peace for a while." Then the leaflet asked: "But does he really want peace? Or does he wish to gain time and then sacrifice more North Korean and Chinese soldiers in another useless attack?"

A Chinese-language leaflet shows two hairy hands from the North reaching down to tear Manchuria and Outer Mongolia away from China. "Protect your country and family?" it asks. "If so, why don't you do it at home?" After reciting Russia's seizures of Chinese possessions and sacrifice of Chinese lives to her own ambitions, it says: "From the so-called Sino-Korean friendship, you get nothing but abundance of cold water. From the so-called Sino-Russian friendship, death is your only fate. * * *"

Another psychological warfare leaflet in Chinese shows a Chinese figure cramming Chinese troops into the breach of a cannon, while Russia applauds. It is titled: "Be Not Cannon Fodder for Others!"

Similar messages in both languages are poured down on Chinese and North Korean lines from loudspeakers mounted in low-flying planes, causing many desertions.

These, it should be reiterated, are military psychological warfare operations, but they form a consistent pattern with USIE operations against the Communist "home front".

USIE Hong Kong, in cooperation with the regional production center at Manila and the Department, serves as a center for production of Chinese publications to be read both inside and outside Red China. A biweekly Chinese language magazine, "America Today" is distributed in 125,000 copies among Chinese professional, business, and school groups throughout the area. A special small newsletter is produced weekly in 10,000 copies, numbers of which find their way into Red China as previously described. Posters, leaflets, and cartoon pamphlets also carry out the "cannon fodder" theme.

For example, a single recent issue of "America Today" carried the following cartoons:

> Russian offering a Chinese a dinner of bomb, hammer, and sickle.
> Schoolmaster Stalin standing over his pupil Mao.
> Chinese Red ordering civilians to don uniforms and march into a cannon mouth, from which they emerge as skeletons. Caption: "This is what is called 'The People's Volunteer Forces'."
> The dove of peace spitted on a sickle.
> Stalin, Red China, and North Korea tossing peace in a blanket.
> Stalin, acting as prompter to China and North Korea, giving a concert.
> Stalin, as a deer hunter, holding antlers and a hammer and sickle over his head for concealment.

Typical cartoon pamphlets are a cartoon book on the fate of a farm family under North Korean Red rule mentioned elsewhere, which depicts (among other things) the conscription of peaceful North Korean farm boys into the Red army (appendix 5–A) and one which tells the experience of a Chinese doctor in the Red army who was deceived into thinking he was defending North Korea from invading Americans, but learned that the Russians had instigated the war and that Chinese Reds under Moscow orders were recklessly sacrificing their armies. . . .

Individual cartoons, from the American press and locally drawn, reiterate the theme again and again. A cartoon showing Mao shoveling regiment after regiment of Chinese into the cannon's mouth, while Stalin stands by approvingly, was serviced by the Department to all posts in contact with Chinese populations, for use in Chinese-language newspapers, and was also converted by Hong Kong into a striking poster. Another poster shows Stalin herding Chinese into a box from which they emerge as lambs and are cast into the flames. A third, for Chinese populations in southeast Asia, uses a collection of 13 cartoons from the United States press on Russia's sacrifice of lives and destruction of world peace.

From prisoners of war close behind the lines in Korea, USIE radio and press reporters are obtaining a stream of voluntary interviews which are played back to Chinese on both sides of the Asian iron curtain. Some recent interview themes were:

"Reds Use Chinese as Cannon Fodder, says U. N. P. O. W."
"Chinese Prisoner of War Urges China to 'Wake Up'."
"Chinese Soldier Denounces Communists."
"Captured Chinese Says Real Enemy is Russia."
"Communists Plan to Enslave China, Chinese Army Doctor Tells His People."
"Chinese Prisoner Wants to Fight for United Nations."
"Chinese Physician, Prisoner of War in Korea, Recounts Red Betrayal of China."

QUESTION 6

What effort is being made to inform colonial countries especially in the Far and Near East, that Soviet domination has nothing in common with national independence and that only the democracies can guarantee such independence?

As all the world knows, the biggest and most successful use the Kremlin makes of the "technique of the big lie" in the expansion of Soviet imperialism is Moscow's adoption of the theme that international communism stands for freedom, for escape from exploitation, and for anticolonialism.

This lie has been glaringly exposed over and over again, but it does not die easily. It remains—and will remain—one of our greatest problems in colonial and newly independent areas.

To Asians and Africans, we are part of the white-skinned "West" from which the colonial masters of the last few centuries have come. Some of our chief allies in resisting Communist expansion throughout the world are also the chief colonial powers. When we step in to prevent Communist penetration of any area, we are misrepresented by Communist propaganda as seeking to perpetuate colonial rule or substitute ourselves for the old rulers.

Of course, the United States has one special asset, which has won us friendship and trust among colonial peoples: the fact that we ourselves emerged from colonial status through revolution. This was well demonstrated, for example, by recent editorials in Iran, which though independent now sees itself as throwing off the economic imperialism of Great Britain. These editorials welcomed American participation in oil negotiations because—

* * * Mr. Harriman represents a nation well acquainted with the evils of foreign imperialism—

and, again:

* * * Mr. Harriman will not leave the path trod by his forebears * * * who knew how to get rid of their British overlords.

But valuable as it is, this "asset" has a corresponding major liability: Colonial peoples and peoples who believe themselves oppressed by any form of foreign exploitation can easily look to American for "revolutionary" assistance. If our aim were mere popularity, rather than an integrated defense of the free world, it would be easy to win that popularity by encouraging the reckless throwing off of bonds and breaking of foreign ties by peoples without sufficient military strength or governmental experience. But by so doing we would simply expose them to being gobbled up by the new Soviet imperialism.

To promote the proper course of evolution toward independence, without being suspected of proimperialism on the one hand or recklessly exposing innocent peoples to Communist domination on the other, is one of our most difficult and challenging tasks.

Nonetheless, we meet the challenge frontally, and have applied the full force of all media available to us to countering the cynical Soviet appeal to the colonial desire for freedom, "helped" by Stalin.

Primarily, our attack has been through turning the full glare of publicity on recent history, setting the record of the western democracies side by side with the record of nations "helped" by Moscow. An example of the implementation of this theme is a graphic pamphlet, prepared in pilot model in America and furnished USIE posts for local reproduction, which documents with colored maps and simple facts the glaring truth that since 1939 Russia has annexed or taken control of more than 13 million square kilometers of land containing 574 million people, while the United States, Britain, and the Netherlands have given independence to more than 6 million square kilometers and 545 million people. . . .

To demonstrate the true nature of Communist "liberation" in gripping human terms, for people of minimum literacy, the Department and USIE Korea collaborated in producing a true-to-life cartoon story. Based on interviews with North Koreans, this cartoon book tells a dramatic story of a Korean farmer and his family and their sufferings—how the Russians drove out the Japanese and set up a North Korean "People's Republic" which seized crops, forced young men into the Army, introduced thought control, and finally plunged North Korea into a bloody aggressive war. More than 700,000 copies are printed or in production.

A leaflet now being printed in many countries proves communism guilty of deliberate aggression in Korea by quoting battle orders, issued before June 25, 1950, to the North Korean Army and Soviet observers.

The same picture is presented, in documentary but readable form by the text, "North Korea: Soviet Satellite," which has been forwarded to all USIE offices abroad for use in pamphlets, magazine articles, and for newspaper serialization. Based on North Korean Government documents, court decisions, and correspondence plus the testimony of North Koreans, collected during the U. N. advance into North Korea in the fall of 1950, it provides a gripping broadside view of Moscow-directed police rule, thought control, religious persecution, oppression of farmers and labor, and Russian economic domination which the North Korean Red regime had inflicted on the "liberated" former Japanese colony.

To show how the free world helps its dependencies to assume self-rule and build a better life, another pamphlet tells the story of Puerto Rico

—"A People Moves Ahead." Describing how the United States has helped and encouraged Puerto Ricans to solve their economic problems, improve housing, education, and health, and assume more and more self-government, it concludes with an inspiring statement by the island's first native Governor.

Again, to dramatize the attitude of the democracies (and the United States in particular) toward underdeveloped areas, the pamphlet "Point Four" shows how this country is cooperating with local authorities in colonial, newly independent and free countries throughout the world in improving standards of living and health.

These pamphlets are, of course, only a part of the story. We use all available media to pound home to colonial countries, or countries that have acquired national independence in recent times, that the Soviet regime has not the remotest desire to strengthen the independence of those nations that have recently acquired independence, or to bring about the independence of those entities not now free—that their future as free nations is threatened by Russian imperialism and Communist tyranny, and that native Red leaders who claim to be patriots actually are Russia's servants and stooges.

Simultaneously we use all media to show the very real progress made by various peoples in acquiring and strengthening their independence with the aid of the democracies, including, of course, the United States. All our output seeks to inform and persuade all peoples who have recently acquired independence, and dependent peoples generally, that their future is best assured by the enlightened and humane policies and practices of the democracies.

How these and similar themes are spread to colonial and excolonial areas by various media is summarized below:

Radio broadcasting (Voice of America)

We broadcast to the Far and Near East in English, in Arabic, in Urdu and Hindi, in Thai, Vietnamese, Burmese, Russian, Indonesian, Malayan, in four major dialects of China, and in Korean. The broadcasts are transmitted in short wave, some are rebroadcast at relaying bases in medium wave. In addition, a great deal of material is placed by our information officers in the foreign service posts with the local radio stations.

In West Africa, for example, a nightly local broadcast has been set up on a Liberian station which reaches the British colonies of Nigeria and Gold Coast and offsets a Soviet broadcast to these areas. VOA is also being beamed southward from Tangier to be picked up and rebroadcast from Liberia. In Libya, the one-time Italian colony just attaining independence, local USIE broadcasts in Arabic, French, and English go out over Army transmitters, supplemented by printed news bulletins distributed into the desert to tribal chieftains.

The burden of our radio programs is that with the help of the United States Government's policy and influence, backed by the public opinion and the material and moral support of the American people, "colonial countries," especially in the Far East, have all but disappeared. In Burma, Thailand, Indonesia, the Philippines complete independence has been achieved and guaranteed through the good will of the Western Powers, the telling influence of American diplomacy, and by peaceful development and political negotiations.

Because this record is so clear, communism's new "line" is that the old colonial powers and the old colonialism is being replaced by a new, American colonialism. But Voice of America broadcasts counter this effectively by stressing the traditional Lincolnian American stand in regard to the independence of our own Nation and of other nations (government of the people, by the people, and for the people); and by informing the audiences about ECA and point 4 aid rendered to "underdeveloped" (not backward) countries. We contrast this to the practices of Soviet colonialism in Soviet subjugated countries which include not only a domination over the economic life of the subjugated areas but over the spiritual, educational, and family life as well.

Here is how one such broadcast, "Facts Behind the News No. 4," echoed the "Who Is The Imperialist?" theme:

> Look how the world map has changed since 1939. Of course, you are talking about the way the Soviet Union has taken more and more land. But many changes on the map are victories for freedom. We see the new and independent Republics of India, Pakistan, Indonesia, Burma, and the Philippines. Yes; and remember that England freely agreed to India's independence. The United States also freely promised independence to the Philippines, and kept that promise in 1946. But now look at the Soviet Union's borders in Europe. In 1938 Soviet troops invaded little Finland. In 1939 the Red Army joined Nazi troops in conquering Poland. After the war the Soviet Union took land from Rumania, Poland, and Czechoslovakia. The Soviet Union also took all of the three Baltic States: Estonia, Latvia, and Lithuania. But what about the satellite countries, the rest of the land behind the iron curtain? These countries have also fallen under Soviet control. Yes; of course. The head of the Communist Army in Poland is a Soviet citizen, General Rokosovsky. The armies of the other satellite countries are also controlled by Soviet officers. In Manchuria, Soviet troops control the ports and railways. Yes; the map tells the story of Soviet expansion by conquest of weaker neighbors. Those are facts.

Other radio programs broadcast around the same period were: "Soviet Statements on War and Peace," "No Strings to United States Aid," "Soviet Imperialism Plunders Asia," "The Birth of Soviet Slavery," and "The Stalinist System of Progressive Domination Over the Peasants."

Special Commentary No. 566, "Comrades Stalin and Mao," broadcast August 17, 1951, again underlined Soviet imperialism:

> * * * This subservience of Peiping to Moscow will continue to exist as long as the Chinese continue to honor the Sino-Soviet Friendship Pact, which firmly cements their economy to the needs of the Soviet Union and simultaneously cuts them off from contact—whether economic or cultural—with the free world.
>
> Under the terms of this pact * * * there was imposed upon China a system of "joint" exploitation of major Chinese industrial

resources and enterprises and a pattern of trade lopsidedly favorable to the Soviet Union. Likewise, the practice was begun of funelling all Chinese exports into the Soviet Union for resale.

Until lately, Chinese resentment for the Soviets was expressed by slow and silent resistance, passive dodging, and subtle frustration. More recently, however—and especially since the knowledge has spread of China's enormous losses in the Soviet-inspired Korean war —this resentment has changed to overt hostility.

"Press Opinion U. S. A.," August 13, 1951, quoted a "New Orleans Times Picayune" editorial based on a statement by I. Lubin, United States delegate to UNESCO, to demonstrate Moscow's true disinterest in the cause of human need:

> For the U. N. Children's Emergency Fund—"exactly zero." For the Palestine refugee organization—"precisely nothing." For the International Refugee Organization—"the Soviet Union has made no contribution." For the World Health Organization—"the Soviet Union failed to pay its assessment." For the International Bank for Reconstruction and Development—"not a single cent." For Korean relief— "not a penny." For the U. N. technical assistance program—"not a single ruble," is the record of the Soviet Union in the United Nations program for underdeveloped and distressed areas. And instead of aiding U. N. causes—the editorial remarks—the Moscow Government has been the largest contributor to human misery and suffering since the elimination and defeat of the Axis powers.

The "New York Herald Tribune" was quoted in connection with the same issue:

> Countless beneficiaries of United Nations aid mistakenly assume that—because the Soviet Union is a United Nations member—it is also a contributor to the help they are receiving. They should be set right. Dr. Lubin's statement should be carried around the world.[1] It answers a dangerous Soviet myth in a way that the most underprivileged person can understand. In short—any resemblance between Stalin and Santa Claus is purely imaginary.

Voice of America programs to the Near East repeatedly deal specifically with particular dangers confronting that area as a result of Soviet policies and practices—the territorial, political, cultural, and economic designs of the Kremlin, etc.

Thus, VOA's Arabic service, reaching both the Arabic-speaking African colonies and the newly independent states, such as Syria and Transjordan, said September 7, 1951:

> I discussed with various members of the Arab delegation attending the San Francisco Conference the brilliant statement made by the representative of Ceylon, Mr. Jayewardeme, attacking Soviet imperialism and intrigues and debunking Gromyko and Company assertions that the Soviet Union is the champion of democracy and the people.

[1] It was—by radio broadcasts, the Wireless Bulletin, and a leaflet. . . .

The Arab delegations, prominent among whom were the Egyptian Ambassador, the Ambassador of Saudi Arabia, the Lebanese Minister, and the Iraqui Chargé d'Affairs, gave me a reply which was unanimous. The substance of the reply was as follows:

We are not surprised that Mr. Jayewardeme rose to the occasion in answering the Soviet allegations, because the Asiatic peoples, if they don't know now, will soon realize that (it is quite audacious) on the part of the Kremlin to pose as the champion of the Asiatic peoples, as if these peoples had no life of their own, nor any officially designated representatives. We are here representing independent, sovereign countries. As Arab states, most of our countries are in Asia and even we think it very bad taste on the part of Gromyko to self-style himself as spokesman of the whole of Asia.

Exchange of persons

This program, although numbers exchanged are necessarily small, is of special importance in colonial areas. People relatively untrained in democratic practices need that training in order to build soundly toward independence. And because they have seen fewer examples of democracy and of how democratic institutions work successfully, they are more susceptible to the lure of pretended magic, overnight solutions to all problems which the Communists offer.

Because there is so much for colonial peoples to learn, special attention is paid to selecting candidates who are receptive and who will be able to express themselves and pass on what they have learned to others.

For example, the Nigerian labor leader, Adioh Moses, was brought to this country to visit American labor unions and attend a major union convention. He expressed himself as very much impressed by the responsibility accorded to labor organizations and the corresponding sense of responsibility which their leaders felt—a lesson which will obviously serve as an antidote for Communist propaganda that only under the so-called "rule of the proletariat" can labor maintain its rights.

From the British Gold Coast came a leading journalist who, in addition to observing democracy in general, made a study of United States principles of honest journalism—a step toward developing, in this colony, the kind of press which any people needs for effective self-rule.

A teacher has been supplied, under the Smith-Mundt Act, to a private American school in Tangier, the crossroads of the north African colonial area, and USIE is negotiating with a private foundation for additional aid. The USIE public-affairs officer inspired the founding of the school by a group of local Moroccans and Americans, and it already has pupils from 11 countries and dependencies, including all the French African colonies.

Motion pictures

The motion-picture program in colonial areas is a powerful means of bridging gaps of experience. It gives the people of these generally remote and underprivileged areas a visual image of the far-off American people and how they think and live. With this background image, they can begin to conceive of America's interest in their independence, and of what this independence might mean for them. Without it, they would remain dangerously susceptible to the magic cures which local Communist agitators offer them on their own soil, in their own terms.

Such films as "Blue Ribbon," the story of 4-H Club activities, "Ohio Town," "The Doctor," and "The School" show them United States democracy in action, in rural and small-town settings they can grasp, and in terms of agricultural progress, health, and education which touch on their own immediate needs.

Newsreel stories of Communist obstruction and Soviet imperialistic aims and actions are fed into newsreel channels for overseas distribution at every opportunity. Such stories include positions taken by Soviet Union and satellite nations on issues before the U. N., stories of refugees from the U. S. S. R. and the satellite countries, and similar items that serve to show that communism and national independence are incompatible.

United States information centers

In United States information centers in each of the colonial and formerly colonial countries of the Far and Near East, materials exposing the true nature of communism generally, and of the imperialist policies and practices of the Soviet policy in particular are available in quantity, both in book and in pamphlet form. Contrasting with the story they tell are other books, pamphlets, and exhibits, lectures, film and filmstrip showings, demonstrating the American philosophy and actual practice of democracy at home and abroad.

This story was already being carried, in colonial Asia and Africa, at Honk Kong, Nairobi (Kenya), Singapore, Accra (Gold Coast), and in two Indochina centers. With the stepped-up program, centers were added at two other Indochina posts, at Kowloon (Hong Kong territory), Lagos (Nigeria), Leopoldville (Belgian Congo), Dakar (Senegal), and Luanda (Portuguese Angola), and loans and special showings extended to more schools and local libraries in colonial areas.

A striking example of the direct effect of providing such information to colonial and newly independent peoples occurred in Burma. As that nation attained its independence, one regular user of the USIE library in Rangoon was the Honorable U Chan Htoon, attorney general of Burma, who has been called the "father of the Burmese Constitution." From USIE's collection of books on American government, he was able to study the reasoning followed by the writers of the American Constitution and the factors which influenced them in creating the constitutional system of checks and balances and the Bill of Rights, and apply this knowledge to the shaping of Burma's own constitution. He expressed deep appreciation for the help he received.

Press and publications

Examples from the various pamphlets and leaflets which carry our dual message to colonies and newly independent ex-colonies are given at the beginning of this question.

Greatly increased attention has been given to press materials for all colonial areas within the last year. Newspapers, although their circulation seems relatively small, do reach the very group of literate, active political leaders, educators, and relatively advanced city dwellers who are planning for future independence and will lead each country as it attains self-rule.

The Wireless Bulletin, although transmitted to all independent areas in Asia and Africa, until a year ago went direct to only four of the colonies and dependencies—Indochina, Hong Kong, Malaya, and Tangier. With the aid of Campaign of Truth resources, direct monitoring and rapid local distribution have been established in Algiers, Tripoli (Libya), and Nairobi (Kenya), and arrangements have been completed to start in Lagos (Nigeria) and Accra (Gold Coast). Installation in Liberia has also improved relaying by mail to nearby colonial areas, as well as contributed to the west African broadcasts from Liberia previously mentioned.

Features, articles, photographs, and plastic printing plates of photographs, and picture exhibits also go to all colonial areas with good effect. In the central African colonies especially, Communist propaganda has attempted to arouse doubt about the good intentions of the United States by stressing the "color line"—by exaggerating and distorting race relations problems in this country and implying that a nation which (allegedly) mistreats its own Negro population can hardly be a sincere friend to Negro peoples in Africa. We have countered this with a continuous flow of materials about United States Negroes and their place and achievements in the United States—Dr. Ralph Bunche and Mrs. Edith Sampson, Negroes in the Armed Forces, in science, education, and business. For example, one set of exhibit photos, "A Southern United States Farmer," showed how Stokes King and his family live near Greenville, Miss., with their own 80-acre farm, farm machinery, and a comfortable house. There is no emphasis—in fact, no mention—of the fact that the King family are Negroes; the pictures tell the story.

Plastic-plate photo engravings, with which even the poorest small newspaper can afford to print our photographs, are invaluable in colonial areas. The USIE officer at Luanda, in Portuguese Angola, reported:

> The Luanda press, which has limited wire-service material, has given 100 percent coverage in plastic plates relating to the Soviet menace.

Typical of such material is a cartoon from the "Akron Beacon Journal," showing Stalin secretly writing up his timetable for world conquest. Such cartoons are distributed at the rate of several a week, as plastic plates in English and six other languages.

Typical of recent news material and articles especially pertinent for colonial areas used during the period of the Senator's question were:

Wireless Bulletin:

> Truman Commends Writing of Puerto Rican Constitution.
> Soviet Satellites Compared with Former Western Colonies.
> Acheson Says Strong Defense Would Enable U. S. to Aid Mid-East More.
> Soviet Banishes and Liquidates Minorities, Says N. Y. Times.
> Soviet Colonization Brings Harvest of Ill Will, Says N. Y. Times.
> Bombay Chronicle Cites Soviet Ruthlessness (With Satellites).
> U. S. Senator (Douglas) Tells of American People's Friendship for Asia.

Mailed articles:

The Philippines.

Puerto Rico.

The Hawaiian Islands.

Alaska.

U. S. Seeks Asian Friendship, Senator (Green) Says.

The Moscow-Peiping Plot Against Asia's Freedom—Reprint from "The American Federationist."

The New Frontiers of the Soviet Union—Reprint from "Foreign Affairs" Magazine.

Sinkiang's Plight Under Chinese Communist Regime Depicted.

Communist Imperialism Drops Its Cloak in Indo-China.

"Familiar Pattern"—staff column on "liberation" of Tibet.

QUESTION 10

What is the explanation of our apparent abject failure in convincing India of our aims relative to Japan, Formosa, Nationalist China, as reflected in India's attitude toward us in Korea and as regards the Japanese Peace Treaty?

At the outset, we must reject the premise that—

India's attitude toward us in Korea and as regards the Japanese Peace Treaty * * * reflect * * * apparent abject failure in convincing India of our aims relative to Japan, Formosa [and] Nationalist China.

Despite the very real difficulties that have handicapped us in our Indian program, and despite admitted shortcomings in this program, there is ample evidence that, while we have not effected total Indian support for American moves in Asia, we have succeeded to a significant degree in "convincing India of [the rightness of] our aims" relative to Asia.

Throughout this discussion it should be borne in mind that our information activities represent only one facet of the influences bearing on Indo-American relations. The international political and economic activities of the United States in general, domestic events in America, and conflicting views among Americans on many issues—all reported through commercial communications channels of several nations in frequently sensational form—also affect India's understanding of the United States. They do not lessen USIE's responsibility for bringing about better relations, but they must be taken into account as part of our problem.

Before examining the USIE program to India, and seeking explanation for the relative weakness of the program's effect on the shape of Indian policy, it may be fruitful to review the facts of India's "attitude toward us in Korea and toward the Japanese treaty," in order to establish just what these attitudes do signify.

With first reference to Korea, India voted with us in support of United Nations measures to resist North Korean aggression, and she herself sent a medical unit to serve U. N. Korean forces, as a manifest of her support. The over-all orientation of Indian policy, as stated September 19 by Madam Pandit, Indian Ambassador to the United States and sister of the Prime Minister, is proclaimed as—

> * * * pro-U. N., pro-free nations. We deplore the word "neutralism" as applied to us in our situation. We are members of the U. N.; we stand with you for freedom, equality, orderly justice, and a world at peace. In recent sessions of the U. N. General Assembly we voted as you did 38 times out of 51, abstaining 11 times and differing from you only twice. * * *

The failure of India to walk in step with us the whole of the course in Korea has stemmed, she has made it plain, from the fact that India, like Great Britain and some other free nations, has chosen to recognize the Communist government of Peiping and to withhold recognition from the Nationalist Government of China now based on Formosa. India was the first non-Communist Government to extend recognition to Communist China; the simple geographic fact that Red China is India's most powerful close neighbor must be borne in mind when evaluating the course of India's foreign policy. India has now seen Tibet, the last buffer between herself and Red China, succumb to Red pressure. The fact of India's geographical location does much to help us understand, though not to agree with, the orientation of India's foreign policy.

India argues that her recognition of Red China is not to be read as a lack of entente with the West. As expressed by Madam Pandit:

> It is important, however, that areas of disagreement among friends should also be understood. As to Chinese recognition, we believe the free nations will be served by our recognition of China, just as the United Kingdom believes this by her recognition. We recognize that this may appear to be a difference, but it is a different approach in attempting to achieve the same goal—a democratic, peaceful world, and our nation as a bulwark of freedom in Asia.

India's course with regard to the Japanese Peace Treaty is a direct outgrowth of Indian recognition of Red China and of the Indian view that a basic prerequisite for long-term peace in Asia is that the Peiping government be party to all arrangements and agreements designed to secure peace. India's attitude toward Formosa is based on the same primary policy factor; nonrecognition of the Nationalist Government on Formosa and recognition of Red China.

That "India's attitude toward * * * the Japanese Peace Treaty" did not reflect "abject failure in convincing India of our aims" was evidenced by the very note in which, on August 28, Prime Minister Nehru declined to sign the treaty. In this note, Nehru reaffirmed India's community of aims with America, saying:

> The Government of India hopes that the observations made in the foregoing paragraphs reveal a unity of outlook between them and the Government of the United States in many vital matters that affect the future of the people of Asia and of humanity in general. The differences that exist between them are differences of method and

approach. Such divergencies of opinion are bound to occur even amongst the friendliest nations and should not be allowed to cause resentment that might come in the way of mutual understanding and community of effort.

That India's failure to attend at San Francisco gave no aid and comfort to the Indian Communist was apparent. Shortly after the announcement of the Prime Minister's decision, the Communist Party of India issued a statement condemning failure to send Indian delegates to the treaty ceremony. Delegates should be sent, this statement argued, so that they might insist that Formosa be turned over to Red China, might demand that United States troops leave Japan, and might agitate for restrictions on Japanese armament. In short, Indian Communists should have preferred to follow the course taken by Moscow—to send delegates, as did the U. S. S. R., to use the San Francisco Conference as a rostrum for Red propaganda.

Despite its absence from San Francisco, India has only recently announced its intention of entering into a bilateral treaty with Japan which will not contain provisions contrary to those of the Japanese Peace Treaty concluded at San Francisco. In this bilateral treaty the Indian Government intends to stipulate provisions which will secure to it and to the nationals of India all rights, privileges, indemnities, and advantages, together with the right to enforce them, which, under the treaty of San Francisco, have been stipulated in favor of the allied powers and their nationals.

Summarizing the above examination of question 10, we believe it fair to conclude that—

1. India's attitude toward American policy in Korea and toward the Japanese Peace Treaty cannot fairly be taken as evidence of "abject failure in convincing India of our aims relative to Japan, Formosa, and Communist China."

2. There is ample evidence that both the Indian leadership and the great majority of the masses of the Indian people understand, respect, and concur in American aims in Asia; that they accept these aims as nonimperialist, and believe them honestly devoted to achieving the cause of world peace, freedom, and democracy.

3. In two respects we have not succeeded:

(a) We have yet to convince Indian leadership and peoples that the policies we have adopted in Asia are in all cases wise and best calculated to achieve our objectives, which are fundamentally the same as those of India.

(b) We have not completely destroyed the hard-dying stereotype of "western imperialism" as applied to the United States, and have not fully convinced India that Soviet imperialism is the true and deeply real threat over India today.

Having granted that we have fallen short of these two objectives, we must seek explanations.

It is our sincere convicion that both these matters are failures of degree, not of direction. We believe that our program to India has been "right" across the boards—and has been effective—but that it has been insufficient. Our failure has not been failure to do—but failure to do enough.

The United States is endeavoring, through diplomatic channels as well as in its information activities, to bring India closer to our point of view. The USIE program has delivered an ever-increasing flow of motion pictures, news stories, photos, posters, magazines, and cartoons to India exposing the hand of the U. S. S. R. in China and Korea; demonstrating the strength of collective action against aggression and alerting India to the imminent threats to her own security—increasing her awareness that she may be next on Moscow's timetable.

In discussing and reporting on topics such as Korea, the threat of Red China and Soviet imperialism, USIE places emphasis on the steadfast determination of the United States, working in cooperation with the free nations of the world, to resist aggression. USIE constantly points up the threat of Communist expansionism, discloses the emptiness of Communist promises of well-being for its subjects, and denies the sincerity of Communist pretensions that they are "peacemakers."

One effective method used is giving currency to the testimony of Indians and other Asians. A steady flow of material by Indian and other eastern authors putting forward America's story, is maintained. Typical of these were a recent article contrasting American and Soviet treatment of far-eastern peoples; a series of articles on Red China by an Indian journalist, and an interview with a Soviet defector widely known to Indians. All such articles are given widest possible placement.

This Indian-speaking-to-Indian technique attains even more enduring effects through the exchange-of-persons program and through USIE assistance in privately sponsored tours of the United States. One Indian journalist who visited the United States recently under private auspices, and who was aided by USIE's Washington staff, later forwarded clippings of editorials he had written since his return.

> My fortnight tour in the United States　*　*　*　helped me a lot in understanding a great country—

he wrote.

> Since my return, I have been trying my best to place my views about the U. S. A. vis-à-vis India before our people.

Radio, press materials, pamphlets, and local USIE activities have kept up a steady stream of patient, temperate explanations of United States goals and attitudes in world affairs. To supplement placement of such materials in the Indian press, and insure that they reach all government officials and other leaders, the USIE offices in India prepare a weekly printed news review, "American Reporter" in the nine chief languages. A typical issue of the Marathi-language edition reports that "America has shipped 400,000 tons of loan wheat to India in 3 months"; reprints a statement by the Indian Ambassador to the United States, Mrs. Pandit, titled "India Stands With Free Nations for Peace"; reports on other United States help to India; and explains the terms of the Japanese Peace Treaty: "New Japan pledged to work for world peace and prosperity."

Pamphlets recently distributed in India include "Atomic Energy—for War or Peace?", the President's Fourth of July "Message to All Freedom Lovers," "What America Stands For," and "America's Foreign Policy."

Meanwhile, USIE has shown films to more than 400,000 persons per month—films which illustrate the strength and stability of American society, and increase confidence in our ability to meet our international commitments.

The USIE library program, which makes available books on current issues and publications such as Time, the New York Times, and Newsweek, as well as United States Government publications, reaches other important groups with American interpretations of international events. On a person-to-person basis, and by mail, material explaining the United States position on issues such as recognition of Red China, the Stockholm peace petition, and Korea—including speeches made by Department of State spokesmen and other representatives in the U. N.—are distributed to numerous individuals and organizations. Many of these are primary "targets" in our information program planning, such as university political societies.

This broad confidence-building effort does not preclude plain talk. When the issue of the Japanese treaty arose, the American point of view on the Japanese treaty was presented frankly and forcefully, before the Conference, by VOA broadcasts and through USIE press releases, and our reaction to the Prime Minister's decision against attending was made unmistakably clear. Within the first 5 days after the Indian announcement, for example, press material to India included the full text of the stiff United States reply to Prime Minister Nehru's letter; a round-up of largely adverse American editorial comment on India's position; a second round-up of American editorial reaction; a story of Senator McCarran's criticism of the Indian position; another quoting Mrs. Roosevelt's "regrets"; and a reemphasis of Secretary Acheson's statement that the Treaty Conference would be a test of the desire for peace held by the nations invited.

This is the sort of thing we have been doing, to the limit of our present staff potential. Yet, we fully recognize that our impact on India falls far short of our goal. Why?

The sheer immensity of the Indian target must be borne in mind—and the limitations inherent in any program aimed at India. India's land mass and population are staggering in scale. To carry a message to the Indian people, one must speak dozens of tongues; must literally create communications media; and must cover vast areas. Economic and literacy factors, too, put severe handicaps on use of the usual media of the printed word, radio, and films. Face-to-face operation is almost essential.

With missions at Bangalore, Bombay, Calcutta, Hyderabad-Daccan, Lucknow, Madras, New Delhi, and Old Delhi, and with mobile operations in provincial areas, USIE recognizes that it is only beginning to scratch the surface. We know that although our expanding film program now reaches 400,000 persons per month, there are millions each month who still do not see our films—and that it would, at this rate, take us more than 70 years to reach all of India's 342,000,000—further expansion is a "must." Similarly, we recognize that the impact of press material is limited by the factors of literacy and the Indian press medium itself. We are building display activities and simple-text publications programs to get around literacy limitations. All these things are being done—but there is a limit to the speed with which we can accomplish them.

The sheer magnitude of our USIE problem in India is one explanation of our limited success to date. A second lies in the suddenness with which this problem has been thrust upon America.

Until 1947 India was an integral part of the British world. As such, it was not a prime "target country" for the USIE program in the sense that this term is used in our program.

Overnight it became imperative that America tell its own story on India direct; it became simultaneously urgent that we open up channels of communication to the peoples of India—and that we exploit these channels to the utmost to put our own story across. The immediacy of the world situation made it impossible for us to move in orderly fashion through the usual processes of opening offices, building friendships, carefully selecting and training personnel, creating an audience, and then building upon this foundation—we were forced to run before ever we were prepared to walk.

In our attempt to expand USIE operations throughout India, we have been hampered by a very real difficulty in recruiting personnel of sufficient background to undertake the USIE task in this delicate area. Staffing has been a slow process, and, quite candidly, we have not yet obtained a full staff of the type we should like to see on duty.

A third major inhibitory factor limiting the effectiveness of our program in India can be found in the nature of the target and of the task itself. Our problem in India has been complex and difficult.

It must be remembered that India, as a new nation, is as proud of its independence and as wary of foreign domination as was the United States in 1790. It views the activities of any western power in Asia with a suspicion akin to that which Americans accord to European intervention in the Western Hemisphere.

Americans, deeply laced into the world's affairs today through such programs as the Marshall plan, the Truman doctrine, NATO, and the like, can still recall the century when the Republic avoided "all foreign entanglements." The same desire to forswear too-close alinement with any single foreign power now motivates the infant Indian nation.

India's independence is so new that Indians tend to see every evidence of foreign interest or influence in Asia, regardless of motivation, as a drive toward imperialist domination. India finds it difficult to break the habit of battling against "western imperialism," and to accept that this war is won.

For this reason, USIE has had to carry out all its activities in such wise that they will not "oversucceed"—will not be of such drive, fervor, and intensity that the Indian will read into them an "imperialist" push. While it is urgent that we make America's aims, actions, and ideals eminently clear to India, it is equally urgent that we avoid any semblance of "putting on an imperialistic propaganda drive." All of our expansion has had to be effected with careful recognition of the fact that India, with centuries of thinking colored by yesterday's western imperialism, finds it hard to believe in a dispassionately humanitarian, freedom-loving West fighting for a free world, a West without territorial ambition or desire to dominate.

Indians have been accustomed, in the past, to hearing western imperialism advancing moral and political arguments for maintaining troops and political administrators on Asian soil—arguments more convincing to westerners than to Indians themselves. Thus today, although the United States is associated with the United Nations in Korea to repel aggression and to permit Asians to run their own affairs, this fact is difficult for Asians and Indians to accept at face value, in the light of their experience.

To recapitulate, in reply to question 10, we feel that there has been far from "abject failure" in convincing India of our aims relative to Japan, Formosa, and Nationalist China. We feel that, to a remarkable degree, we have maintained and extended the Indian belief in America's lack of imperialist aims and America's support of independence and freedom for all peoples.

We believe we have failed, so far, simply because the time has been too brief, the target too diffuse, the task too huge, the message too alien to India's experience, to permit of overnight success. We feel that, within the limitations of time and potentials, we are succeeding. We are encouraged by the emergence of thinking such as the following, from Indian press editorials written by the recipient of a USIE leader grant after his return from America:

* * * By alienating the Anglo-American bloc have we won the good opinion of the Communist Powers? We don't think so. * * * It is not enough to say that India stands for peace and for nonalinement with any power bloc. Statesmanship dictates chalking out a course which will not leave us wholly friendless if a conflict is forced on us * * *

* * * On the issue of Formosa our sympathy with Red China, our most powerful neighbor, is understandable. But is it necessary to go out of our way to take sides on a vital issue affecting the two rival power blocs? The extent to which Red China respects our sentiments can be gaged by her "peaceful" annexation of Tibet despite our pained protests * * * Now we have gratuitously estranged further our relations with the Western World by refusing to participate in the San Francisco Conference where at least we would have had a forum to clarify our stand and dissipate the misgivings of the powers from whom no aggression is apprehended.

Recommended Reading

Persuade or Perish, by Wallace Carroll. Houghton Mifflin Company, Boston, 1948

Sykewar, by Daniel Lerner. (Library of Policy Sciences) George W. Stewart, Publisher, Inc., New York, 1949

Overseas Information Service of the United States Government, by Charles A. H. Thomson. The Brookings Institution, Washington, D. C., 1948

The True Believer, by Eric Hoffer. Harper & Brothers, New York, 1951

Psychological Warfare, by Paul M. A. Linebarger. Infantry Journal Press, Washington, D. C., 1948

How to Make Friends for the U. S., by Vera Micheles Dean. Headline Series of Foreign Policy Association, No. 93, May-June, 1952

War and the Minds of Men, by Frederick S. Dunn. Published for the Council on Foreign Relations by Harper & Brothers, New York, 1950

Other source books that were particularly helpful to the author:

Secret Missions, by Captain Ellis M. Zacharias, USN. G. P. Putnam's Sons, New York, 1946

War or Peace, by John Foster Dulles. The Macmillan Company, New York, 1950

The Big Change, by Frederick Lewis Allen. Harper & Brothers, New York, 1952

The Psychological Warfare Division Supreme Headquarters Allied Expeditionary Force. An account of its operations in the Western European Campaign, 1944-45

Unwritten Treaty, by James P. Warburg. Harcourt Brace & Co., New York, 1946

Human Relations in a Changing World, by Alexander Hamilton Leighton. E. P. Dutton & Co., Inc., New York, 1949

Words That Won the War, by James R. Mock and Cedric Larson. Princeton University Press, Princeton, N. J., 1939

My Three Years in Moscow, by Walter Bedell Smith. J. P. Lippincott Company, Philadelphia, 1950

Peace Can be Won, by Paul G. Hoffman. Doubleday & Company, Garden City, New York, 1951

The Revolt of the Masses, by Jose Ortega y Gasset. W. W. Norton & Company, Inc., New York, 1932

How to Co-Exist, by James P. Warburg. The Beacon Press, Boston, 1952

The Coming Defeat of Communism, by James Burnham. The John Day Company, Inc., New York, 1950

A Window on Red Square, by Frank Rounds, Jr. Houghton Mifflin Company, Boston, 1953

Index

347